MARIJUANA FEDERALISM

MARIJUANA FEDERALISM

Uncle Sam and Mary Jane

EDITED BY
JONATHAN H. ADLER

BROOKINGS INSTITUTION PRESS
Washington, D.C.

The Brookings Institution is a private nonprofit organization devoted to research, education, and publication on important issues of domestic and foreign policy. Its principal purpose is to bring the highest quality independent research and analysis to bear on current and emerging policy problems. Interpretations or conclusions in Brookings publications should be understood to be solely those of the authors.

Library of Congress Cataloging-in-Publication data.
Names: Adler, Jonathan H., editor.
Title: Marijuana federalism : Uncle Sam and Mary Jane / edited by
    Jonathan H. Adler.
Description: Washington, D.C. : Brookings Institution Press, [2020] |
Identifiers: LCCN 2019048656 (print) | LCCN 2019048657 (ebook) | ISBN
    9780815737896 (paperback) | ISBN 9780815737902 (epub)
Subjects: LCSH: Drug legalization—United States. | Marijuana—
    Government policy—United States. | Marijuana—Law and legislation—
    United States. | Federal government—United States. | Conflict of
    laws—United States.
Classification: LCC HV5825 .M354 2020 (print) | LCC HV5825 (ebook) |
    DDC 362.29/55610973—dc23
LC record available at https://lccn.loc.gov/2019048656
LC ebook record available at https://lccn.loc.gov/2019048657

9 8 7 6 5 4 3 2 1

Typeset in Granjon LT

Composition by Elliott Beard

CONTENTS

ACKNOWLEDGMENTS

This book grew out of a November 2014 conference at the Case Western Reserve University School of Law, the proceedings of which were published in the *Case Western Reserve Law Review*. That conference helped stimulate greater discussion of how the United States's distinct federalist system should influence and shape the debate over marijuana policy reform. Thanks are due to those who helped make that program possible—both those who have contributed to this volume directly and those who did not, including many people at the law school, not least of whom our co-deans, Jessica Berg and Michael Scharf. Special thanks are due to the late Peter Lewis, for the financial support that made the program possible, as well as to Graham Boyd.

In addition to the above, I would like to thank Joseph Sabo and Lisa Peters for their research assistance, Bill Finan at the Brookings Institution Press for believing this project was worthwhile, Cecilia González for overseeing production at the press, and all of those (not least of whom my family) who have had to put up with me while I was completing this and other projects.

Introduction

OUR FEDERALISM ON DRUGS

Jonathan H. Adler

Just twenty-five years ago, marijuana was illegal throughout the United States. Beginning in the 1990s, several states, led by California, began to allow the cultivation, possession, and use of cannabis for medicinal purposes, but they remained the exception. In the past decade, however, the legal landscape for marijuana has been radically transformed as an increasing number of states have rejected marijuana prohibition.

Colorado and Washington were the first states to withdraw fully from the federal war against marijuana. In 2012, voters in both states approved ballot initiatives legalizing possession of marijuana for recreational use and authorizing state regulation of marijuana production and commercial sale.[1] Over the next six years, eight more states and the District of Columbia followed suit.[2] Meanwhile, the possession and use of medical marijuana for medicinal purposes, with a doctor's recommendation, became legal in a majority of states,[3] while another dozen states largely decriminalized personal possession of small amounts of marijuana. By 2019, only a handful of states had failed to loosen legal restrictions on marijuana in some way.

These rapid changes in state marijuana policy both exploit and challenge American federalism. While many states have rejected marijuana prohibition, the use, possession, cultivation, and sale of marijuana remain illegal under federal law.[4] Marijuana is listed in Schedule I of the Controlled Substances Act (CSA), where it was placed by Congress in 1970.[5] Cultivation and distribution of marijuana are felonies, and CSA violations may authorize asset seizure.[6] Those who use marijuana, even for medicinal purposes, may lose their ability to purchase firearms[7] or dwell in public housing,[8] without regard for whether their use of marijuana is sanctioned under state law. Marijuana-related businesses may not deduct the costs of running their businesses for federal income taxes[9] and may be vulnerable to civil RICO suits.[10] Banks and financial institutions, in particular, face tremendous legal uncertainty about the extent to which they may provide services to marijuana-related businesses without exposing themselves to legal jeopardy,[11] and it is unclear whether lawyers may counsel clients engaged in marijuana-related business ventures without running afoul of state rules of professional responsibility.[12] Some also fear that the legalization of marijuana sales in some jurisdictions could feed the black market in other states.

The constitutional authority of the federal government to prohibit the possession and distribution of marijuana was affirmed by the Supreme Court,[13] but the ability of the federal government to enforce this policy on the ground is largely dependent on state cooperation. The federal government is not responsible for the local cop on the beat, and federal law enforcement agencies have neither the resources nor the inclination to try to enforce the federal marijuana prohibition nationwide.

While the federal government has not prioritized enforcement of marijuana prohibition in states that have adopted more permissive marijuana policies, it has not sought to preempt state initiatives either, including those that affirmatively license and regulate a growing marijuana industry. Congress, for its part, has made clear that it does not want federal law enforcement efforts to interfere with state-level medical marijuana programs. While failing to enact legislation to authorize or decriminalize medical marijuana where permissible under state law, Congress has repeatedly prohibited federal law enforcement agencies from taking actions that could prevent states from "implementing" their own medical marijuana programs. As interpreted by federal courts, these "appropriations riders" bar the federal prosecution of individuals for conduct that is expressly permitted by state medical marijuana laws.[14] This is not a permanent condition, however, as appropriations riders must be reenacted each year to remain effective.

Even before Congress limited federal enforcement efforts, state and local law enforcement agencies were responsible for the overwhelming majority of marijuana law enforcement. Whatever course federal policy takes, this is unlikely to change. There are approximately four times as many state and local law enforcement officers within just two states—Washington and Colorado—as there are Drug Enforcement Administration (DEA) agents across the globe.[15] Nor can Congress or the executive branch compel state cooperation.[16] If state and local governments do not cooperate, the federal government must wage its war on drugs without many foot soldiers.

For the most part, federal agencies have not shown much interest in interfering with state-level reforms. In a series of memoranda issued during the Obama administration, the Department of Justice (DOJ) sought to clarify federal enforcement priorities, deemphasizing federal enforcement in states where marijuana possession is legal for some or all purposes. In 2009, Deputy Attorney General David Ogden issued a memorandum indicating that the Justice Department would focus its enforcement efforts on the production and distribution of marijuana in an effort to curb trafficking, but would not devote significant resources to pursue those who used or possessed marijuana in compliance with state laws allowing the use and possession of marijuana for medicinal purposes.[17] A follow-up memorandum issued by Ogden's successor, James Cole, reaffirmed that, while the Justice Department was clarifying its enforcement priorities, the possession, cultivation, and distribution of marijuana remained illegal under federal law.[18]

After Colorado and Washington voters passed their respective marijuana legalization initiatives, the Justice Department maintained this position. In August 2013, Deputy Attorney General Cole announced that the department would make no effort to block the implementation of either initiative, nor was it the federal government's position that state-level regulations of marijuana were preempted by the CSA.[19] According to this memorandum, it was the Justice Department's view that the cultivation, distribution, sale, and possession of marijuana in compliance with state laws was "less likely to threaten" federal priorities, such as curbing interstate trafficking and preventing youth access. So long as this assumption holds, the second Cole memorandum explained, "enforcement of state law by state and local law enforcement and regulatory bodies should remain the primary means of addressing marijuana-related activity."[20] Meanwhile, the DEA denied multiple petitions to reschedule marijuana under the CSA and ease its treatment under federal law.[21]

Attorney General Jeff Sessions rescinded the Cole memoranda in January 2018, but it is unclear how much this changed things on the ground. While issuing a new memorandum announcing "a return to the rule of law," Attorney General Sessions disavowed any intention to depart from traditional enforcement priorities. Federal prosecutors "haven't been working small marijuana cases before, they are not going to be working them now," Sessions explained in a 2018 speech at the Georgetown University Law Center.[22] As he acknowledged, the Justice Department could not take over routine enforcement of the federal marijuana prohibition even if it so desired.

In early 2019, Sessions's successor, Attorney General William Barr, reaffirmed that the Justice Department has little interest in trying to enforce marijuana prohibition in jurisdictions that have chosen to legalize or decriminalize marijuana in some way. While personally opposed to marijuana legalization, Barr told Congress that he did not wish to "upset settled expectations and the reliance interest" that arose in the wake of the Cole memos.[23] At the same time, Barr noted that the status quo was "untenable" and suggested federal legislation was necessary to smooth out potential conflicts between state and federal law.

The insistence of multiple states on experimenting with various levels of marijuana decriminalization or legalization raises a host of important and difficult legal questions, not the least of which is how states can adopt marijuana polices preferred by local residents without running afoul of federal law.[24] As a theoretical matter, the federalist structure of American government would enable different jurisdictions to adopt laws in line with local conditions and local preferences. As a practical matter, however, things have been more complicated.

DUAL SOVEREIGNTY AND COMPETITIVE FEDERALISM

The constitutional structure of the United States is often referred to as one of "dual sovereignty"[25]—a system in which there are two distinct levels of government. The U.S. Constitution creates a federal government of limited and enumerated powers. All other powers, including the so-called "police power" to protect public health, safety, and the general welfare, are left in the hands of state governments.[26] Federal law is supreme, but the scope of federal power is limited.

This federalist structure leaves states with substantial latitude to enact laws and regulations that conform with the needs and preferences of their citizens, thereby accounting for the diversity of views and preferences across the country.[27] California, Texas, Vermont, and Alabama differ in many respects. Each of these states has a different climate, different geography, and different demographics and populations with different policy preferences. It should be no surprise that each of these jurisdictions has adopted a different set of policies with regard to the use and distribution of marijuana.

In a large, heterogeneous republic in which different groups of people have different priorities and preferences with regard to how the law should treat marijuana, setting a single national policy increases the number of people who live under laws with which they disagree.[28] As Alexis de Tocqueville observed, "In large centralized nations the lawgiver is bound to give the laws a uniform character which does not fit the diversity of places and of mores."[29] On the other hand, allowing each jurisdiction to adopt policies in line with the preferences of its citizens makes it more likely that more people will live in jurisdictions with policies that match their preferences.[30]

Alabama made precisely this point when California sought to defend the viability of its medical marijuana laws in federal court. In *Gonzales v. Raich*, the state of Alabama filed briefs urging the Supreme Court to hold that the federal government could not prohibit the possession of marijuana for medicinal purposes where authorized by state law.[31] While pointedly refusing to endorse the substance of California's law allowing medical marijuana use, Alabama urged the Court to allow different states to adopt different marijuana policies. Although Alabama maintained some of the most punitive marijuana possession laws in the country, it supported the ability of California to make a different policy choice.[32]

Where allowed to operate, dual sovereignty creates a system of competitive federalism in which states are under pressure to innovate in public policy. This may encourage innovation, as states experiment with providing different bundles of policies and services. At the same time, competitive federalism provides a means to discipline states that overreach.[33] Those states that are more successful in providing a mix of laws and amenities that are appealing to different groups of people will attract residents (who are also taxpayers) and investment from other jurisdictions. States that impose policies that are too costly or too restrictive will lose population and investment to other jurisdictions on the margin as well.[34]

These competitive pressures provide a potentially powerful discovery mechanism to reveal the relative benefits and costs of different policy measures. In Justice Louis Brandeis's famous formulation, allowing states to enact competing policy measures frees them to serve as "laboratories of democracy" in which policymakers may attempt "novel social and economic experiments without risk to the rest of the country."[35] Allowing private possession and consumption of marijuana for medicinal or recreational purposes may enhance individual welfare, or it may not. Such policies may expand human freedom in meaningful ways without jeopardizing other public concerns, or they may not. Reasonable people may disagree on these points. Allowing states to adopt different policies can generate the empirical evidence necessary to inform, if not also resolve, such disputes.

This discovery process may inform policymakers about the costs and benefits of legalizing or decriminalizing marijuana. Legislators considering changing the marijuana laws in their state can base their decision, in part, on the consequences of similar measures adopted in other jurisdictions. Perhaps more important, the practical experiences of competing jurisdictions can reveal the relative costs and benefits of adopting different approaches to marijuana law reform. The contours of a legal regime and its implementation can be just as important as the underlying legal rule, and the consequences of different rules, on the margin, can be particularly difficult to predict without first putting them into practice.

While much of the policy debate centers on the binary choice between legalizing use and maintaining prohibition, there are multiple margins along which existing laws and policies may be reformed. How a given jurisdiction chooses to legalize or decriminalize marijuana may be as important as whether a state chooses to move in this direction. Not only do jurisdictions face choices about whether to legalize marijuana, and for what uses, they also face choices about whether marijuana production and distribution is to be a private commercial enterprise; whether the state will license retailers or producers and, if so, under what conditions; how sales and use are or are not to be regulated or taxed; how potential risks to children or vulnerable populations will be addressed; how the consequences of reform will be measured and assessed; and so on. Allowing different jurisdictions to experiment with different combinations of reforms generates information about the benefits and costs of different measures, thereby allowing marijuana policy discussions to proceed on a more informed basis. Whatever the end result of this process will be, marijuana policy will be better the more we allow this federalism-based discovery process to operate.

While federalism, in principle, should create a framework for interjurisdictional competition and discovery, federal law often gets in the way. The expansion of federal law, and federal criminal law in particular, has constrained the choices left to state policymakers and foreclosed meaningful experimentation in many policy areas, dampening the discovery mechanism competitive federalism can provide.[36] Insofar as federal law prohibits particular conduct, states have less ability to experiment with different legal regimes and are less able to discover whether alternative rules or restrictions would produce policy results more in line with local preferences.

STRIKING A BALANCE

Questions about the proper balance between federal and state government have endured since the nation's founding. Marijuana policy is just the latest battleground in this long-standing conflict. It is also an issue that could cut across traditional right-left political lines.

Drug policy reform is often seen as a "liberal" issue. Conservatives are expected to be "tough on crime," and voters who support marijuana legalization are more likely to support Democratic political candidates. Yet many Democrats continue to oppose changes to marijuana laws,[37] and it is those on the political right who are more likely to call for allowing states to deviate from one-size-fits-all federal policies. On everything from environmental regulation to education policy, Republican officeholders often argue that individual states should be free from federal interference to adopt their own policy priorities.

In December 2014, Nebraska and Oklahoma both filed suit seeking to force the preemption of Colorado's Amendment 64. Both these states have been active champions of state prerogatives, regularly challenging federal regulatory initiatives in other policy areas. Here, however, the two states sought federal support to suppress Colorado's experiment with marijuana, arguing that Colorado's decision to allow a legal market in marijuana threatened to impose a nuisance on neighboring jurisdictions.[38] Colorado's experience to date, however, suggests that state governments are capable of effectively regulating intrastate marijuana markets.[39]

Some of the more difficult legal questions confronting state efforts to legalize marijuana involve the intersection between state law and the existing federal prohibition. Even if the federal government decides to scale back marijuana law enforcement in non-prohibition states, federal law remains federal law and it continues to have an effect. Banks, attorneys, and others are bound to respect federal law even in the absence of conforming state laws, as the legalization of a product by state law does not eliminate the federal prohibition.[40] Legalizing the possession and use of marijuana by adults poses the risk that marijuana will become more accessible to juveniles.[41] Just as some states may disagree with federal prohibition, some localities may disagree with their states' marijuana policy decisions, raising the question of whether marijuana federalism should become marijuana localism.[42]

The federal government has a legitimate interest in controlling interstate drug trafficking, but no particular interest in prosecuting those who seek to provide medical marijuana to local residents pursuant to state law. So it only makes sense for the Justice Department to tell federal prosecutors to focus their efforts on those who are not in compliance with state law, such as those who use medical marijuana distribution as a cover for other illegal activities, particularly interstate drug trafficking. California should be free to set its own marijuana policy, but the federal government retains an interest in preventing California's choice from adversely affecting neighboring states.

One possibility is for the federal government to treat marijuana like alcohol, retaining a federal role in controlling illegal interstate trafficking but leaving each state entirely free to set its own marijuana policy, whether it be prohibition, decriminalization, or somewhere between.[43] Another alternative would be for the federal government to offer states waivers or enter into cooperative agreements with states that seek to adopt alternative approaches to marijuana policy.[44]

When alcohol prohibition was repealed, states retained the ability to prohibit or regulate alcohol, and the federal government focused on supporting state-level preferences by prohibiting interstate shipment of alcohol in violation of applicable state laws. There is no clear reason why a similar approach to marijuana would be less effective, though any such step would require legislative reform.

UNCLE SAM AND MARY JANE

The aim of this book is to help inform the emerging debate over marijuana federalism by identifying and clarifying many of the legal and policy issues that are at stake as these issues work their way through our federal system.

The marijuana policy debate is rapidly evolving. As John Hudak and Christine Stenglein detail, public opinion on marijuana has changed quite dramatically in a relatively short period of time, driven in part by a widespread perception that marijuana is less dangerous than other illicit substances.[45] As they note, public opinion may change as more people experience the consequences of legalization—or it may not. According to Angela Dills, Sietse Goffard, and Jeffrey Miron, the effects of marijuana legalization in legalizing states, thus far, have been less significant than both supporters and opponents had predicted.[46]

The fact that marijuana can be legal in some states while prohibited under federal law may seem odd, but this is a key aspect of how our federalist system operates. As Ernest Young and Robert Mikos each explain, the federal government lacks the power to "commandeer" state governments or police forces to implement federal law or policy priorities.[47] The Supreme Court has repeatedly reaffirmed this principle, which is why so much of marijuana policy "on the ground" reflects state and local choices, and state resistance to federal priorities can be quite profound. One might think that federal officeholders are obligated to make greater efforts to enforce federal prohibition, but as Zachary Price explains, the executive branch retains ample flexibility regarding how to deploy law enforcement resources—and this flexibility that has been utilized by both the Obama and Trump administrations.[48]

Even if the federal government is not actively enforcing the federal prohibition on the possession, distribution, and sale of marijuana, the mere existence of the federal prohibition has effects on businesses and professionals with their own obligations to comply with federal law. As Julie Hill explains, federal marijuana prohibition has made it more difficult for banks to provide banking services to marijuana-related businesses due to the demands of compliance with banking laws.[49] And as Cassandra Robertson explains, the persistence of a federal prohibition has forced attorneys, and those who evaluate and enforce rules of professional responsibility for lawyers, to consider whether attorneys may provide legal services to marijuana-related businesses without running afoul of their ethical obligations.[50]

As noted above, much of the legal and policy tension between the federal and state governments is a consequence of current constitutional doctrine, under which the scope of federal power is determined independent of the actions taken by states. But need this be so? A congressionally enacted statute could reorient the federal-state balance concerning marijuana, but so could a shift in Supreme Court doctrine. As William Baude suggests, perhaps existing constitutional doctrine should be more solicitous of state actions and recognize limits on federal power in circumstances where states have productively occupied the field.

Whatever approach the federal government takes in the years ahead—and whether legal reforms come from Congress or the courts—the marijuana policy debate today extends well beyond whether to legalize cannabis for some or all purposes. Unless the federal government takes action to remove legal obstacles to state-level reforms, various interjurisdictional conflicts and legal quandaries will continue to arise. Administrative action, however popular with recent presidents, is unlikely to be sufficient to resolve these conflicts. Legislative action of some sort will be required eventually. Until then, this is our federalism on drugs, and it is going to be an interesting trip.

NOTES

1. Colorado Constitution, Amendment 64; Washington Initiative 502, No. 63-502, Reg. Sess. (November 6, 2012).

2. National Conference of State Legislatures, "Marijuana Overview," December 14, 2018 (www.ncsl.org/research/civil-and-criminal-justice/marijuana-overview.aspx). This site is updated regularly as state laws change.

3. National Conference of State Legislatures, "Marijuana Overview," March 5, 2019 (www.ncsl.org/research/health/state-medical-marijuana-laws.aspx). This site is updated regularly as state laws change.

4. For an overview of federal and state laws and how they potentially conflict, see

Lisa N. Sacco and others, "The Marijuana Policy Gap and the Path Forward," *Congressional Research Service* 7-5700, March 10, 2017.

5. Comprehensive Drug Abuse Prevention and Control Act of 1970, Pub. L. No. 91-513, 84 Stat. 1236 (codified as amended at 21 U.S.C. §§ 801–889 (2006)). For a brief history, see John Hudak, *Marijuana: A Short History* (Washington, DC: Brookings Institution Press, 2016).

6. See, for instance, 21 U.S.C. § 841 (prison terms for marijuana cultivation); § 881(a) (7) (property "used, or intended to be used, in any manner or part" to violate the CSA may be subject to forfeiture).

7. The U.S. Court of Appeals for the Ninth Circuit upheld portions of the federal Gun Control Act and implementing regulations that effectively criminalize the possession of a firearm by the holder of a state marijuana registry card. See *Wilson v. Lynch*, 835 F.3d 1083 (9th Cir. 2016).

8. Because marijuana is listed under Schedule I of the Controlled Substances Act, the Quality Housing and Work Responsibility Act prohibits public housing agencies from allowing current users of marijuana to participate in public housing programs. See 42 U.S.C. §13661.

9. 28 U.S.C. §280E.

10. In *Safe Streets Alliance v. Hickenlooper*, the U.S. Court of Appeals for the Tenth Circuit held that neighboring landowners could file a civil claim under the federal Racketeer Influenced and Corrupt Organizations Act (RICO) against a marijuana grower alleging that the cultivation of marijuana contributed to a common law nuisance. 859 F.3d 865 (10th Cir. 2017).

11. See Chapter 6, this volume.

12. See Chapter 7, this volume

13. See *Gonzales v. Raich*, 545 U.S. 1 (2005). For a critique of this ruling, see Jonathan H. Adler, "Is *Morrison* Dead? Assessing a Supreme Drug (Law) Overdose," *Lewis & Clark Law Review* 9 (2005); Chapter 8, this volume.

14. See, for example, *United States v. McIntosh*, 833 F.3d 1163 (9th Cir. 2016); *United States v. Marin Alliance for Medical Marijuana*, 139 F. Supp. 3d 1039 (E.D. Cal. 2015).

15. See Mark Kleiman, "How Not to Make a Hash Out of Cannabis Legalization," *Washington Monthly*, April/May 2014.

16. See *Printz v. United States*, 521 U.S. 898 (1997) (the federal government may not "commandeer" state and local governments to implement or enforce federal law); *New York v. United States*, 505 U.S. 144 (1992) (the federal government may not force a state to legislate in accord with federal policy).

17. Memorandum from David W. Ogden, Deputy Attorney General, to U.S. Attorneys, October 19, 2009 (www.justice.gov/sites/default/files/opa/legacy/2009/10/19/medical-marijuana.pdf).

18. Memorandum from James M. Cole, Deputy Attorney General, Guidance Regarding the Ogden Memo in Jurisdictions Seeking to Authorize Marijuana for Medical Use, June 29, 2011 (www.justice.gov/oip/docs/dag-guidance-2011-for-medical-marijuana-use.pdf).

19. Memorandum for All U.S. Attorneys from James M. Cole, Deputy Attorney

General, Guidance Regarding Marijuana Enforcement, August 29, 2013 (www.justice. gov/iso/opa/resources/3052013829132756857467.pdf).

20. Ibid.

21. Drug Enforcement Administration, "Denial of Petition to Initiate Proceedings to Reschedule Marijuana," 81 *Federal Register*, 53767-53845, August 12, 2016; Drug Enforcement Administration, "Denial of Petition to Initiate Proceedings to Reschedule Marijuana," 81 *Federal Register*, 53687-53766, August 12, 2016; Drug Enforcement Administration, "Denial of Petition to Initiate Proceedings to Reschedule Marijuana," 76 *Federal Register*, 40552-40589, July 8, 2011.

22. Quoted in Max Greenwood, "Sessions says despite rules change federal prosecutors will not take 'small marijuana cases'," *The Hill*, March 10, 2018.

23. Dominic Holden, "Bill Barr Says He's 'Not Going After' Marijuana in States Where It's Legal," *Buzzfeed News*, Jan. 15, 2019 (www.buzzfeednews.com/article/dom inicholden/bill-barr-attoreny-general-marijuana-legal-enforcement).

24. See Alex Kreit, "Beyond the Prohibition Debate: Thoughts on Federal Drug Laws in an Age of State Reforms," *Chapman Law Review* 13 (2010), pp. 555–56 ("when it comes to federal drug law, traditional debates about prohibition, legalization, or decriminalization turn out to be surprisingly unimportant. Instead, as states begin to enact new policies the key question facing federal lawmakers and administration officials will be how to harmonize federal law with state reforms").

25. See, for example, *Federal Maritime Commission v. South Carolina State Ports Authority*, 535 U.S. 743, 751 (2002) ("Dual sovereignty is a defining feature of our Nation's constitutional blueprint"); *Gregory v. Ashcroft*, 501 U.S. 452, 457 ("As every schoolchild learns, our Constitution establishes a system of dual sovereignty between the States and the Federal Government").

26. See *Chicago, B & Q Railway C., v. People of State of Illinois*, 200 U.S. 561, 592 (1906) (defining the police power to include "regulations designed to promote the public convenience or the general prosperity, as well as regulations designed to promote the public health, the public morals, or the public safety").

27. Michael W. McConnell, "Federalism: Evaluating the Founders' Design," *University of Chicago Law Review* 54 (1987), p. 1493.

28. F. A. Hayek, "The Economic Conditions of Interstate Federalism," in *Individualism and Economic Order* (University of Chicago Press, 1948), pp. 264–65.

29. Alexis de Tocqueville, *Democracy in America* (J. P. Mayer, ed. 1969), p. 161.

30. McConnell, "Federalism," p. 1493.

31. Brief of the States of Alabama, Louisiana, and Mississippi as Amici Curiae in Support of Respondents, *Ashcroft v. Raich*, No. 03-1454, Supreme Court of the United States, October 13, 2004. Note that this case was styled *Ashcroft v. Raich* when Alabama filed the amicus brief, but was *Gonzales v. Raich* when the case was decided.

32. At the time of the litigation, individuals convicted three times for marijuana possession could be jailed for fifteen years. Ethan Nadelman, "An End to Marijuana Prohibition," *National Review*, July 12, 2004, p. 28.

33. Hayek, "Interstate Federalism," p. 268.

34. For an extended discussion of the role of mobility in competitive federalism, see

Ilya Somin, "Free to Move: Foot Voting, Federalism, and Political Freedom," in *NOMOS LV: Federalism and Subsidiarity*, James Fleming and Jacob Levy, eds. (NYU Press, 2014), pp. 110–154.

35. See *New State Ice Co. v. Liebmann*, 285 U.S. 262, 311 (1932) (Brandeis, J., dissenting) ("It is one of the happy incidents of the federal system, that a single courageous state may, if its citizens choose, serve as a laboratory; and try novel social and economic experiments without risk to the rest of the country").

36. As Justice Kennedy noted, federal law often "forecloses the States from experimenting and exercising their own judgment" in areas traditionally left within state hands. *United States v. Lopez*, 514 U.S. 549, 583 (1995).

37. Democratic National Committee Chair Debbie Wasserman Shultz, for instance, opposed Florida's medical marijuana initiative. See Marc Caputo, "Behind Wasserman Schultz's Marijuana Feud," *Politico*, February 24, 2015 (www.politico.com/story/2015/02/behind-wasserman-schultzs-marijuana-feud-115442.html).

38. See Jonathan H. Adler, "Are Nebraska and Oklahoma Just Fair-Weather Federalists?" *The Volokh Conspiracy*, December 19, 2014 (www.washingtonpost.com/news/volokh-conspiracy/wp/2014/12/19/are-nebraska-and-oklahoma-just-fair-weather-federalists/).

39. See Chapter 4 of this volume.

40. See Chapter 6 of this volume.

41. See Steven Davenport, Jonathan P. Caulkins, and Mark A. R. Kleiman, "Controlling Underage Access to Legal Cannabis," *Case Western Reserve Law Review* 65 (2015).

42. See Robert A. Mikos, "Marijuana Localism," *Case Western Reserve Law Review* 65 (2015).

43. For an argument that this should be the approach to all illicit drugs, see Daniel K. Benjamin and Roger Leroy Miller, *Undoing Drugs: Beyond Legalization* (New York: Basic Books,1993).

44. See, for example, the proposal outlined in Erwin Chemerinsky, Jolene Forman, Allen Hopper, and Sam Kamin, "Cooperative Federalism and Marijuana Regulation" *UCLA Law Review*, 62 (2015).

45. Chapter 2 of this volume.

46. Chapter 3 of this volume.

47. Chapters 4 and 5 of this volume.

48. Chapter 6 of this volume.

49. Chapter 7 of this volume.

50. Chapter 8 of this volume.

1

PUBLIC OPINION AND AMERICA'S EXPERIMENTATION WITH CANNABIS REFORM

John Hudak | Christine Stenglein

Before the first adult-use cannabis reform ballot initiatives passed in 2012, it was not a sure bet that cannabis's status as an illicit drug would change any time soon. Public support for legalization had grown slowly but steadily over the 2000s, but that followed a solid twenty years of stagnation from the late 1970s through the late 1990s.[1] Despite that increased support, most polls found the public split nearly evenly between those for and those against legalizing cannabis. Although it was widely believed that generational turnover would inevitably lead to increased support for legalization, as support was highest in younger age cohorts, there was no guarantee that those trends would bear out both over time and in potentially shifting political contexts.[2]

But the ensuing seven years have brought about tremendous change. Now legal for medical use in thirty-four states and the District of Columbia and for adult recreational use in eleven states and the District of Columbia, cannabis has shifted from broad prohibition to a patchwork of regulatory and decriminalization approaches across the states. At the federal level, the current picture is more complicated. The rescission of the Cole Memo in 2018 signaled an interest in a more conservative approach to federal enforcement. Meanwhile, in Congress, numerous measures have been introduced to resolve the ambiguities resulting from the Cole rescission, allow hemp cultivation, and expand research, among other reforms.

During this rapid increase in the availability of cannabis to more Americans, public attitudes toward cannabis legalization have also changed rapidly. Two in three Americans now support legalizing cannabis, according to Gallup, following record-breaking increases in support for three consecutive years. Since 2012, support for legalization has increased by 12 percent, and opposition has fallen by 16 percent.[3]

WHITHER THE RISKS OF CANNABIS?

Part of the reason for the breadth of support for cannabis reform may stem from the perception of the risks of use relative to other drugs. A 2018 NBC News/*Wall Street Journal* poll asked respondents to select the substance they thought was the most harmful to an individual's overall health from the following options: alcohol, tobacco, cannabis, and sugar. Only 9 percent chose cannabis—about half the number who chose sugar.[4] About four times as many respondents chose tobacco as chose cannabis. Also in 2018, CBS News asked people to compare alcohol and cannabis and choose which was more harmful to a person's health: 51 percent chose alcohol as the most harmful, and 28 percent ranked them equally harmful.[5] When CBS asked people whether they thought cannabis was more or less dangerous than other drugs, 63 percent said it was less dangerous and 28 percent said it was just as dangerous. Less than 5 percent said it was more dangerous than other drugs.

THE LANGUAGE OF LEGALIZATION

Often in discussions around cannabis reform, confusing terminology is thrown about, and some use the jargon improperly. So, it is important to get on the same page with the lingo used in this chapter. First, legalization is the most far-reaching type of cannabis reform. It removes legal penalties around cannabis. The removal of those penalties can and does vary significantly in the United

States. Legalization can describe a system in which the cultivation, production, processing, sale, purchase, and possession of cannabis is legal in a given jurisdiction for all adults of a certain age (in the United States, that age is universally over twenty-one, but this varies in places like Uruguay and certain provinces in Canada). Colorado, Washington, California, Nevada, and others have taken this step. This type of legalization is often called "recreational," "adult-use," or sometimes "non-medical" legalization. Those three terms are used interchangeably.

In one U.S. state with adult-use cannabis legalization, Vermont, the sale of cannabis is prohibited, and there is no commercial market for cannabis. However, Vermont's state legislature approved a 2018 law that legalized home cultivation of a limited number of cannabis plants and allows residents of that state to give away or "gift" cannabis to others, so long as cash is not exchanged. Other states put restrictions on the amount of cannabis that can be purchased at one time, how much an individual can possess at a given time, whether "homegrows" are allowed, the number of plants allowed in a homegrow, as well as a bevy of other regulations around private, personal, and commercial cannabis activity.

Medical legalization is different. While many of the medical systems in the United States look similar to the adult-use legalization systems—cannabis is grown commercially and sold to consumers (patients) at dispensaries—there are differences between the two. First, states with medical cannabis put restrictions in place on who can access it. Those restrictions include age and an individual's medical illness or condition. To access medical cannabis, one must have a medical condition that qualifies for entry into the program (this is called a "qualifying condition"), and that condition must be recognized by a licensed medical professional. In some states, like California and Colorado, the number and/or types of qualifying conditions allow for permissive entry into the medical cannabis system. Other states, like Connecticut and Delaware, list only a few qualifying conditions, severely restricting residents' access to the system.

In addition to accessing medical cannabis from the commercial market, several states allow qualifying medical patients to grow at home or join a cooperative in which another individual (typically called a "caregiver") cultivates cannabis for a patient.

"Decriminalization" is a term that is often most confusing in this space; it is also one of the terms that the public most frequently uses improperly. Decriminalization refers to a reform in which criminal penalties are removed for the possession of cannabis (meaning it no longer qualifies as a felony or misdemeanor); however, possession still remains illegal under the law. Rather than arresting and locking up an individual caught possessing cannabis, a decriminalization system treats possession similar to a speeding or parking ticket. You are issued a ticket and have to pay a fine (often around $100 for a first offense). Subsequent offenses can increase the fine required, and repeated offenses, in some states, can become a misdemeanor. There are additional limitations imposed by decriminalization systems. Typically, there is a maximum amount that an individual can possess (a set number of grams, or an ounce) beyond which he or she can be charged with a crime (such as a misdemeanor or felony).

One of the challenges with public polling (though decreasingly so as cannabis policy becomes more mainstream) is that various terms may be used interchangeably, making it difficult to understand what the public is actually saying. For example, some pollsters use "decriminalization" when they really mean "adult-use legalization." As we will see, the most effective means of polling involves a description of precisely what is meant in the question.

LIMITATIONS AND CAVEATS OF CANNABIS POLLING

The polling data we have on cannabis reform is limited in a few ways. One of the main limitations is that when the data come from national samples they cannot provide precise insight into the disaggregated, state-by-state structure of cannabis reform. Another is that when pollsters do conduct surveys within a given state, they may be capturing the public's perception of a specific piece of legislation rather than their underlying attitudes about cannabis reform.

State versus National Polling

Since Gallup first began asking about cannabis legalization in 1969, polling on this issue has developed and matured significantly. Pollsters have since begun tracking age groups and cohorts, partisanship, gender, and ideology with regard to support.[6] Polling has taken a deep dive into the details of different types of cannabis reform, and some have even explored why individuals support or oppose cannabis reform.[7] In addition, polling continues at the national level, but state-level polls have informed much about how different areas of the country, in different political settings, feel about the issue. Finally, polling has even examined how specific population subsets feel about cannabis legalization, including Latinos[8] and veterans.[9]

National-level polling has made important contributions to understanding Americans' views on the issue. Each poll offers a snapshot into the worldview of the U.S. public and, taken together, can offer additional confidence regarding where the public stands on an issue. A single poll can provide odd results, given margins of error and the nature of polling. On the other hand, a group of polls—or an average of polls—can offer a better perspective on the true nature of public opinion. In addition, polling over time helps us understand changes in public opinion and changes within similar age cohorts over time.[10] While comparing different polls with differently worded questions taken at different points in time can potentially generate faulty analysis, the best longitudinal comparisons involve the same polling outlet using the same phrasing. We have that from Gallup, who has been asking the same question for half a century, and other organizations that have been asking questions consistently for some time.

However, national-level polling tells only so much, and there are multiple limitations as to its effect. First, cannabis reform in the United States, through 2018, has happened at the state level. National-level polling can describe the percentage of the public that supports reform; however, that support is not evenly distributed among states. Some states have significantly higher-than-average levels of support for reform, while others have lower levels of support.[11]

In addition, many advocates point to national-level polling—much of which shows support for cannabis reform exceeding 60 percent—and seem confused as to why national-level reform has not occurred. One of the many challenges to that line of logic assumes that individual elected officials respond to national-level polling. In reality, no elected official in the United States has a political constituency that is nationwide, not even the president.[12, 13] For members of the House and Senate who would be the initial source of national-level cannabis reform, their constituencies are significantly concentrated to the state or substate levels, making national-level polling irrelevant to their considerations. If legislators were responsive to national-level polling on cannabis, Hal Rogers, a Republican from Kentucky's 5th congressional district—who represents one of the most rural and the most conservative districts in the country—would mirror Earl Blumenauer, a Democrat from Oregon's 3rd congressional district that includes Portland. He does not.

Polling on Initiatives versus Issues

Another area of public opinion used to demonstrate public support for cannabis reform involves ballot initiatives. In advance of an initiative appearing on the ballot, advocates field polls to understand where the public stands—and, often, what work the campaigns for or against the initiative need to do. But pre-election polling is not the only data that reflect opinion. The outcome of the vote is heralded as the public's view on cannabis reform, and post-passage reflection on how the public feels about the new reforms provides relevant information as well.

However, those data should not be confused with broader public support for cannabis reform for a few reasons. First, pre-election polling, post-passage reflection, and election day results reflect the public's opinion of a specific cannabis reform initiative and the system that initiative seeks to put in place. That initiative may underestimate public support for broader cannabis reform—or even different reform systems. For a variety of reasons, voters may support cannabis reform but oppose a specific ballot initiative.

Election day results of a ballot initiative are all that ultimately matter in terms of getting reform in place. However, arguing that those results reflect what the broader public believes about reform is not necessarily valid. Turnout in a given election is not a representative sample of the broader public; the constituency that turns out to vote tends to be older, whiter, and wealthier than the general population. Those demographic realities may underestimate support for reform—even one specific to an initiative.

However, polling on a given initiative and the results of an initiative can be important and informative for the cannabis reform community. Although differences exist among state systems, many state-based cannabis reform ballot initiatives build upon others, and there is a degree of policy learning from the experiences of other states. Understanding why a ballot initiative passes in Colorado with 55 percent of the vote and in Maine with just over 50 percent of the vote helps inform other states that are considering initiatives.

The general takeaway is that while any public opinion data regarding cannabis reform is critically important, carelessness and imprecision in the discussion of these data can be damaging to an advocacy movement. It is incumbent upon those working with and discussing polling to understand those data in context and with the necessary caveats.

MEDICAL CANNABIS

While the medical use of cannabis has been around for millennia, the U.S. government effectively outlawed cannabis in all forms in 1937 and formally outlawed it in 1970. Since 1996, however, states have begun reforming their laws around medical cannabis, and now a large majority of Americans live in states with medical cannabis systems in place. Medical cannabis has exploded in popularity since California passed the first medical cannabis initiative, and that support extends across age groups, races and ethnicities, partisanship, ideology, and gender.

Americans embrace the idea that cannabis can be used for medical purposes—to relieve pain, quell the seizures associated with epilepsy, reduce inflammation, ease the suffering associated with chemotherapy, induce hunger for those with auto-immune disorders, and treat anxiety, among other symptoms and conditions. As medical cannabis programs have expanded, so, too, has Americans' experience with the substance. Millions of Americans have found therapeutic relief from cannabis and tens of millions know someone who has, transforming this once taboo issue into one that is mainstream.

Since 2014, CBS News has been asking if doctors should be able to prescribe (recommend) cannabis to patients with serious illnesses. As figure 1-1 shows, that support has remained stable, never dropping below 84 percent, and rising as high as 88 percent in 2017.[14]

Similarly, the Quinnipiac poll asked a random sample of Americans whether individuals should be able to legally access cannabis with a doctor's prescription.[15] Quinnipiac fielded this question twice each year in 2017 and 2018 and, as figure 1-2 shows, support for medical cannabis is quite high—between 91 percent and 94 percent, making it one of the most popular policy proposals in the United States.[16]

That public support has transformed into real results. Since 2008, twelve medical cannabis initiatives have appeared on ballots across the United States.

FIGURE 1-1. *Do you think doctors should be allowed to prescribe smalls amounts of marijuana for patients suffering from serious illnesses or not? (CBS News)*

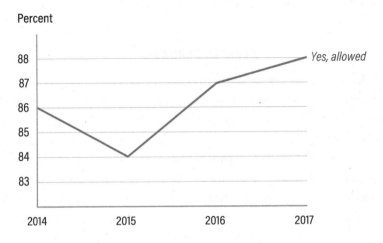

FIGURE 1-2. *Do you support or oppose allowing adults to legally use marijuana for medical purposes if their doctor prescribes it? (Quinnipiac)*

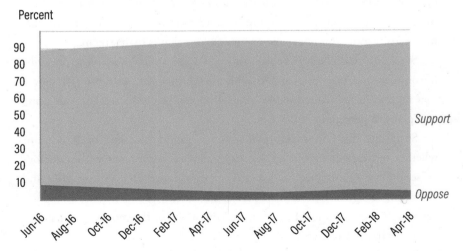

Of those initiatives, nine passed. Diving into the success and failure of initiatives is important. Initiatives passed both in liberal states like Massachusetts (2012) and conservative places like Utah and Oklahoma (2018). The three states in which they failed—South Dakota, Arkansas, and Florida—have unique histories as well. Sixty-three percent of voters opposed South Dakota's medical cannabis initiative. Arkansas defeated a medical cannabis initiative in 2012 only to vote on it again four years later. In 2012, the measure was defeated by fewer than 3 percent but passed by more than 6 percent in 2016.

In 2014, Florida voted on a constitutional amendment to legalize and regulate medical cannabis. In Florida, constitutional amendments require 60 percent support to pass. Although a majority of voters supported reform, it fell short of the 60 percent threshold, with 57.6 percent of voters approving. More than 900,000 more Floridians voted yes than voted no. Just two years later, Floridians voted on another medical cannabis constitutional amendment. The result was quite different—the measure passed 71 percent to 29 percent. More than 3.9 million more voters voted in favor of reform than those who voted to oppose. In fact, the 2016 cannabis ballot initiative received about 2 million more votes in Florida than either Donald Trump or Hillary Clinton.

Medical Cannabis and Key Constituencies

Beyond broad support for medical cannabis, there are a series of subgroups and related issues that have been the focus of much attention of late. First, veterans are a critical part of the medical cannabis conversation, in part because of federal restrictions on their access to cannabis via VA hospitals as well as their increased likelihood to have a qualifying condition. According to the National Institutes of Health (NIH), veterans are significantly more likely than non-veterans to experience severe chronic pain,[17] and veterans (especially combat veterans) have disproportionately high levels of post-traumatic stress disorder (PTSD).[18]

Veterans' organizations, including the American Legion,[19] Iraq and Afghanistan Veterans of America (IAVA),[20] and Veterans of Foreign Wars (VFW),[21] have come out in support of expanded, federally-funded medical cannabis research. Additionally, some veterans' organizations have polled their members on the issue. The results have been definitive. A 2017 poll by IAVA asked members whether they supported medical cannabis legalization. In a

2017 poll, 63 percent of IAVA members supported medical legalization, with another 22 percent neutral. Only 15 percent of members opposed the move. A 2017 poll from the American Legion asked veterans, veterans' family members, and veterans' caregivers about medical cannabis. Although the poll showed that only 22 percent of respondents used cannabis medically, 82 percent said they would "want to have cannabis as a federally-legal treatment," and 83 percent stated they "believe the federal government should legalize medical cannabis." Fully 92 percent supported research into medical cannabis.

The opioid crisis has become an issue that has influenced the cannabis policy debate. With some medical research suggesting that cannabis could be used to treat opioid use disorder (OUD),[22] some states considered OUD as a qualifying condition. The public is ready for a solution to the opioid crisis, and many believe medical cannabis may be a path forward. In a 2018 Harris Poll/HealthDay survey, 85 percent of Americans supported the legalization of medical cannabis, and a majority—53 percent—said they believe "if cannabis were legal, fewer people would die from opioid overdoses."[23] Other polls have shown more mixed results on the topic. An April 2018 Quinnipiac poll showed that 20 percent of Americans believe legalization could increase opioid use, 20 percent of Americans believe it could ease use, and another 56 percent believe it would have no effect.[24] Yet, even among Americans most skeptical of cannabis legalization—those over the age of fifty—there is agreement on the relative dangers of cannabis and opioids. In a University of Michigan/AARP poll, respondents age fifty to eighty, 48 percent believed that prescription pain medication is more addictive than cannabis, whereas only 14 percent believed the opposite.[25][26]

LEGALIZATION

Since 1969, Gallup has been asking Americans "Do you think the use of cannabis should be made legal, or not?" Just 12 percent of respondents said yes on that first survey. Support grew somewhat in the 1970s, then hovered around 20 percent for the next thirty years. For the first decade of the millennium, it grew steadily toward 50 percent. Then, as seen in figure 1-3, it began to rise rapidly after 2012 to reach two-thirds support.

Increasing support for legalization is typically interpreted as an effect of generational replacement, with younger people much more likely to support

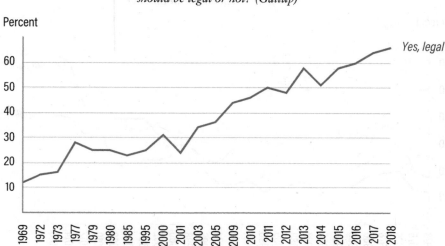

FIGURE 1-3. *Do you think the use of marijuana should be legal or not? (Gallup)*

legalization than older generations. That does seem to be taking place, but so, too, are increases in support over the last several years extending to older Americans. For the first time, in 2018, those fifty-five and older in Gallup's cannabis legalization poll were in favor of legalization by a majority. However, older Americans remain much less likely to support legalization than younger Americans.

There has been a persistent, although shrinking, gender gap in support for cannabis legalization. As recently as 2012, Quinnipiac found that, while men supported legalization at 59 percent, women opposed it at 52 percent.[27] YouGov found a similar five-point gap in 2015, with fewer women agreeing that cannabis should be legalized.[28] In a 2018 Quinnipiac poll, however, women supported legalization at 60 percent, just five points behind male respondents.[29]

Although Republicans trail Democrats in their support for legalization, support has increased among members of all major political affiliations over the last decade. As figure 1-4 shows, using data from the General Social Survey, Democrats have seen the sharpest increase in support, with Independents a few points lower.

One demographic category where Gallup found that differences in support have more or less disappeared was geographic region. In 2009–2010, support

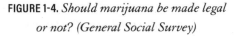

FIGURE 1-4. *Should marijuana be made legal
or not? (General Social Survey)*

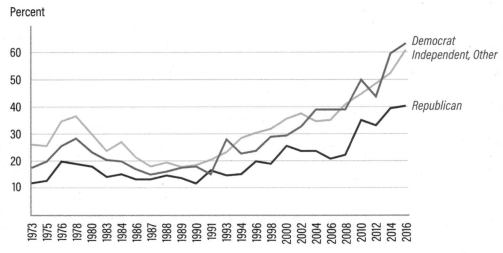

for legalization was lowest in the South and Midwest, where it trailed behind the East by five to six points and the West by fifteen to sixteen points. But by 2017–2018, all regions had reached two-thirds support; in the Midwest, that increase was a twenty-five-point jump.

There may be some variation in the favorability of different regulatory regimes that is not captured in the legalize-or-not polling that is most commonly deployed. One poll conducted by Mason-Dixon in 2018 asked in more detail about types of cannabis regulation. They asked registered voters to choose between keeping cannabis illegal, legalizing it for medical use, keeping sale of cannabis illegal but removing jail time as a penalty, and legalizing it for recreational use. Approximately half of respondents selected legalization for recreational use, and another 29 percent chose legalizing medical cannabis.[30] Similarly, a 2017 Harvard-Harris poll found 49 percent in favor of legalization for medical and personal use, and 37 percent in favor of medical use only. One criticism of a survey like this is that citizens need not choose between each of those. For example, some states have a medical cannabis system in place and have decriminalized its use. In addition, every state that has legalized adult-use cannabis already had a pre-existing medical cannabis program.

THE GATEWAY EFFECT

A key aspect of the rhetoric opposing cannabis legalization has been the perception of a gateway effect—the progression of cannabis users to more dangerous drugs. When Gallup asked this question in 1977, 60 percent of respondents agreed that "for most people the use of cannabis leads to the use of hard drugs." When Pew Research Center asked the same question in 2013, that number dropped to 38 percent.[31] Quinnipiac's respondents in 2018 were even less convinced of the gateway effect, with 31 percent agreeing that cannabis is a "gateway drug" and 61 percent disagreeing, as figure 1-5 shows. Republicans were approximately fifty-fifty on the question, whereas only 18 percent of Democrats believed cannabis is a gateway drug. As figure 1-5 shows, the eighteen-to-thirty-five age group was much less likely to believe in the gateway effect than older age groups.[32]

Data from CBS News present somewhat different opinions on the gateway effect. In 2018, they asked whether people thought the legalization of cannabis would make people more or less likely to use other drugs. About half responded that it would not have much of an effect, 28 percent said it makes them more likely to use other illegal drugs, and 20 percent said it makes them less likely.[33]

FIGURE 1-5. *Do you consider marijuana a so-called "gateway drug" or not? (Quinnipiac)*

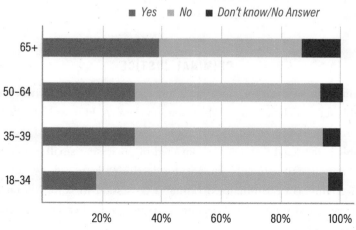

FEDERALISM

Americans generally support a federalist approach to cannabis regulation. When polled about which should regulate cannabis—the individual states or the federal government—a majority of Americans say it should be left to the states. This was the case in 2014, according to a CBS News poll, with 59 percent saying that state governments should decide whether cannabis should be legal or not and 33 percent answering that it should be the federal government.[34] When they asked the same question in 2018, the total response remained basically the same but with an interesting partisan shift: the number of Republicans on the side of state control shrank this time around, going from 70–27 to 64–32.[35] Morning Consult also polled on this issue in 2018 and found majority support for states to decide on legalization: 56 percent supporting the state option with only 26 percent agreeing that the federal government should decide.[36] Their results echo the slightly higher support for federal control among Republicans: 32 percent of them support federal control versus 23 percent of Democrats and Independents. In fact, Republican respondents supported federal regulation of cannabis more than any other subgroup measured in the poll.

Most American voters oppose the government enforcing federal laws in states that have legalized cannabis for medical or recreational purposes, according to polls by Quinnipiac in 2017[37] and 2018.[38] Across most subgroups, 70 percent oppose federal enforcement in states that have legalized. There is a partisan divide on this question, with a thirty-point gap between Democrats and Republicans. Respondents were similarly supportive of legislation to protect states from federal prosecution.

CRIMINAL JUSTICE

In addition to legalization, there are a few criminal justice reforms related to cannabis for which we have public opinion data. A Harvard-Harris poll of registered voters conducted in 2017 found that 72 percent agreed that even if cannabis is not legalized, people convicted of possessing small amounts of it should not serve time in jail—support for decriminalization.[39]

After Illinois decriminalized cannabis possession in 2016, Mason-Dixon polled registered voters about the current policy and other alternatives. They found 47 percent of respondents were in favor of keeping the current policy and 23 percent were in favor of legalizing for recreational use. Only 18 percent were in favor of making all cannabis use illegal.[40] (In 2019, shortly before Illinois governor J. B. Pritzker signed full-scale legalization into law, the *Chicago Sun-Times* reported that when given the choice simply to support or oppose adult-use cannabis, 60 percent statewide supported the policy.[41])

Clean slate legislation, which seals the records of those convicted of nonviolent crimes and who do not commit further crimes, also intersects with cannabis policy. A 2018 Center for American Progress poll in two states where such legislation was being considered—South Carolina and Michigan—found that 70 percent of voters supported such legislation, and 68 percent favored cannabis legalization.[42]

THE REVENUE RATIONALE

Now that public support for legalization has grown and more than eleven states have legalized cannabis, pollsters have begun asking more specific questions about American's attitudes toward cannabis reform. Rather than a complete inventory, these responses provide a look at a few of the issues that intersect cannabis reform, as well as the values or cost-benefit assessments that contribute to Americans' views.

During the fiscal year 2018, Colorado collected over $20 million in taxes, licenses, and fees on cannabis every month. The potential for revenue gains was presented to respondents in the April 2018 Quinnipiac poll as follows: Is revenue a good reason to make cannabis legal for recreational use, or a bad one? Responses diverged along partisan and age group lines. In aggregate, 54 percent replied that it was a good reason and 42 percent that it was a bad one. Two-thirds of Democrats thought it was a good reason; in almost the same proportion, a majority of Republicans thought it was a bad reason. Younger respondents were more open to legalization for revenue benefits: 76 percent of eighteen-to-thirty-four-year-olds said it was a good reason, with that number dropping off in successive age groups, until 62 percent of those aged over sixty-five said that revenue was a bad reason to legalize cannabis for recreational use.[43]

SUPPORT VERSUS SALIENCE

Often, supporters of cannabis reform cannot fathom why politicians have not yet embraced the issue *en masse* and reform has not gotten traction at the national level given that cannabis reform is as popular as it is at the national, state, and local levels. Although there are a variety of factors as to why such policy reform has faced inertia, one important—and somewhat hidden—reason is a lack of salience. This distinction is an important one. Support for an issue is defined as the percentage of the public that believes in a given idea. That issue could be cannabis reform, universal health care, middle class tax cuts, expanded gun rights, or union rights. However, salience is how passionately the public feels about a given issue. A combination of significant public support and significant salience is key to reforming policy.

The challenge for cannabis is that, while it became dramatically more popular over the past two decades, its importance as an issue in the broader public has remained muted. Some polling results offer insight into this lack of salience. A January 2018 poll by NBCNews/*Wall Street Journal* showed that fewer than 10 percent of the public considered cannabis reform to be their number one issue of importance.[44] The same outlets fielded a poll in 2014 asking the public whether they were more or less likely to support a candidate if that candidate supported cannabis legalization. A plurality of the public—40 percent—said that it did not matter.[45] In fact, for decades, Gallup has been asking Americans about the issues most important to them, and cannabis reform has never once been in the top twenty issues.[46]

This generates a simple reality: Americans support cannabis reform, but they really do not care about it.

The 2018 midterm elections may have marked a turning point on this issue, however. For the first time, cannabis was presented not as an albatross around the necks of potential candidates but as an important issue to embrace. Successful gubernatorial candidates in states with existing recreational systems, including California, Colorado, and Nevada, supported cannabis reform. But successful candidates in states without reform in place, including Connecticut, Illinois, Michigan, and Minnesota, also embraced reform.[47]

Some candidates in other races seized on cannabis policy as a means of connecting with voters, even in states where such a position would have been unheard of a few years ago. Beto O'Rourke was the 2018 Democratic nominee for Senate in Texas. He openly embraced national-level cannabis reform in a state that has not embraced even medical cannabis. He ultimately lost by about 2.5 percent; however, in the twenty-two years (and eight Senate elections) prior to that contest, the closest a Democrat came to national office in Texas was an eleven-point loss, in 1996. Candidates for office may not see cannabis as an issue that will propel them to a win, but 2018 may mark a moment in which candidates understood that support for cannabis is no longer the liability it once was.

CONCLUSION

Americans' support for cannabis reform has reached an all-time high. Support is highest for medical cannabis treatment by doctors, but a majority of Americans across age groups, and across all regions, support legalization. They also view cannabis as a safer substance than other drugs; only a minority see it as leading to the use of other, more dangerous drugs. Despite the breadth of that support, and urgent campaigns for reform among interest groups like veterans, the salience of the issue continues to be low—Americans are largely not inclined to base their votes for elected officials on their views regarding cannabis reform and do not rank the issue as a high priority. Polling data show that the status quo of a federalist approach is acceptable to most Americans, but as ballot initiatives are contested in the states, strong support measured at the national level can be a poor indicator of their chances for success. It remains to be seen how Americans' views will evolve as cannabis continues to become more widely available both for medical and recreational purposes.

NOTES

The authors would like to thank Leslie Aguilar for her invaluable research assistance.

1. See Gallup, "Americans' Views on Marijuana Legalization (Trends)," 2018 (https://news.gallup.com/poll/243917/americans-views-marijuana-legalization-trends.aspx); J. P. Caulkins and others, "Marijuana Legalization: Certainty, Impossibility, Both, or Neither?" *Journal of Drug Policy Analysis* 5, no. 1 (2012), pp. 1–27.

2. Caulkins and others (2012); A. L. Nielsen, "Americans' Attitudes toward Drug-Related Issues from 1975–2006: The Roles of Period and Cohort Effects," *Journal of Drug Issues* 40, no. 2 (2010), pp. 461–93; L. Schnabel and E. Sevell, "Should Mary and Jane

Be Legal? Americans' Attitudes toward Marijuana and Same-Sex Marriage Legalization, 1988–2014," *Public Opinion Quarterly* 81, no. 1 (2017), pp. 157–72; H. Toch and K. Maguire, "Public Opinion regarding Crime, Criminal Justice, and Related Topics: A Retrospect," *Journal of Research in Crime and Delinquency* 51, no. 4 (2014), pp. 424–44.

3. Caulkins and others, "Marijuana Legalization, pp. 1–27; Nielsen, "Americans' Attitudes," pp. 461–93.

4. "Study #18033," NBC News/*Wall Street Journal* Survey, January 2018 (www.wsj. com/public/resources/documents/18033NBCWSJJanuaryPoll01192018Complete.pdf).

5. "CBS News Poll: Support for Legal Marijuana Use Remains High," CBS News, April 2018 (www.cbsnews.com/news/support-for-legal-marijuana-use-remains-high-cbs-news-poll/).

6. Caulkins and others, "Marijuana Legalization," pp. 1–27; Nielsen "Americans' Attitudes," pp. 461–93; Toch and Maguire, "Public Opinion."

7. Caulkins and others, "Marijuana Legalization," pp. 1–27; Toch and Maguire "Public Opinion," pp. 424–44.

8. "NALEO Educational Fund State Poll," October 2016 (www.naleo.org.)

9. "IAVA 2017 Annual Member Survey," Iraq and Afghanistan Veterans of America, 2017 (https://iava.org/).

10. For example, we can trace baby boomers' public opinion on cannabis over time by examining that group (individuals born between 1945 and 1964) throughout periods of time. Rather than simply considering how a twenty-five-year-old feels in 1970 and how a twenty-five-year-old feels in 1990, we can consider what a twenty-five-year-old feels in 1970 and how a forty-six-year-old feels in 1990. This shows not just how an age group changes the electorate but how an age cohort—voters born in the same time period—evolves on an issue.

11. Caulkins and others, "Marijuana Legalization," pp. 1–27.

12. John Hudak, *Presidential Pork: White House Influence over the Distribution of Federal Grants* (Washington: Brookings Press, 2014).

13. While the president does represent all Americans, he is elected not by a national plebiscite but by fifty-one individual subnational elections that are aggregated, and presidents and presidential candidates are responsive to the needs and demands of constituencies according to the Electoral College (see Hudak 2014).

14. "CBS News Poll: American Oppose Federal Crackdown in States with Legalized Marijuana, as Support for Legalization Reaches a New High," CBS News, April 2017.

15. "Prescription" is used here, likely as an efficient way to convey physician approval of medical cannabis use. In reality, it is illegal for doctors to prescribe cannabis because it is a Schedule I substance and is not recognized as having medical use. Thus, a DEA-regulated prescription pad cannot be used to authorize an illegal substance. Instead, doctors must write a "recommendation" that notes that cannabis will likely help a patient's condition.

16. "U.S. Voters Believe Comey More Than Trump, Quinnipiac University National Poll Finds; Support for Marijuana Hits New High," April 2018, Quinnipiac University Poll (https://poll.qu.edu/national/release-detail?ReleaseID=2539).

17. "Pain: U.S. Military and Veterans," Bethesda, MD: National Center for Com-

plementary and Integrative Health, September 24, 2017 (https://nccih.nih.gov/health/pain/veterans).

18. Miriam Reisman, "PTSD Treatment for Veterans: What's Working, What's New, and What's Next," *Pharmacy and Therapeutics*, October 2016 (www.ncbi.nlm.nih.gov/pmc/articles/PMC5047000/).

19. Medical Marijuana Research, The American Legion (www.legion.org/mmj research).

20. Julie Howell, "Get With The Times: Veterans Desire Cannabis Research," *Iraq and Afghanistan Veterans of America,* October 18, 2018 (https://iava.org/blogs/get-with-the-times-veterans-desire-cannabis-research/).

21. Resolution No. 627: Research on Medical Cannabis Treatments, Veterans of Foreign Wars of the United States (www.vfw.org).

22. Beth Wiese and Adrienne R. Wilson-Poe, "Emerging Evidence for Cannabis' Role in Opioid Use Disorder," *Cannabis and Cannabinoid Research*, 2018 (www.ncbi.nlm.nih.gov/pmc/articles/PMC6135562/).

23. Dennis Thompson, "Majority in U.S. Support Medical Pot, Think It Could Fight Opioid Crisis," *HealthDay*, July 30, 2018 (https://consumer.healthday.com/public-health-information-30/marijuana-news-759/majority-in-u-s-support-medical-pot-think-it-could-fight-opioid-crisis-736216.html).

24. "U.S. Voters Believe Comey More Than Trump."

25. Barbara A. Gabriel, "Most Older Americans Support Medical Marijuana," *AARP*, April 4, 2018 (www.aarp.org/health/drugs-supplements/info-2018/medical-marijuana-pain-prescription-fd.html).

26. In that same University of Michigan/AARP poll, 80 percent of respondents age fifty to eighty supported medical cannabis use with a doctor's recommendation, and 64 percent favored government funded research into medical cannabis.

27. "American Voters Back Legalized Marijuana, Quinnipiac University National Poll Finds; Voters Split On Gay Marriage, But Catholics Back It," Quinnipiac University Poll, December 2012 (https://poll.qu.edu/national/release-detail?ReleaseID=1820).

28. December 16–17, 2015, YouGov, December 2015 (https://today.yougov.com).

29. "U.S. Voters Believe Comey More Than Trump."

30. "National Poll, January 10–January 13, 2018," Mason Dixon and Smart Approaches to Marijuana (SAM), January 2018 (https://learnaboutsam.org/wp-content/uploads/2018/01/SAMNationalPollResults.pdf).

31. "Majority Now Supports Legalizing Marijuana," Pew Research Center, April 4, 2013 (www.people-press.org/2013/04/04/majority-now-supports-legalizing-marijuana/).

32. "U.S. Voters Believe Comey More Than Trump."

33. "CBS News Poll: Support for Legal Marijuana Use Remains High," CBS News, April 2018 (www.cbsnews.com/news/support-for-legal-marijuana-use-remains-high-cbs-news-poll/).

34. "For the First Time, Most Americans Think Marijuana Use Should be Legal," CBS News Poll, January 2014 (www.cbsnews.com/news/majority-of-americans-now-support-legal-pot-poll-says/).

35. "CBS News Poll: Support for Legal Marijuana Use Remains High."

36. "National Tracking Poll #180724," Morning Consult, July 2018 (https://mor ningconsult.com/wp-content/uploads/2018/07/180724_crosstabs_MARIJUANA_V1_ HS.pdf).

37. "U.S. Voter Support For Marijuana Hits New High; Quinnipiac University Poll Finds; 76 Percent Say Their Finances Are Excellent Or Good," Quinnipiac University Poll, April 2017 (https://poll.qu.edu/national/release-detail?ReleaseID=2453).

38. "U.S. Voters Believe Comey More Than Trump."

39. Monthly Harvard-Harris Poll: July 2017, Harvard CAPS/ Harris Poll, July 2017 (https://harvardharrispoll.com/).

40. National Poll, January 10–January 13, 2018." Mason Dixon and Smart Approaches to Marijuana (SAM), January 2018 (https://learnaboutsam.org).

41. Tina Sfondeles, "Six in 10 Illinoisans want recreational pot treated 'just like alcohol,' poll shows," *Chicago-Sun Times,* May 20, 2019 (https://chicago.suntimes.com /2019/5/20/18632868/illinois-recreational-pot-marijuana-poll).

42. John Halpin and Karl Agne, "Voters Across Party Lines Support Clean Slate Legislation," Center for American Progress, June 20, 2018 (www.americanprogress.org/ issues/criminal-justice/news/2018/06/20/451624/voters-across-party-lines-support-clean-slate-legislation/).

43. "U.S. Voters Believe Comey More Than Trump."

44. "Study #18033," NBC News/*Wall Street Journal* Survey, January 2018 (www.wsj .com/public/resources/documents/18033NBCWSJJanuaryPoll01192018Complete.pdf).

45. Rebecca Ballhaus, "WSJ/NBC Poll: Solid Support for Legal Marijuana," *Wall Street Journal*, January 28, 2014 (https://blogs.wsj.com/washwire/2014/01/28/wsjnbc-poll-broad-support-for-legal-marijuana/).

46. John Hudak, *Marijuana: A Short History* (Washington: Brookings Press, 2016).

47. In Michigan, candidate Gretchen Whitmer embraced cannabis reform in a state with adult-use cannabis legalization in the ballot; she even endorsed the measure, which ultimately passed on the same day she was elected governor.

2

THE EFFECT OF STATE MARIJUANA LEGALIZATIONS

An Update

Angela Dills | Sietse Goffard | Jeffrey Miron

In November 2012, Colorado and Washington approved ballot initiatives that legalized marijuana for recreational use under state law. Two years later, Alaska and Oregon followed suit.[1] Since then, five additional states—California, Nevada, Maine, Vermont, and Massachusetts—along with the District of Columbia have legalized recreational marijuana either by ballot initiative or legislative action. At least two other states, Michigan and North Dakota, voted on legalization in November 2018, with Michigan legalizing medical and recreational use of marijuana and North Dakota medical use.[2]

Supporters and critics make numerous claims about the effects of state-level marijuana legalization. Advocates think legalization reduces crime, raises revenue, lowers criminal justice expenditures, improves public health, improves traffic safety, and stimulates the economy.[3] Critics argue that legalization spurs marijuana and other drug or alcohol use, increases crime, diminishes traffic safety, harms public health, and lowers teen educational achievement.[4] Systematic evaluation of those claims, however, has been limited, particularly for states that have more recently legalized marijuana.[5]

This chapter assesses the effects to date of marijuana legalization and related policies in Colorado, Washington, Oregon, Alaska, California, Nevada, Maine, and Massachusetts; this is an update of an earlier paper on the first four of these states.[6] Each of those legalizations occurred recently, and each rolled out gradually over several years. The data available for before-and-after comparisons are, therefore, limited, so our assessments of legalization's effects are tentative. Yet some post-legalization data are available, and considerable data exist regarding earlier marijuana policy changes—such as legalization for medical purposes—that plausibly have similar effects. Thus, available information provides a useful if incomplete perspective on what other states should expect from legalization or related policies. Going forward, additional data may allow stronger conclusions.

Our analysis compares the pre- and post-policy change paths of marijuana use, other drug or alcohol use, marijuana prices, crime, traffic accidents, teen educational outcomes, public health, tax revenues, criminal justice expenditures, and economic outcomes. These comparisons indicate whether the outcomes display obvious changes in trend around the time of changes in marijuana policy.

Our conclusion is that state-level marijuana legalizations to date have been associated with, at most, modest changes in marijuana use and related outcomes. Our estimates cannot rule out small changes, and related literature finds some effects from earlier marijuana policy changes such as medicalization. But the strong claims about legalization made by both opponents and supporters are not apparent in the data. The absence of significant adverse consequences is especially striking given the sometimes-dire predictions made by legalization opponents.

The following section of this chapter outlines the recent changes in marijuana policy in the states of interest and discusses the timing of those changes. Subsequent sections examine the trends in marijuana use and related outcomes before and after those policy changes. A final section summarizes and discusses implications for upcoming legalization debates.

HISTORY OF STATE-LEVEL MARIJUANA LEGALIZATIONS

Until 1913, marijuana was legal throughout the United States under both state and federal law.[7] Beginning with California in 1913 and Utah in 1914, however, states began outlawing marijuana, and by 1930, thirty states had adopted marijuana prohibition.[8] Those state-level prohibitions stemmed largely from anti-immigrant sentiment and, in particular, from racial prejudice against Mexican migrant workers, who were often associated with the use of the drug. Prohibition advocates attributed terrible crimes to marijuana and the Mexicans who smoked it, creating a stigma around marijuana and its purported "vices."[9] Meanwhile, film productions like *Reefer Madness* (1936) presented marijuana as "Public Enemy Number One" and suggested that its consumption could lead to insanity, death, and even homicidal tendencies.[10]

Starting in 1930, the Federal Bureau of Narcotics pushed states to adopt the Uniform State Narcotic Act and to enact their own measures to control marijuana distribution.[11] Following the model of the National Firearms Act, in 1937 Congress passed the Marijuana Tax Act, which effectively outlawed marijuana under federal law by imposing a prohibitive tax; even stricter federal laws followed thereafter.[12] The 1952 Boggs Act and the 1956 Narcotics Control Act established mandatory sentences for drug-related violations; a first-time offense for marijuana possession carried a minimum sentence of two to ten years in prison and a fine of up to $20,000.[13] Those mandatory sentences were mostly repealed in the early 1970s but reinstated by the Anti-Drug Abuse Act under President Ronald Reagan. The current controlling federal legislation is the Controlled Substances Act, which classifies marijuana as Schedule I. This category is for drugs that, according to the Drug Enforcement Administration, have "no currently accepted medical use and a high potential for abuse" as well as a risk of "potentially severe psychological or physical dependence."[14]

Despite this history of increasing federal action against marijuana (and other drugs), individual states have been backing away from marijuana prohibition since the 1970s. Beginning with Oregon, eleven states decriminalized possession or use of limited amounts of marijuana between 1973 and 1978.[15] [16] A second wave of decriminalization began with Nevada in 2001; nine more states and the District of Columbia have since joined the list.[17] Fully twenty-five states and the District of Columbia have gone further by legalizing marijuana for medical purposes. In some states, these medical regimes approximate de facto legalization.

The most dramatic cases of undoing state prohibitions and departing from federal policy have occurred in the states that have legalized marijuana for recreational as well as medical purposes (Colorado, Washington, Oregon, Alaska, California, Nevada, Maine, and Massachusetts). The subsections below illustrate the typical paths these states took in decriminalizing, medicalizing, and, ultimately, legalizing marijuana.

Decriminalization

In October 1973, Oregon became the first state to decriminalize marijuana upon passage of the Oregon Decriminalization Bill. The bill eliminated criminal penalties for possession of up to an ounce of marijuana and downgraded the offense from a "crime" to a "violation" with a fine of $500 to $1,000.[18] State law continued to outlaw using marijuana in public, growing or selling marijuana, and driving under the influence. In 1997, state lawmakers attempted to recriminalize marijuana and restore jail sentences as punishment for possessing less than one ounce, and Oregon's governor signed the bill. Activists gathered swiftly against the new law, however, and forced a referendum; the attempt to recriminalize failed by a margin of two to one.[19]

Alaska's experience with decriminalization was less straightforward. A 1972 court case sparked the state's shift. Irwin Ravin, an attorney, was pulled over for a broken taillight and found to be in possession of marijuana. Ravin refused to sign the traffic ticket while he was in possession of marijuana so he could challenge the law. Ultimately, the Alaska Supreme Court deemed marijuana possession in the privacy of one's home to be constitutionally protected, and *Ravin v. State* established legal precedent in Alaska for years to come.[20]

Alaska's legislature officially decriminalized marijuana in 1975. Persons possessing less than one ounce in public—or any amount in one's own home—could be fined no more than $100; that fine was eliminated in 1982. However, unlike in Oregon, Alaska's new drug regime would be short-lived. Marijuana opponents mobilized later in the 1980s as law enforcement busted several large, illegal cultivation sites hidden in residences. A voter initiative in November 1990 proposed banning the possession and use of marijuana even in one's own home, punishable by ninety days of jail time and a $1,000 fine. The initiative passed with 54 percent support.[21]

Medicalization

By the mid-1990s, mounting scientific evidence pointed to marijuana's potential medicinal benefits. Around this time, various states legalized medical marijuana but restricted access to only patients who satisfied strict criteria. Over the past two decades, however, the number of eligible patients has grown significantly. Restrictions on medical marijuana have become somewhat laxer, and access to it has become much more expansive. In states without full legalization, medical dispensaries have helped certain users bypass state restrictions and procure marijuana for personal use.

Washington legalized medical marijuana in 1998 after a court case involving a terminal cancer patient being treated with marijuana brought extra attention to the issue and set the stage for a citizen-driven ballot initiative. In November 1998, state voters approved Initiative 692, known as the Washington State Medical Use of Marijuana Act, with 59 percent in favor. Use, possession, sale, and cultivation of marijuana became legal under state law for patients with certain medical conditions that had been verified by a licensed medical professional. Initiative 692 also imposed dosage limits on the drug's use. By 2009, an estimated 35,500 Washingtonians had prescriptions to buy medical marijuana legally.

Oregon also medicalized marijuana by ballot initiative in November 1998, with 55 percent support. The Oregon Medical Marijuana Act legalized cultivation, possession, and use of marijuana by prescription for patients with specific medical conditions.[22] A new organization was set up to register patients and caregivers. In 2004, voters turned down a ballot proposal to increase to six pounds the amount of marijuana a patient could legally possess. Six years later, voters also rejected an effort to permit medical marijuana dispensaries, but the state legislature legalized them in 2013.[23] As of July 2016, Oregon's medical marijuana program counted nearly 67,000 registered patients, the vast majority claiming to suffer severe pain, persistent muscle spasms, and nausea.[24]

In November 2000, Colorado legalized medical marijuana through a statewide ballot initiative. The proposal, known as Amendment 20, or the Medical Use of Marijuana Act, passed with 54 percent voter support. It authorized patients and their primary caregivers to possess up to two ounces of marijuana and up to six marijuana plants. Patients also needed a state-issued Medical Marijuana Registry Identification Card with a doctor's recommendation. State regulations limited caregivers to prescribing medical marijuana to no more than five patients each.

The number of licensed medical marijuana patients initially grew at a modest rate. Then, in 2009, after Colorado's Board of Health abandoned the caregiver-to-patient ratio rule, the medical marijuana industry took off.[25] That same year, in the so-called "Ogden Memo,"[26] the U.S. Department of Justice signaled it would shift resources away from state medical marijuana issues and refrain from targeting patients and caregivers.[27] Thus, although medical marijuana remained prohibited under federal law, the federal government would tend not to intervene in states where it was legal. Within months, medical marijuana dispensaries proliferated. Licensed patients rose from 4,800 in 2008 to 41,000 in 2009. More than 900 dispensaries were operating by the end of 2009, according to law enforcement.[28]

Legalization and Regulation

Although recreational legalization is a relatively recent development, efforts to legalize marijuana have been ongoing for the past decade and a half. In many states, marijuana advocates made multiple failed attempts at legalization before finally earning victory at the voting booths. Nearly every state that has legalized marijuana thus far has done so through citizen-driven ballot initiatives. After formally legalizing marijuana, states normally take one to two years to set up regulatory regimes, establish licensing guidelines, and impose marijuana taxes; only then can the first marijuana shops open.

Colorado provides a good example. In fall 2006, Colorado voters considered Amendment 44, a statewide ballot initiative to legalize the recreational possession of up to one ounce of marijuana by individuals age twenty-one or older. Amendment 44 failed, with 58 percent of voters opposed. In November 2012, however, Colorado voters passed Amendment 64 with 55 percent support, becoming one of the first two states to re-legalize recreational marijuana. The ballot initiative authorized individuals age twenty-one and older with valid government identification to grow up to six plants and to purchase, possess, and use up to one ounce of marijuana.[29] Colorado residents could now buy up to one ounce of marijuana in a single transaction, whereas out-of-state residents could purchase 0.25 ounces.[30]

In light of Amendment 64, Colorado's government passed new regulations and taxes to prepare for legalized recreational marijuana use. A ballot referendum dubbed Proposition AA that was passed in November 2013 imposed a 15 percent tax on sales of recreational marijuana from cultivators to retailers and a 10 percent tax on retail sales (in addition to the existing 2.9 percent state sales tax on all goods). Local governments in Colorado were permitted to impose additional taxes on retail marijuana.[31] Following about a year of planning, Colorado's first retail marijuana businesses opened on January 1, 2014. Each business was required to pay licensing fees of several hundred dollars and to adhere to other requirements.

In November 2012, Washington joined Colorado in legalizing recreational marijuana. Voters passed ballot Initiative 502 with 56 percent in support amid an 81 percent voter turnout at the polls. The proposal removed most state prohibitions on marijuana manufacture and commerce, permitted limited marijuana use for adults age twenty-one and over, and established the need for a licensing and regulatory framework to govern the state's marijuana industry. Initiative 502 further imposed a 25 percent excise tax levied three times (on marijuana producers, processors, and retailers) and earmarked the revenue for research, education, healthcare, and substance abuse prevention, among other purposes.[32]

Legal possession of marijuana took effect on December 6, 2012. A year and a half later, Washington's licensing board began accepting applications for recreational marijuana shops. After some backlog, the first four retail stores opened on July 8, 2014. As of June 2016, several hundred retail stores were open across the state.

In Alaska, advocates tried to legalize marijuana three separate times over fourteen years. A ballot initiative in 2000 proposed legalizing use for anyone eighteen years and older and regulating the drug "like an alcoholic beverage." The initiative failed, with 59 percent of voters opposed. Voters considered a similar ballot measure in 2004 but again rejected it. A third ballot initiative on recreational marijuana legalization passed in November 2014, with 53 percent of voters in support. It permitted adults age twenty-one and over to possess, use, and grow marijuana. It also legalized manufacture and sale. The law further created a Marijuana Control Board to regulate the industry and establish excise taxes.

In Oregon, recreational marijuana suffered several defeats before eventual approval. In 1986, the Oregon Marijuana Legalization for Personal Use initiative failed, with 74 percent of voters opposed.[33] In November 2012, a similar measure also failed, even as neighboring Washington passed its own legalization initiative. Oregon Ballot Measure 80 would have allowed personal marijuana cultivation and use without a license, plus unlimited possession for those over age twenty-one. To oversee the new market, the measure would have established an industry-dominated board to regulate the sale of commercial marijuana. This proposal failed, with more than 53 percent of the electorate voting against it.[34]

Full legalization in Oregon finally passed on November 4, 2014, when voters approved Measure 91, officially known as the Oregon Legalized Marijuana Initiative. This measure legalized recreational marijuana for individuals over age twenty-one and permitted possession of up to eight ounces of dried marijuana, along with four plants, with the Oregon Liquor Control Commission regulating sales of the drug. More than 56 percent of voters cast ballots in favor of the initiative, making Oregon the third state in the nation (along with Alaska) to legalize recreational marijuana.[35]

Oregon's legislature then adopted several laws to regulate the marijuana industry. Legislators passed a 17 percent state sales tax on marijuana retail sales and empowered local jurisdictions to charge their own additional 3 percent sales tax.[36] Later, the state legislature gave individual counties the option to ban marijuana sales if at least 55 percent of voters in those counties opposed Measure 91.[37] Legal sales went into effect on October 1, 2015. As of June 2016, Oregon had 426 locations where consumers could legally purchase recreational marijuana.[38]

KEY DATES

To determine the effect of marijuana legalization and similar policies on marijuana use and related outcomes, we examine the trends in use and outcomes before and after key policy changes. We focus mostly on recreational marijuana legalizations, because earlier work has covered other modifications of marijuana policy, such as medicalization.[39] The specific dates we consider, derived from the discussion above, are as follows:

Colorado
- 2001, after legalization of medical marijuana
- 2009, after liberalization of the medical marijuana law

- 2012, after legalization of recreational marijuana
- 2014, after the first retail stores opened under state-level legalization

Washington
- 1998, after legalization of medical marijuana
- 2012, after legalization of recreational marijuana
- 2014, after the first retail stores opened under state-level legalization

Oregon
- 1998, after legalization of medical marijuana
- 2013, after the state legislature legalized medical marijuana dispensaries
- 2014, after legalization of recreational marijuana
- 2015, after the first retail stores opened under state-level legalization

Alaska
- 1990, after voters recriminalized marijuana
- 1998, after legalization of medical marijuana
- 2014, after legalization of recreational marijuana

California
- 1996, after legalization of medical marijuana
- 2016, after legalization of recreational marijuana

Nevada
- 2000, after legalization of medical marijuana
- 2016, after legalization of recreational marijuana

Maine
- 1999, after legalization of medical marijuana
- 2016, after legalization of recreational marijuana

Massachusetts
- 2008, after decriminalization of marijuana
- 2012, after legalization of medical marijuana
- 2016, after legalization of recreational marijuana

Our analysis examines whether the trends in marijuana use and related out-comes changed substantially after these dates. Observed changes do not necessarily implicate marijuana policy, because other factors might have changed as well. Similarly, the absence of changes does not prove that policy changes had no effect; the abundance of potentially confounding variables makes it possible that, by coincidence, a policy change was approximately offset by some other factor operating in the opposite direction. Thus, our analysis focuses on the factual outcomes of marijuana legalization, rather than on causal inferences. (The figures that are referenced in the sections that follow are all gathered as an appendix to this chapter.)

DRUG USE

Arguably, the most important potential effect of marijuana legalization is on marijuana use or other drug or alcohol use. Opinions differ on whether increased use is problematic or desirable, but because other outcomes depend on use, a key step is to determine how much policy affects use. If such effects are small, then other effects of legalization are also likely to be small.

Figure 2-1 shows past-year use rates in Colorado for marijuana and cocaine, along with past-month use rates for alcohol.[40] The key fact is that marijuana use rates increased modestly for several years before 2009, when medical marijuana became readily available in dispensaries, and continued this upward trend through legalization in 2012. Post-legalization use rates deviate from this overall trend, but only to a minor degree. The data do not show dramatic changes in use rates corresponding either to the expansion of medical marijuana or legalization. Similarly, cocaine exhibits a mild downward trend over the time period but shows no obvious change after marijuana policy changes. Alcohol use shows a pattern similar to marijuana: a gradual upward trend but no obvious evidence of a response to marijuana policy.

Figure 2-2 graphs the same variables in Washington. As in Colorado, marijuana, cocaine, and alcohol use proceed along preexisting trends after changes in marijuana policy.

Figures 2-3 through 2-8 present analogous data for Oregon, Alaska, California, Nevada, Maine, and Massachusetts, respectively. As in other legalizing states, past-year marijuana use has been rising since the mid-2000s, and policy changes do not appear to have significantly influenced that trend, although in some states we have limited observations of drug use post-legalization.

Figure 2-9 presents data on current (past month) marijuana use by youth from the Youth Risk Behavior Survey, a survey of health behaviors conducted in middle schools and high schools. Data are unavailable for Washington and Oregon. The available data for remaining states show no obvious effect of legalization on youth marijuana use. All those observed patterns in marijuana use might provide evidence for a cultural explanation behind legalization: as marijuana becomes more commonplace and less stigmatized, residents and legislators become less opposed to legalization. In essence, rising marijuana use may not be a consequence of legalization, but a cause of it.

Consistent with this possibility, figure 2-10 plots, for all legalizing states, data on perceptions of "great risk" from smoking marijuana monthly.[41] All states exhibit a steady downward trend, indicating that fewer people associate monthly marijuana use with high risk. These downward trends predate legalization, consistent with the view that changing attitudes toward marijuana fostered both policy changes and increasing use rates. Interestingly, risk perceptions rose in Colorado in 2012–2013, immediately following legalization; the same is true for both California and Massachusetts in 2015–2016. This rise may have resulted from public safety and anti-legalization campaigns that cautioned residents about the dangers of marijuana use.

Data on marijuana prices may also shed light on marijuana use. One hypothesis before legalization was that use might soar because prices would plunge. For example, Dale Gieringer, director of California's NORML (National Organization for Reform of Marijuana Laws) branch, testified in 2009 that in a "totally unregulated market, the price of marijuana would presumably drop as low as that of other legal herbs such as tea or tobacco—on the order of a few dollars per ounce—100 times lower than the current prevailing price of $300 per ounce."[42] A separate study by the Rand Corporation estimated that marijuana prices in California would fall by 80 percent after legalization.[43, 44] Using data from Price of Weed (priceofweed.com), which crowd-sources real-time information from thousands of marijuana buyers in each state, we derive monthly average prices of marijuana in Colorado, Washington, and Oregon.[45] See figures 2-11, 2-12, and 2-13.

In Colorado, monthly average prices were declining even before legalization and have remained fairly steady since. The cost of high-quality marijuana hovers around $230 per ounce, while that of medium-quality marijuana remains around $190. The opening of shops in January 2015 seems to have had little effect. In Washington, marijuana prices have been similarly steady and have converged almost exactly to Colorado prices—roughly $230 for high-quality marijuana and $200 for medium-quality marijuana. Oregon prices show a rise after legalization, catching up to Colorado and Washington levels. Although we cannot draw a conclusive picture on the basis of consumer-reported data, the convergence of prices across states makes sense. This convergence is also consistent with the idea that legalization helped divert marijuana commerce from the black market to legalized retail shops.[46] Overall, these data suggest no major drop in marijuana prices after legalization and, consequently, less likelihood of soaring use because of cheaper marijuana.

HEALTH AND SUICIDES

Previous studies have suggested a link between medicalization of marijuana and a lower overall suicide rate, particularly among demographics most likely to use marijuana in general (males age twenty to thirty-nine).[47] In fact, supporters believe marijuana can be an effective treatment for bipolar disorder, depression, and other mood disorders—not to mention a safer alternative to alcohol. Moreover, the pain-relieving element of medical marijuana may help patients avoid more harmful prescription painkillers and tranquilizers.[48] Conversely, certain studies suggest excessive marijuana use may increase the risk of depression, schizophrenia, unhealthy drug abuse, and anxiety.[49] Some research also warns about long-lasting cognitive damage if marijuana is consumed regularly, especially at a young age.[50]

Figure 2-14 displays the overall yearly suicide rate per 100,000 people in each of the legalizing states between 1999 and 2016.[51,52] Suicide rates in all states trend slightly upward during the seventeen-year-long period, but it is difficult to see any association between marijuana legalization and any changes in these trends. Previous research has suggested a link between medical marijuana and a lower suicide rate; it is not obvious that recreational marijuana would necessarily lead to the same result or that legalization of recreational marijuana after medical marijuana is already legalized would have much of an extra effect.[53]

Data on treatment center admissions provide a proxy for drug abuse and other health hazards associated with misuse. Figures 2-15 and 2-16 plot rates of annual admissions involving marijuana and alcohol to publicly funded treatment centers in Colorado and King County, Washington (which encompasses Seattle).[54, 55] Marijuana admissions in Colorado were fairly steady over the past decade but began falling in 2013 and 2014, just as legalization took effect. Alcohol admissions began declining around the same time. In King County, admissions for marijuana and alcohol continued their downward trends after legalization. These patterns suggest that extreme growth in marijuana abuse has not materialized, as some critics had warned before legalization.

CRIME

In addition to substance use and health outcomes, legalization might affect crime. Opponents think these substances cause crime through psychopharmacological and other mechanisms, and they note that such substances have long been associated with crime, social deviancy, and other undesirable aspects of society.[56] Although those perspectives first emerged in the 1920s and 1930s, marijuana's perceived associations with crime and deviancy persist today.[57] Before referendums in 2012, police chiefs, governors, policymakers, and concerned citizens spoke up against marijuana and its purported links to crime.[58] They also argued that expanding drug commerce could increase marijuana commerce in violent underground markets and that legalization would make it easy to smuggle the substance across borders to locations where it remained prohibited, thus causing negative spillover effects.[59]

Proponents argue that legalization reduces crime by diverting marijuana production and sale from the black market to legal venues. This shift may be incomplete if high tax rates or significant regulation keeps some marijuana activity in gray or black markets, but this merely underscores that more legalization means less crime. At the same time, legalization may reduce the burden on law enforcement to patrol for drug offenses, thereby freeing budgets and staff to address larger crimes. Legalization supporters also dispute the claim that marijuana increases neurological tendencies toward violence or aggression.[60]

Figure 2-17 presents monthly crime rates from Denver, Colorado, for all reported violent crimes and property crimes.[61] Both metrics remain essentially constant after 2012 and 2014; we do not observe substantial deviations from the illustrated cyclical crime pattern. Other cities in Colorado mirror those findings. Analogous monthly crime data for Fort Collins, for example, reveal no increase in violent or property crime.[62] Figure 2-18 shows monthly violent and property crime rates as reported by the Seattle Police Department.[63] Both categories of crime have declined steadily over the past twenty years, with no major deviations after marijuana liberalization. Property crime does appear to spike in 2013 and early 2014, and some commentators have posited that legalization drove this increase.[64] That connection is not convincing, however, since property crime starts to fall again after the opening of marijuana shops in mid-2014. All told, crime in Seattle has neither soared nor plummeted in the wake of legalization.[65]

Monthly violent and property crime remained steady after legalization in Portland, Oregon, as seen in figure 2-19.[66] Portland provides an interesting case because of its border with Washington. Between 2012 and 2014, Portland (and the rest of Oregon) prohibited the recreational use of marijuana, while marijuana sales and consumption were fully legal in neighboring Washingtonian towns just to the north. This situation creates a natural experiment that allows us to look for spillover effects in Oregon. Figure 2-19 suggests that legalization in Washington and the opening of stores there did not produce rising crime rates across the border. Elsewhere in Oregon, we see no discernible changes in crime trends before and after legalization or medical marijuana liberalization.[67]

ROAD SAFETY

We next evaluate how the incidence of traffic accidents may have changed in response to marijuana policy changes. Previous literature and political rhetoric suggest two contrasting hypotheses. One holds that legalization increases traffic accidents by spurring drug use and, thereby, incidents of driving under the influence. This hypothesis presumes that marijuana impairs driving ability.[68] The opposing theory argues that legalization improves traffic safety because marijuana substitutes for alcohol, which some studies say impairs driving ability even more.[69] Moreover, some consumers may be able to drive better if marijuana serves to relieve their pain.

Rhetoric from experts and government officials has been equally divided. Kevin Sabet, a former senior White House drug policy adviser, warned that potential consequences of Colorado's legalization could include large increases in traffic accidents.[70] A recent Associated Press article noted that "fatal crashes involving marijuana doubled in Washington after legalization."[71] Yet Coloradan law enforcement agents are themselves unsure whether legal marijuana has led to an increase in accidents.[72] Research by Radley Balko, an opinion blogger for the *Washington Post* and an author on drug policy, claims that, overall, "highway fatalities in Colorado are at near-historic lows" in the wake of legalization.[73]

Figure 2-20 presents the monthly rate of fatal accidents and fatalities per 100,000 residents in Colorado.[74] No spike in fatal traffic accidents or fatalities followed the liberalization of medical marijuana in 2009.[75] Although fatality rates have reached slightly higher peaks in recent summers, no obvious jump occurs after either legalization in 2012 or the opening of stores in 2014.[76] Likewise, neither marijuana milestone in Washington appears to have substantially affected the fatal crash or fatality rate, as illustrated in figure 2-21.[77] In fact, more granular statistics reveal that the fatality rate for drug-related crashes was virtually unchanged after legalization.[78]

Figure 2-22 depicts the crash fatality rate in Oregon.[79] Although few post-legalization data were available at the time of publication, we observe no signs of deviations in trend after the opening of medical marijuana dispensaries in 2013. We can also test for possible spillover effects from neighboring Washington. Legalization there in 2012 and the opening of marijuana shops in 2014 do not seem to materially affect road fatalities in Oregon in either direction. Figures 2-23 through 2-26 present annual data on crash fatality rates in Alaska, Nevada, Maine, and Massachusetts; these show no discernible increase after legalization.[80]

YOUTH OUTCOMES

Much of the concern surrounding marijuana legalization relates to its possible effect on youths. Many observers, for example, fear that expanded legal access—even if officially limited to adults age twenty-one and over—might increase use by teenagers, with negative effects on intelligence, educational outcomes, or other youth behaviors.[81, 82]

Figure 2-27 displays the total number of school suspensions and drug-related suspensions in Colorado public high schools during each academic year.[83] Total suspensions trend downward over time, with a slight bump after 2014, but that bump was not one driven by drug-related causes. Drug-related suspensions appear to rise after medical marijuana commercialization in 2009 but drop after full legalization and the opening of retail shops. Figure 2-28 shows public high school expulsions, both overall and drug-related. It reveals a parallel bump in drug-related expulsions right after marijuana liberalization in 2009, but expulsions drop steeply thereafter. In fact, by 2014, expulsions drop back to their previous levels. Figures 2-29 and 2-30 show analogous numbers from California; these data clearly reveal that the downward trend of suspensions and expulsions remains unchanged in the wake of marijuana legalization. Data from Massachusetts paint a similar picture; see figure 2-31.

We also consider potential effects on academic performance. Standardized test scores measuring the reading proficiency of 8th and 10th graders in Washington show no indication of significant positive or negative changes caused by legalization, as illustrated in figure 2-32.[84] Although some studies have found that frequent marijuana use impedes teen cognitive development, our results do not suggest a major change in use, thereby implying no major changes in testing performance.

ECONOMIC OUTCOMES

Changing economic and demographic outcomes are unlikely to be significant effects of marijuana legalization, simply because marijuana is a small part of the overall economy. Nevertheless, we consider this outcome for completeness. Before legalization, many advocates thought legalization could drive a robust influx of residents, particularly young individuals enticed to move across state lines to take advantage of loose marijuana laws. More recently, various news articles say housing prices in Colorado (particularly around Denver) are soaring at growth rates far above the national average, perhaps as a consequence of marijuana legalization. One analyst went so far as to say that marijuana has essentially "kick-started the recovery of the industrial market in Denver" and led to record-high rent levels.[85]

Figure 2-33 sheds doubt on these extreme claims by presenting the Case-Shiller Home Price Index for Denver, Seattle, and Portland, along with the national average.[86] Data show that home prices in all three cities have been rising steadily since mid-2011, with no apparent booms after marijuana policy changes. Housing prices in Denver did rise at a robust rate after January 2014, when marijuana shops opened, but this increase was in step with the national average. Furthermore, marijuana legalization in all legalizing states had, at most, a trivial effect on population growth.[87] Whereas some people may have moved across states for marijuana purposes, any resulting growth in population has been small and unlikely to cause noticeable increases in housing prices or total economic output.

Advocates also argue that legalization boosts economic activity by creating jobs in the marijuana sector, including "marijuana tourism" and other support industries, thereby boosting economic output.[88] Marijuana production and commerce do employ many thousands of people, and Colorado data provide some hint of a measurable effect on employment. As figure 2-34 indicates, the seasonally adjusted unemployment rate began to fall more dramatically after the start of 2014, which coincides with the opening of marijuana stores.[89] One hypothesis may be that Colorado, as the first state to open retail shops, benefitted from a "first mover advantage." If more states legalize, any employment gains will become spread out more broadly, and marijuana tourism may diminish. The impact of legalization, however, was still small relative to the entire state economy.

Data from the Bureau of Economic Analysis show little evidence of significant gross domestic product (GDP) increases after legalization in any state.[90] Although it is hard to disentangle marijuana-related economic activity from broader economic trends, the surges in economic output predicted by some proponents have not yet materialized. Similarly, no clear changes have occurred in GDP per capita.

One area where legal marijuana has reaped unexpectedly large benefits is state tax revenue. Colorado, Washington, and Oregon all impose significant excise taxes on recreational marijuana, along with standard state sales taxes, other local taxes, and licensing fees. As seen in figure 2-35, Colorado now collects over $20 million per month from recreational marijuana alone.[91] In 2015, the state generated a total of $135 million in recreational marijuana revenue, $35 million of which was earmarked for school construction projects. These figures are above some pre-legalization forecasts, although revenue growth was disappointingly sluggish during the first few months of sales.[92] A similar story has unfolded in Washington, as illustrated in figure 2-36, where recreational marijuana generated approximately $70 million in tax revenue in the first year of sales[93]—double the original revenue forecast.[94] Oregon, which began taxing recreational marijuana only in January 2016, has reported revenues of $10 million per month, far above the initial estimate of $2.0 million to $3.0 million for the entire calendar year.[95] Figure 2-37 documents Oregon's marijuana tax revenues. The tax revenues in these states may moderate as legalizations continue.

CONCLUSION

Limited post-legalization data prevent us from ruling out small changes in marijuana use or other outcomes. As additional post-legalization data become available, expanding this analysis will continue to inform the debate. The data so far, however, provide little support for the strong claims about legalization made by either opponents or supporters. The absence of significant adverse consequences is especially striking given the sometimes dire predictions made by legalization opponents.

FIGURE 2-1. *Substance Use Rates in Colorado*
(NSDUH, Respondents Ages 12+ Years)

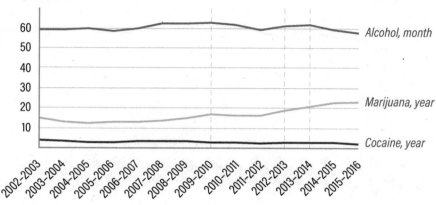

Percent of population
using substance

Source: National Survey on Drug Use and Health, Substance Abuse and Mental Health Services Administration (SAMHSA) (www.samhsa.gov/data/nsduh/state-reports-NSDUH-2016) and Interactive NSDUH State Estimates (https://pdas.samhsa.gov/saes/state).

FIGURE 2-2. *Substance Use Rates in Washington*
(NSDUH, Respondents Ages 12+ Years)

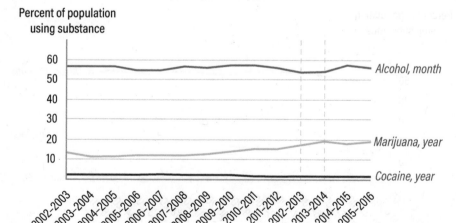

Percent of population
using substance

Source: National Survey on Drug Use and Health, Substance Abuse and Mental Health Services Administration (SAMHSA) (www.samhsa.gov/data/nsduh/state-reports-NSDUH-2016) and Interactive NSDUH State Estimates (https://pdas.samhsa.gov/saes/state).

FIGURE 2-3. *Substance Use Rates in Oregon*
(NSDUH, Respondents Ages 12+ Years)

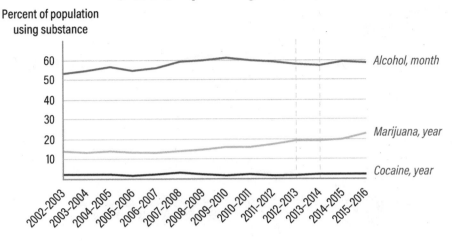

Source: National Survey on Drug Use and Health, Substance Abuse and Mental Health Services Administration (SAMHSA) (www.samhsa.gov/data/nsduh/state-reports-NSDUH-2016) and Interactive NSDUH State Estimates (https://pdas.samhsa.gov/saes/state).

FIGURE 2-4. *Substance Use Rates in Alaska*
(NSDUH, Respondents Ages 12+ Years)

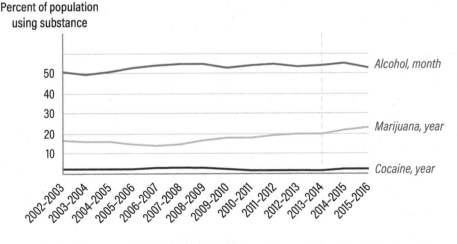

Source: National Survey on Drug Use and Health, Substance Abuse and Mental Health Services Administration (SAMHSA) (www.samhsa.gov/data/nsduh/state-reports-NSDUH-2016) and Interactive NSDUH State Estimates (https://pdas.samhsa.gov/saes/state).

FIGURE 2-5. *Substance Use Rates in California*
(NSDUH, Respondents Ages 12+ Years)

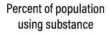

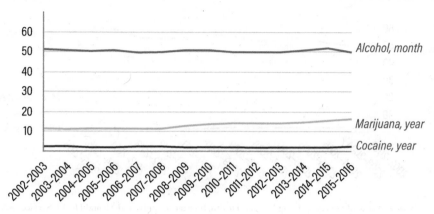

Source: National Survey on Drug Use and Health, Substance Abuse and Mental Health Services Administration (SAMHSA) (www.samhsa.gov/data/nsduh/state-reports-NSDUH-2016) and Interactive NSDUH State Estimates (https://pdas.samhsa.gov/saes/state).

FIGURE 2-6. *Substance Use Rates in Nevada*
(NSDUH, Respondents Ages 12+ Years)

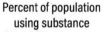

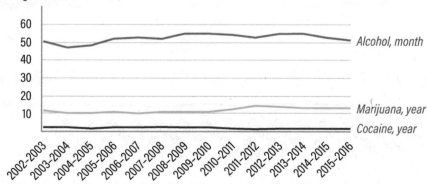

Source: National Survey on Drug Use and Health, Substance Abuse and Mental Health Services Administration (SAMHSA) (www.samhsa.gov/data/nsduh/state-reports-NSDUH-2016) and Interactive NSDUH State Estimates (https://pdas.samhsa.gov/saes/state).

FIGURE 2-7. *Substance Use Rates in Maine*
(NSDUH, Respondents Ages 12+ Years)

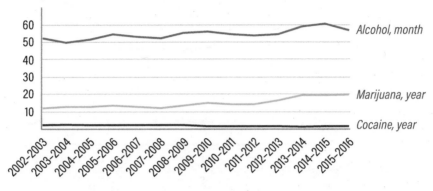

Source: National Survey on Drug Use and Health, Substance Abuse and Mental Health Services Administration (SAMHSA) (www.samhsa.gov/data/nsduh/state-reports-NSDUH-2016) and Interactive NSDUH State Estimates (https://pdas.samhsa.gov/saes/state).

FIGURE 2-8. *Substance Use Rates in Massachusetts*
(NSDUH, Respondents Ages 12+ Years)

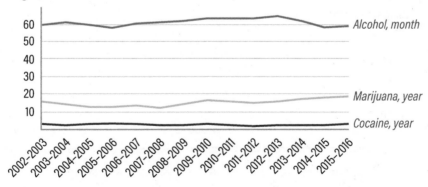

Source: National Survey on Drug Use and Health, Substance Abuse and Mental Health Services Administration (SAMHSA) (www.samhsa.gov/data/nsduh/state-reports-NSDUH-2016) and Interactive NSDUH State Estimates (https://pdas.samhsa.gov/saes/state).

FIGURE 2-9. *Current Use Rates of Marijuana among Youths (YRBS)*

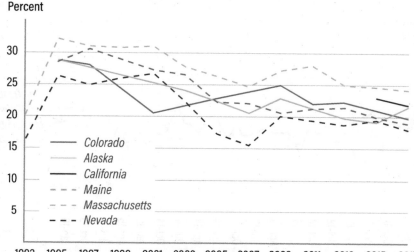

Percent

Source: Youth Risk Behavior Survey, Centers for Disease Control and Prevention: www.cdc.gov/
healthyyouth/data/yrbs/data.htm, https://nccd.cdc.gov/youthonline/app/Results.aspx?LID=CO, and
www.cdc.gov/healthyyouth/data/yrbs/results.htm.

FIGURE 2-10. *Perception of Great Risk in Regular Marijuana Use (NSDUH)*

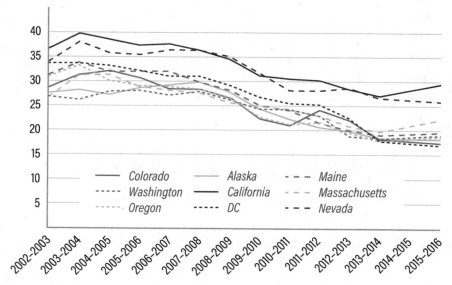

Percent of respondents
perceiving great risk

Source: National Survey on Drug Use and Health, Substance Abuse and Mental Health Services Administration (SAMHSA) (www.samhsa.gov/data/data-we-collect/nsduh-national-survey-drug-use-
and-health).

FIGURE 2-11. *Monthly Average Price of Marijuana in Colorado*

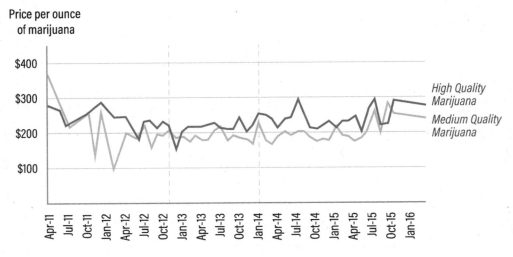

Source: Priceofweed.com (www.priceofweed.com/prices/United-States/Colorado.html).

FIGURE 2-12. *Monthly Average Price of Marijuana in Washington*

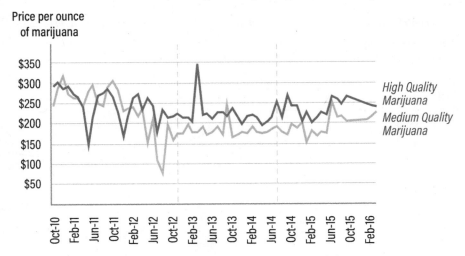

Source: Priceofweed.com (www.priceofweed.com/prices/United-States/Washington.html).

FIGURE 2-13. *Monthly Average Price of Marijuana in Oregon*

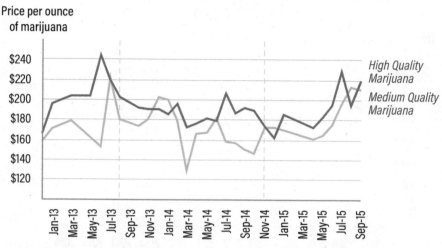

Source: Priceofweed.com (www.priceofweed.com/prices/United-States/Oregon.html).

FIGURE 2-14. *Yearly Suicide Rates per 100,000 People*
(CDC, Overall Population)

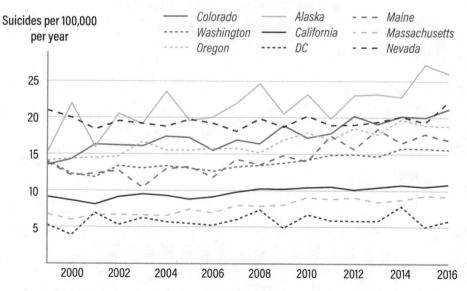

Source: CDC Wonder Portal, Centers for Disease Control and Prevention (http://wonder.cdc.gov/).

FIGURE 2-15. *Marijuana and Alcohol Treatment*
Center Admissions in Colorado

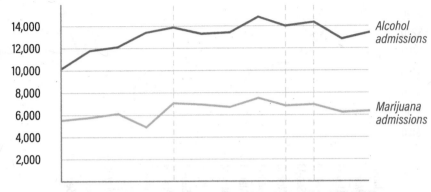

Treatment Admissions

Source: Rocky Mountain High Intensity Drug Trafficking Area (RMHIDTA) report, "The Legalization of Marijuana in Colorado: The Impact," vol. 3, September 2015 (www.rmhidta.org/html/2015%20 final%20legalization%20of%20marijuana%20in%20colorado%20the%20impact.pdf).

FIGURE 2-16. *Marijuana and Alcohol Treatment*
Center Admissions in King County, WA

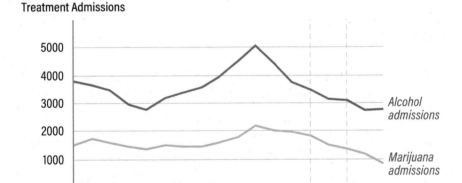

Treatment Admissions

Source: University of Washington Alcohol and Drug Abuse Institute (http://adai.washington.edu/ pubs/cewg/Drug%20Trends_2014_final.pdf).

FIGURE 2-17. *Monthly Crime Rate in Denver, CO*
(Denver County Police Department)

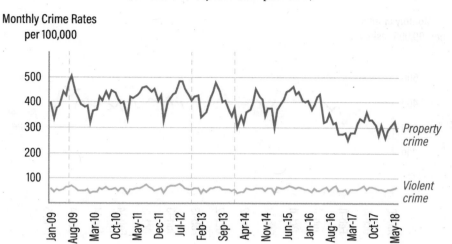

Source: Denver Police Department, Monthly Crime Reports (www.denvergov.org/content/denvergov/
en/police-department/crime-information/crime-statistics-maps.html); Population data source: US
Census Bureau Estimates (www.census.gov/popest/data/intercensal/index.html).

FIGURE 2-18. *Monthly Crime Rate in Seattle,*
WA (Seattle Police Department)

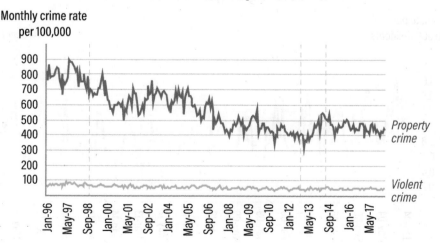

Source: Seattle Police Department, Online Crime Dashboard (www.seattle.gov/seattle-police-depart-
ment/crime-data/crime-dashboard); Population data source: US Census Bureau Estimates (www.
census.gov/popest/data/intercensal/index.html).

FIGURE 2-19. *Monthly Crime Rate in Portland,*
OR (Portland Police Department)

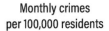

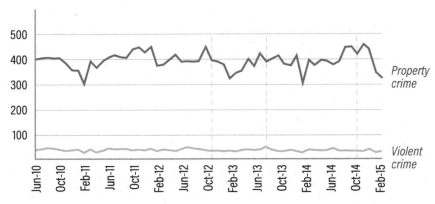

Source: Portland Police Bureau Neighborhood Statistics (www.portlandonline.com/police/crimes-tats/); Population data source: US Census Bureau Estimates (www.census.gov/popest/data/intercen-sal/index.html).

FIGURE 2-20. *Fatal Car Accidents and Fatalities per 100,000 Residents*
in Colorado (Colorado Department of Transportation)

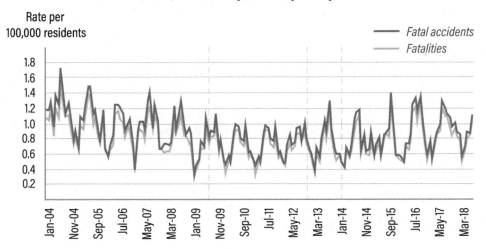

Source: Colorado Department of Transportation (www.coloradodot.info/library/traffic/traffic-manu-als-guidelines/safety-crash-data/fatal-crash-data-city-county/fatal-crashes-by-city-and-county/).

FIGURE 2-21. *Fatal Car Accidents and Fatalities per 100,000 Residents in Washington (Washington Traffic Safety Commission)*

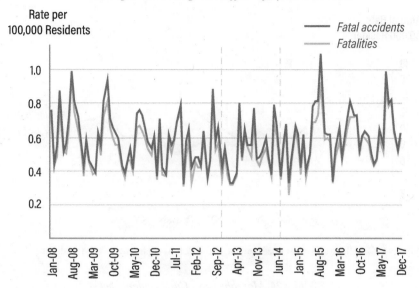

Source: Washington Traffic Safety Commission, Quarterly Target Zero Reports (http://wtsc.wa.gov/research-data/quarterly-target-zero-data/).

FIGURE 2-22. *Car Accident Fatalities per 100,000 Residents in Oregon (Oregon Department of Transportation)*

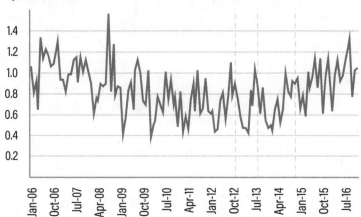

Source: Oregon Department of Transportation, online Crash Summary reports and in-person data request (www.oregon.gov/ODOT/TD/TDATA/pages/car/car_publications.aspx). Special thanks to Theresa Heyn and Coleen O'Hogan.

FIGURE 2-23. *Annual Fatal Car Accidents and Fatalities per 100,000 Residents in Alaska (Alaska Department of Transportation)*

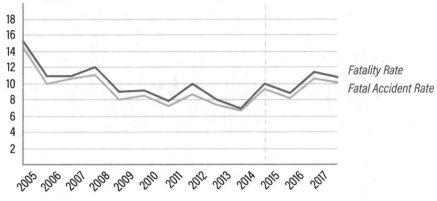

Source: Alaska Highway Safety Office (www.dot.state.ak.us/stwdplng/hwysafety/fars.shtml).

FIGURE 2-24. *Monthly Fatal Car Accidents per 100,000 Residents in Nevada (NHTSA)*

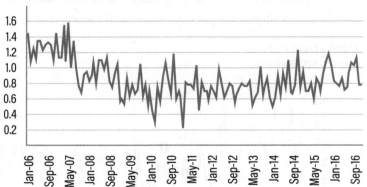

Source: NHTSA, FARS data (www-fars.nhtsa.dot.gov/QueryTool/QuerySection/Report.aspx).

FIGURE 2-25. *Monthly Fatal Car Accidents per 100,000 Residents in Maine (Maine Department of Transportation)*

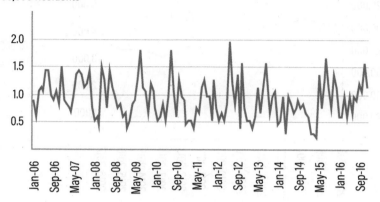

Monthly Fatal Car Accidents
per 100,000 Residents

Source: Maine Department of Transportation, Maine Public Crash Query Tool (https://mdotapps. maine.gov/MaineCrashPublic/PublicQueryStats).

FIGURE 2-26. *Monthly Fatal Car Accidents per 100,000 Residents in Massachusetts (NHTSA)*

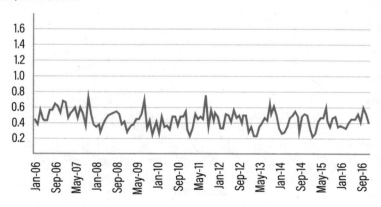

Monthly Fatal Car Accidents
per 100,000 Residents

Source: NHTSA, FARS data (www-fars.nhtsa.dot.gov/QueryTool/QuerySection/Report.aspx).

FIGURE 2-27. *Total and Drug-Related School Suspensions in Colorado (Colorado Department of Education)*

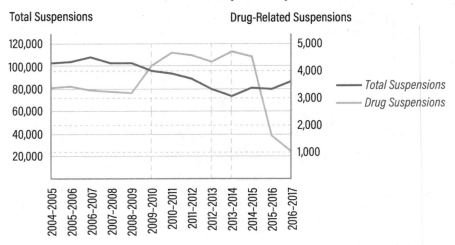

Source: Colorado Department of Education, 10-Year Trend Data (www.cde.state.co.us/cdereval/suspend-expelcurrent).

FIGURE 2-28. *Total and Drug-Related School Expulsions in Colorado (Colorado Department of Education)*

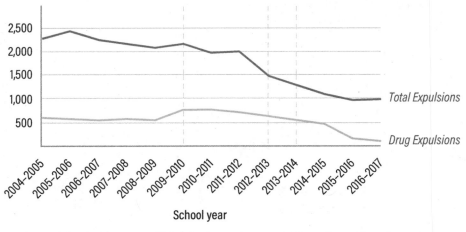

Source: Colorado Department of Education (www.cde.state.co.us/cdereval/suspend-expelcurrent).

FIGURE 2-29. *Total and Drug-Related School Suspensions in California (California Department of Education)*

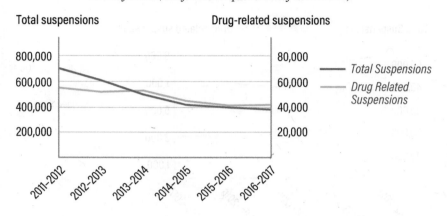

Source: California Department of Education (https://dq.cde.ca.gov/dataquest/).

FIGURE 2-30. *Total and Drug-Related School Expulsions in California (California Department of Education)*

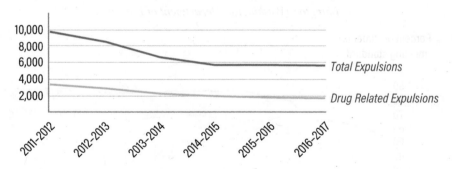

Source: California Department of Education (https://dq.cde.ca.gov/dataquest/).

FIGURE 2-31. *Total and Drug-Related School Suspensions in*
Massachusetts (Massachusetts Department of Education)

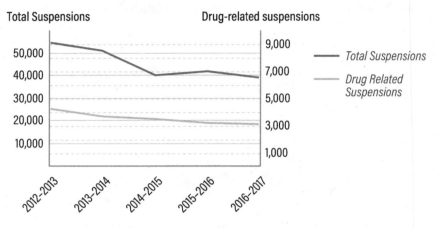

Source: Massachusetts Department of Education (http://profiles.doe.mass.edu/ssdr/default.aspx?orgc
ode=00000000&fycode=2017).

FIGURE 2-32. *Standardized Reading Test Scores in*
Washington (Washington Department of Education)

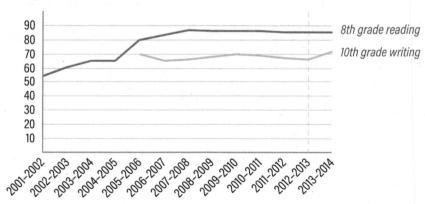

Source: Washington State Office of the Superintendent of Public Instruction (http://reportcard.ospi.
k12.wa.us/).

FIGURE 2-33. *Case-Shiller Home Price Index*

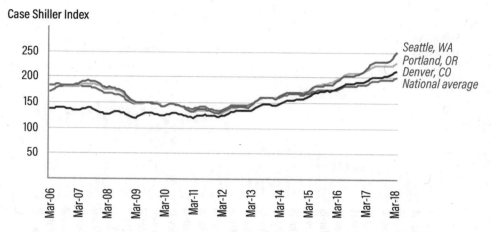

Source: S&P Core Logic Case-Shiller Home Price Indices (http://us.spindices.com/index-family/real-estate/sp-corelogic-case-shiller).

FIGURE 2-34. *Seasonally Adjusted Unemployment Rates (U.S. Bureau of Labor Statistics)*

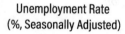

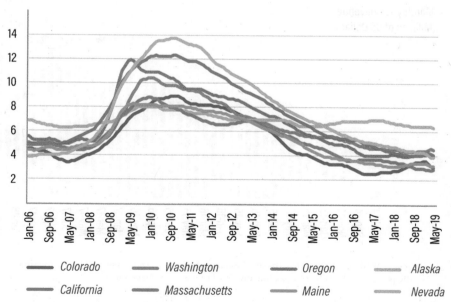

Source: Bureau of Labor Statistics, Local Area Unemployment Statistics (www.bls.gov/lau/).

FIGURE 2-35. *Marijuana Tax Revenues in Colorado*
(Colorado Department of Revenue)

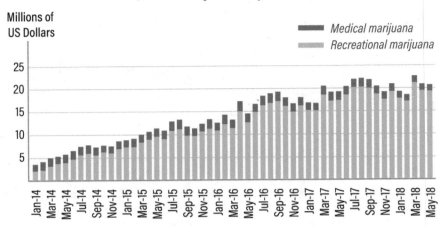

Source: Colorado Department of Revenue (www.colorado.gov/pacific/revenue/colorado-marijuana-tax-data).

FIGURE 2-36. *Marijuana Tax Revenues in Washington*
(Washington Department of Revenue and Washington
State Liquor and Cannabis Board)

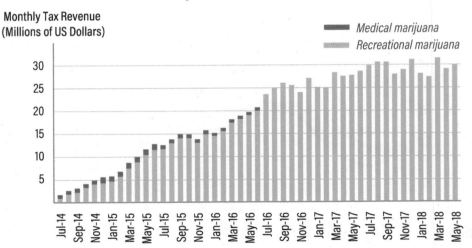

Source: Washington State Department of Revenue (http://dor.wa.gov/Content/AboutUs/StatisticsAndReports/stats_MMJTaxes.aspx); Initiative 502 Data (www.502data.com/).

FIGURE 2-37. *Marijuana Tax Revenues in Oregon*
(Oregon Department of Revenue)

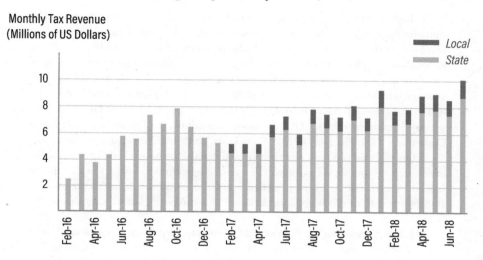

Source: Oregon Department of Revenue (www.oregon.gov/DOR/programs/gov-research/Documents/Financial-reporting-receipts-public.pdf).

NOTES

We thank Erin Partin for her research assistance.

1. In November 2014, the District of Columbia voted overwhelmingly in favor of Initiative 71, which legalized the use, possession, and cultivation of limited amounts of marijuana in the privacy of one's home. It also permitted adults age twenty-one and over to "gift"—or transfer—up to two ounces of marijuana provided no payment or other exchange of goods or services occurred. Selling marijuana or consuming it in public, however, remain criminal violations. In addition, because of ongoing federal prohibition, marijuana remains illegal on federal land, which makes up 30 percent of DC. Therefore, we do not examine data for DC. For more information, see DC Metropolitan Police Department, "The Facts on DC Marijuana Laws," 2018 (http://mpdc.dc.gov/marijuana).

2. Organizations and private citizens in additional states have raised the idea of ballot initiatives but have not yet garnered the requisite signatures to hold a vote. See Bruce Barcott, "Election 2018: A Complete Guide to Cannabis on the Ballot," September 19, 2018 (www.leafly.com/news/politics/election-2018-a-complete-guide-to-cannabis-on-the -ballot).

3. Ethan Nadelmann, for example, has asserted that legalization is a "smart" move that will help end mass incarceration and undermine illicit criminal organizations. See Nadelmann, "Marijuana Legalization: Not If, But When," *Huffington Post*, November 3, 2010 (www.huffingtonpost.com/ethannadelmann/marijuana-legalizationno_b_778222. html). Former New Mexico governor and Libertarian Party presidential candidate Gary Johnson has also advocated marijuana legalization, predicting that the measure will lead to less overall substance abuse because individuals addicted to alcohol or other substances will find marijuana a safer alternative. See Kelsey Osterman, "Gary Johnson: Legalizing Marijuana Will Lead to Lower Overall Substance Abuse," RedAlertPolitics.com, April 24, 2013 (http://redalertpo litics.com/2013/04/24/gary-johnson-legalizing-marijuana-will-lead-to-less-overall-substance-abuse/). Denver police chief Robert White argues that violent crime dropped almost 9 percent in 2012. See Sadie Gurman, "Denver's Top Law Enforcement Officials Disagree: Is Crime Up or Down?" *Denver Post*, January 22, 2014 (www.denver post.com/2014/01/22/denvers-top-law-enforcement-officers-disagree-is-crime -up-or-down/).

4. Colorado governor John Hickenlooper (D) opposed initial efforts to legalize marijuana because he thought the policy would, among other things, increase the number of children using drugs. See Matt Ferner, "Gov. John Hickenlooper Opposes Legal Weed," HuffingtonPost.com, September 12, 2012 (www.huffington post. com/2012/09/12/gov-john-hickenlooper-opp_n_1879248.html). Former U.S. Attorney General Edwin Meese III, who is now the Heritage Foundation's Ronald Reagan Distinguished Fellow Emeritus, and Charles Stimson have argued that violent crime surges when marijuana is legally abundant and that the economic burden of legalization far outstrips the gain. See Meese and Stimson, "The Case against Legalizing Marijuana in California," *Heritage Foundation*, October 3, 2010 (www.heritage.org/research/ commentary/2010/10/thecase-against-legalizing-marijuana-in-california). Kevin Sabet, a former senior White House drug policy adviser in the Obama administration, has called

Colorado's marijuana legalization a mistake, warning that potential consequences may include high addiction rates, spikes in traffic accidents, and reductions in IQ. See Sabet, "Colorado Will Show Why Legalizing Marijuana Is a Mistake," *Washington Times*, January 17, 2014 (www.washingtontimes.com/news/2014/jan/17/sabet-marijuana-legal izations-worst-enemy/). The former director of the DEA, John Walters, claims that "what we [see] in Colorado has the markings of a drug use epidemic." He argues that there is now a thriving black market in marijuana in Colorado and that more research on marijuana's societal effects needs to be completed before legalization should be considered. See Walters, "The Devastation That's Really Happening in Colorado," *Weekly Standard*, July 10, 2014 (www.weeklystandard .com/the-devastation-thats-really-happening-incolorado/article/796308). John Walsh, the U.S. attorney for Colorado, defended the targeted prosecution of medical marijuana dispensaries located near schools by citing figures from the Colorado Department of Education showing dramatic increases in drug-related school suspensions, expulsions, and law enforcement referrals between 2008 and 2011. See John Ingold, "U.S. Attorney John Walsh Justifies Federal Crackdown on Medical-Marijuana Shops," *Denver Post*, January 20, 2012 (www.denver post.com /2012/01/19/u-s-attorney-john-walshjustifies-federal-crackdown-on-medical-mari juanashops-2/). Denver District Attorney Mitch Morrissey points to the 9 percent rise in felony cases submitted to his office during the 2008–2011 period, after Colorado's marijuana laws had been partially liberalized, as evidence of marijuana's social effects. See Gurman, "Denver's Top Law Enforcement Officials Disagree. Other recent news stories that report criticisms of marijuana liberalization include Jack Healy, "After 5 Months of Legal Sale, Colorado Sees the Downside of a Legal High," *New York Times*, May 31, 2014 (www. nytimes.com/2014/06/01/us/after-5-months-of-sales-colorado-sees-the-downside-of-a-legal-high.html), and Josh Voorhees, "Going to Pot, *Slate,* May 21, 2014 (www.slate.com/articles /news_and_politics/politics/2014/05/colorado_s_pot_experiment_the_unintended_ consequences_of_marijuana_legalization.html). Also, White House policy research indicates that marijuana is the drug most often linked to crime. See Rob Hotakainen, "Marijuana Is Drug Most Often Linked to Crime," McClatchy News Service, May 23, 2013 (www.mcclatchydc.com/news/politics-government/article24749413.html).

5. Robert MacCoun and others (2009) review the decriminalization literature from the first wave of decriminalizations in the 1970s, noting that marijuana use did not change in response. See MacCoun and others, "Do Citizens Know Whether Their State Has Decriminalized Marijuana? Assessing the Perceptual Component of Deterrence Theory," *Review of Law and Economics* 5 (2009), pp. 347–71. Analysis of the recent U.S. state legalizations is more limited. Some noteworthy studies include Jeffrey Miron, "Marijuana Policy in Colorado," Cato Institute Working Paper 24 (2014); Andrew A. Monte and others, "The Implications of Marijuana Legalization in Colorado," *Journal of the American Medical Association* 313, no. 3 (2015), pp. 241–42; Stacy Salomonsen-Sautel and others, "Trends in Fatal Motor Vehicle Crashes Before and After Marijuana Commercialization in Colorado," *Drug and Alcohol Dependence* 140 (2014), pp. 137–44, which found a statistically significant uptick in drivers involved in a fatal motor vehicle crash after commercialization of medical marijuana in Colorado; Beau Kilmer and others, "Altered State?: Assessing How Marijuana Legalization in California Could

Influence Marijuana Consumption and Public Budgets," Occasional Paper, Rand Drug Policy Research Center, Santa Monica, CA (2010); Angela Hawken and others, "Quasi-Legal Cannabis in Colorado and Washington: Local and National Implications," *Addiction* 108, no. 5 (2013), pp. 837–38; and Howard S. Kim and others, "Marijuana Tourism and Emergency Department Visits in Colorado," *New England Journal of Medicine* 374 (2016), pp. 797–98. For an analysis of whether Colorado has implemented its legalization in a manner consistent with the law, see John Hudak, "Colorado's Rollout of Legal Marijuana Is Succeeding," *Governance Studies Series*, Brookings Institution, Washington, DC, July 31, 2014 (www.brookings.edu/~/media/research/files/papers /2014/07/colorado-marijuana-legalization-succeeding/cepm mjcov2.pdf). For inter-national evidence from Portugal, see Glenn Greenwald, "Drug Decriminalization in Portugal," Cato Institute White Paper, 2009 (http://object.cato.org/sites/cato.org/files/ pubs/pdf/greenwald_whitepaper.pdf); from the Netherlands, see Robert J. MacCoun, "What Can We Learn from the Dutch Cannabis Coffeeshop System," *Addiction* (2011) pp. 1–12 and Ali Palali and Jan C. van Ours, "Distance to Cannabis Shops and Age of Onset of Cannabis Use," *Health Economics* 24, no. 11 (2015), pp. 1482–1501; for parts of Australia, see Jenny Williams and Anne Line Bretteville-Jensen, "Does Liberalizing Cannabis Laws Increase Cannabis Use?" *Journal of Health Economics* 36 (2014), pp. 20–32; and for parts of London, see Nils Braakman and Simon Jones, "Cannabis Depenalization, Drug Consumption and Crime–Evidence from the 2004 Cannabis Declassification in the UK," *Social Science and Medicine* 115 (2014), pp. 29–37. These all suggest little to no effects of these laws on drug use. See also Jérôme Adda and others, "Crime and the Depenalization of Cannabis Possession: Evidence from a Policing Experiment," *Journal of Political Economy* 122, no. 5 (2014), pp. 1130–1201, who consider depenalization in a London borough, finding declines in crime caused by the police shifting enforcement to non-drug crime.

6. See Angela Dills, Sietse Goffard, and Jeffrey Miron, *Dose of Reality: The Effects of States Marijuana Legalizations*, Cato Institute, 2016. We do not analyze data for Vermont because recreational use was officially legal only as of July 1, 2018, and no retail structure is currently in place.

7. Opium, cocaine, coca leaves, and other derivatives of coca and opium had been essentially outlawed in 1914 by the Harrison Narcotic Act. See C. E. Terry, "The Harrison Anti-Narcotic Act," *American Journal of Public Health* 5, no. 6 (1915), p. 518 (www.ncbi.nlm.nih.gov/pmc/articles/PMC 1286619/?page=1).

8. See "When and Why Was Marijuana Outlawed," *Schaffer Library of Drug Policy*, 2019 (http://druglibrary. org/schaffer/library/mj_outlawed.htm).

9. Ibid.

10. See Mathieu Deflem, ed., Popular Culture, Crime, and Social Control 14, *Sociology of Crime, Law and Deviance* (2010), p. 13 (https://goo.gl/ioAoVY).

11. See Kathleen Ferraiolo, "From Killer Weed to Popular Medicine: The Evolution of Drug Control Policy, 1937–2000," *Journal of Policy History* 19 (2007), pp.147–79 (https://muse.jhu.edu/article/ 217587).

12. See David Musto, "Opium, Cocaine and Marijuana in American History," *Scientific American*, pp. 20–27 (July 1991), www.ncbi.nlm.nih.gov/pubmed/1882226.

13. See United Nations Office on Drugs and Crime, "Traffic in Narcotics, Barbiturates and Amphetamines in the United States," 1956 (www.unodc.org/unodc/en/data-and-analysis/bulletin/bulletin_1956-01-01_3_page005.html).

14. See "Drug Schedules," U.S. Drug Enforcement Administration, 2019 (www.dea.gov/druginfo/ds.shtml).

15. The eleven states were Oregon (1973), Alaska (1975), California (1975), Colorado (1975), Maine (1975), Minnesota (1976), Ohio (1976), Mississippi (1977), New York (1977), North Carolina (1977), and Nevada (1978). See Rosalie Pacula and others, "Marijuana Decriminalization: What Does It Mean for the United States?" Working Paper 9690, National Bureau of Economic Research, January 2004 (www.rand.org/content/dam/rand/ pubs/working_papers/2004/RAND_WR126.pdf).

16. Not all states followed such a straightforward path toward marijuana liberalization. Alaska, for example, decriminalized marijuana use and possession in one's home in 1975. In 1990, however, a voter initiative recriminalized possession and use of marijuana. See the section on Alaska for more details.

17. See "States That Have Decriminalized," National Organization for the Reform of Marijuana Laws, 2019 (http://norml.org/aboutmarijuana/item/statesthat-have-decriminalized).

18. See "State by State Laws: Oregon," National Organization for the Reform of Marijuana Laws, 2006 (http://norml.org/laws/item/oregon-penalties-2).

19. See "Oregon Legislature Ends 24 Years of Marijuana Decriminalization," National Organization for the Reform of Marijuana Laws, news release, July 3, 1997 (https://norml.org/news/1997/07/03/oregon-legislature-ends-24-years-of-marijuana-decriminalization). See also "State by State Laws: Oregon," National Organization for the Reform of Marijuana Laws, 2006 (http://norml.org/laws/item/oregon).

20. See *Ravin v. State*, 537 F.2d 494 (Alaska 1975).

21. See "Alaska Marijuana Criminalization Initiative, Measure 2 (1990)" Ballotpedia (https://ballotpedia.org/Alaska_Marijuana_Criminalization_Initiative_Measure_2_(1990)).

22. See "Medical Marijuana Rules and Statutes: Oregon Medical Marijuana Act," *Oregon Health Authority*, June 2016 (http://public.health.oregon.gov/DiseasesConditions/ChronicDisease/MedicalMarijuanaProgram/Pages/legal.aspx#ors).

23. See "Oregon Medical Marijuana Allowance Measure 33 (2004)," Ballotpedia (https://ballotpedia.org/Oregon_Medical_Marijuana_Allowance_ Measure_33_(2004)).

24. See "Oregon Medical Marijuana Program Statistics," *Oregon Health Authority*, July 2016 (https://public.health.oregon.gov/diseasesconditions/chronicdisease/medicalmarijuanaprogram/pages/data.aspx).

25. See "The Legalization of Marijuana in Colorado: The Impact. A Preliminary Report," *Rocky Mountain HIDTA* 1 (August 2013), p. 3 (www.rmhidta.org/html/final%20legalization%20of%20mj%20in%20colorado%20the%20impact.pdf).

26. David Ogden, the deputy attorney general at the time, issued a memorandum stating it would be unwise to "focus federal resources . . . on individuals whose actions are in clear and unambiguous compliance with existing state law providing for the medical use of marijuana." See "Memorandum for Selected United State Attorneys on Inves-

tigations and Prosecutions in States Authorizing the Medical Use of Marijuana," U.S. Department of Justice, October 19, 2009 (www.justice.gov/opa/blog/ memorandum-selected-united-state-attorneysinvestigations-and-prosecutions-states).

27. The Ogden Memorandum did not permanently resolve confusion about the role of federal law in state marijuana policy. In 2011, the Department of Justice issued another memo, titled the Cole Memo, which somewhat backpedaled on the Ogden Memo's position; it cautioned that "the Ogden Memorandum was never intended to shield such activities from federal enforcement action and prosecution, even where those activities purport to comply with state law." It was not until 2013 when those in the marijuana industry received a clear answer. A third memo unambiguously outlined the eight scenarios in which federal authorities would enforce marijuana laws in states where the substance was legal. Beyond those eight priorities, the federal government would leave marijuana law enforcement to local authorities. For more, see "Guidance Regarding the Ogden Memo in Jurisdictions Seeking to Authorize Marijuana for Medical Use," U.S. Department of Justice, June 29, 2011 (www.justice.gov/sites/default/files/oip/legacy/2014/07/23/dag-guidance-2011-for-medicalmarijuana-use.pdf). See also "Guidance Regarding Marijuana Enforcement," U.S. Department of Justice, August 29, 2013 (www.justice.gov/iso/opa/resources/30520 13829132756857467.pdf).

28. See "The Legalization of Marijuana in Colorado: The Impact. A Preliminary Report," *Rocky Mountain HIDTA* 1 (August 2013), p. 4 (www.rmhidta.org/html/final%20legalization%20of%20mj%20in%20colorado%20the%20impact.pdf).

29. See "Amendment 64: Use and Regulation of Marijuana," City of Fort Collins, Colorado (www.fcgov.com/mmj/pdf/amendment64.pdf).

30. Ibid.

31. Numerous counties, including Denver County, have enacted local taxes on top of state taxes. In Denver, retail marijuana products are subject to a local sales tax of 3.65 percent in addition to a special marijuana tax of 3.5 percent. See "City and County of Denver, Colorado: Tax Guide, Topic No. 95," City of Denver, April 2015 (www.denvergov.org/Portals/571/documents/TaxGuide/Marijuana-Medical_and_Retail.pdf).

32. This system of three separate taxes was eventually replaced by a single 37 percent excise tax levied at the retail point of sale in July 2015. See "FAQs on Taxes," Washington State Liquor and Cannabis Board, 2018 (www.liq.wa.gov/mj2015/faqs-ontaxes). See also Rachel La Corte, "Washington State Pot Law Overhaul: Marijuana Tax Reset at 37 Percent," *The Cannabist*, July 1, 2015 (www.thecannabist.co/2015/07/01/washington-state-pot-law-overhaul-marijuana-tax-reset-at37-percent/37238/).

33. See "Oregon Marijuana Legalization for Personal Use, Ballot Measure 5 (1986)," Ballotpedia (https://ballotpedia.org/Oregon_Marijuana_Legalization_for_Personal_Use,_Ballot_Measure_5_(1986)).

34. See "Oregon Cannabis Tax Act Initiative, Measure 80 (2012)," Ballotpedia (https://ballotpedia.org/Oregon_Cannabis_Tax_Act_Initiative,_Measure_80_(2012)).

35. See "Measure 91," *Oregon Liquor Control Commission* (www.oregon.gov/olcc/marijuana/Documents/Measure91.pdf).

36. Several counties in Oregon have enacted their own local taxes.

37. As of June 2016, eighty-seven municipalities and nineteen counties in Oregon had

prohibited recreational marijuana businesses or producers in their jurisdiction. See "Record of Cities/Counties Prohibiting Licensed Recreational Marijuana Facilities," Oregon Liquor Control Commission, 2019 (www.oregon.gov/olcc/marijuana/Documents /Cities_Counties_RMJ OptOut.pdf).

38. See "Medical Marijuana Dispensary Directory," Oregon Health Authority, 2019 (www.oregon.gov/oha/mmj/Pages/directory.aspx).

39. Recent work includes the following: D. Mark Anderson and others, "Medical Marijuana Laws and Suicides by Gender and Age," *American Journal of Public Health* 104, no. 1 (December 2014), pp. 2369–76; D. Mark Anderson and others, "Medical Marijuana Laws and Teen Marijuana Use," *American Law and Economic Review* 17, no. 2 (2015), pp. 495–528; Esther K. Choo and others, "The Impact of State Medical Marijuana Legislation on Adolescent Marijuana Use," *Journal of Adolescent Health*, forthcoming. Yu-Wei Luke Chu, "Do Medical Marijuana Laws Increase Hard-Drug Use?" *Journal of Law and Economics* 58, no. 2 (May 2015), pp. 481–517; Dennis M. Gorman and J. Charles Huber Jr. "Do Medical Cannabis Laws Encourage Cannabis Use?" *International Journal of Drug Policy* 18, no. 3 (May 2007), pp. 160–67; S. Harper and others, "Do Medical Marijuana Laws Increase Marijuana Use? Replication Study and Extension," *Annals of Epidemiology* 22 (2012), pp. 207–12; Sarah D. Lynne-Landsman and others, "Effects of State Medical Marijuana Laws on Adolescent Marijuana Use," *American Journal of Public Health* 103 (2013), pp. 1500–06; Karen O'Keefe and Mitch Earleywine, "Marijuana Use by Young People: The Impact of State Medical Marijuana Laws," manuscript, Marijuana Policy Project (2011); and Hefei Wen and others, "The Effect of Medical Marijuana Laws on Marijuana, Alcohol, and Hard Drug Use," NBER Working Paper 20085 (2014), which found that medical marijuana laws led to a relatively small increase in marijuana use by adults over age twenty-one and did nothing to change use of hard drugs. Rosalie Liccardo Pacula and others, "Assessing the Effects of Medical Marijuana Laws on Marijuana and Alcohol Use: The Devil Is in the Details," NBER Working Paper 19302 (2015), found that legalizing home cultivation and medical marijuana dispensaries was associated with higher marijuana use, while other aspects of medical marijuana liberalization were not. Choo and others, "The Impact of State Medical Marijuana Legislation on Adolescent Marijuana Use," *Journal of Adolescent Health* 55, no. 2 (2014), pp. 160–66, found no statistically significant differences in adolescent marijuana use after state-level medical marijuana legalization.

40. Data are reported as two-year averages. Data are from "National Survey on Drug Use and Health 2002–2016," Center for Behavioral Health Statistics and Quality, Substance Abuse and Mental Health Services Administration (www.icpsr.umich.edu/ icpsrweb/content/SAMHDA/help/ nsduh-estimates.html).

41. State-level data from "National Survey on Drug Use and Health, 2002–2014," Center for Behavioral Health Statistics and Quality.

42. See Dale H. Gieringer, director, California NORML, "Testimony on the Legalization of Marijuana," Testimony before the California Assembly Committee on Public Safety, October 28, 2009 (http://norml.org/pdf_files/AssPubSafety_Legalization. pdf).

43. See Rand Corporation, "Legalizing Marijuana in California Would Sharply

Lower the Price of the Drug," news release, July 7, 2007 (www.rand.org/news/press/2010/07/07.html).

44. These analyses consider legalization at both the federal and state levels, which would allow additional avenues for lower prices such as economies of scale, although also additional avenues for higher prices because of federal taxation and advertising.

45. The website PriceOfWeed.com allows anyone to submit anonymous data about the price, quantity, and quality of marijuana he or she purchases, as well as where the marijuana was purchased. Founded in 2010, the website has logged hundreds of thousands of entries across the country, and many analysts and journalists look to it as a source of marijuana price data. It has obvious limitations: the data are not a random sample; the consumer reports do not distinguish between marijuana bought through legal means and through the black market; self-reported data may not be accurate; and the data are probably from a self-selecting crowd of marijuana enthusiasts. Nevertheless, Price of Weed provides large samples of real-time data. To reduce the impact of inaccurate submissions, the website automatically removes the bottom and top 5 percent of outliers when calculating its average prices. We were not able to calculate meaningful marijuana price averages from Alaska because of a relatively low number of entries from that state.

46. One further trend we observe in all three states is a widening price gap between high-quality and medium-quality marijuana. Among other things, this gap may be the result of fewer information asymmetries in the marijuana market. On the black market, it can be hard to know the true quality of a product. Marijuana trade is complex, with hundreds of different strains and varieties. Yet in the black market, consumers often have a difficult time differentiating between them and may end up paying similarly high prices for medium- and high-quality marijuana. In all three states, the gap between the prices rose after legalization, suggesting that consumers have had an easier time distinguishing between different qualities and strains of marijuana.

47. See Anderson, Rees, and Sabia, "Medical Marijuana Laws and Suicides by Gender and Age," *American Journal of Public Health* 104, no. 12 (December 2014).

48. See D. Mark Anderson and others, "High on Life?: Medical Marijuana and Suicide," Cato Institute Research Briefs in Economic Policy 17, January 2015 (www.southerncannabis.org/wp-content/uploads/2015/01/marijuana-suicide-study.pdf). See also David Powell and others, "Do Medical Marijuana Laws Reduce Addictions and Deaths Related to Pain Killers?" NBER Working Paper 21345, National Bureau of Economic Research, July 2015.

49. See, for example, Stanley Zammit and others, "Self-Reported Cannabis Use as a Risk Factor for Schizophrenia in Swedish Conscripts of 1969," *British Medical Journal* 325 (2002); Cécile Henquet and others, "Prospective Cohort Study of Cannabis Use, Predisposition for Psychosis, and Psychotic Symptoms in Young People," *British Medical Journal* (December 2004); Carey Goldberg, "Studies Link Psychosis, Teenage Marijuana Use," *Boston Globe*, January 26, 2006; and Matthew Shulman, "Marijuana Linked to Heart Disease and Depression," *U.S. News & World Report*, May 14, 2008. See also Jan C. van Ours and others, "Cannabis Use and Suicidal Ideation," *Journal of Health Economics* 32, no. 3 (2013), pp. 524–37; Jan C. van Ours and Jenny Williams, "The Effects of Cannabis

Use on Physical and Mental Health," *Journal of Health Economics* 31, no. 4 (July 2012), pp. 564–77; van Ours and Williams, "Cannabis Use and Mental Health Problems," *Journal of Applied Econometrics* 26, no. 7 (November 2011), pp. 1137–56; and Jenny Williams and Christopher L. Skeels, "The Impact of Cannabis Use on Health," *De Economist* 154, no. 4 (December 2006), pp. 517–46.

50. See National Institute on Drug Abuse, "What Are Marijuana's Long-Term Impacts on the Brain?" Research Report Series, March 2016 (www.drugabuse.gov/ publications/research-reports/marijuana/how-does-marijuana-use-affect-your-brain-body). Kelly and Rasul evaluate the depenalization of marijuana in a London borough and find large increases in hospital admissions related to hard drug use, particularly among younger men. See Elaine Kelly and Imran Rasul, "Policing Cannabis and Drug Related Hospital Admissions: Evidence from Administrative Records," *Journal of Public Economics* 112 (April 2014), pp. 89–114.

51. See "Detailed Mortality Statistics," Centers for Disease Control and Prevention, WONDER Online Databases (http://wonder.cdc.gov).

52. Ibid.

53. The link between medical marijuana and lower suicide rates may stem partly from the fact that medical marijuana can substitute for other, more dangerous painkillers and opiates. Research by Anne Case and Angus Deaton found suicides and drug poisonings led to a marked increase in mortality rates of middle-aged white non-Hispanic men and women in the United States between 1999 and 2013. Other studies have linked opioid and painkiller overdoses to a recent surge in self-inflicted drug-related deaths and suicides. Medical marijuana, as a less risky pain reliever, may, thus, help lessen the rate of drug deaths and suicides. For more, see Case and Deaton, "Rising Morbidity and Mortality in Midlife among White Non-Hispanic Americans in the 21st Century," *National Academy of Sciences* 112, no. 49 (November 2015).

54. See Kevin Wong and Chelsey Clarke, "The Legalization of Marijuana in Colorado: The Impact," *Rocky Mountain High Intensity Drug Trafficking Area*, September 2015 (www.rmhidta.org/html/2015%20final%20legalization%20of%20marijuana%20 in%20colorado %20the%20impact.pdf).

55. See Caleb Banta-Green and others, "Drug Abuse Trends in the Seattle-King Country Area: 2014," University of Washington Alcohol and Drug Abuse Institute, Seattle, June 17, 2015 (http://adai.washington.edu/pubs/cewg/Drug%20 Trends_2014_ final.pdf).

56. See David Musto, "Opium, Cocaine and Marijuana in American History," *Scientific American* 1 (July 1991), pp. 40–47 (www.ncbi.nlm.nih.gov/pubmed/1882226).

57. See U.S. Drug Enforcement Administration, "The Dangers and Consequences of Marijuana Abuse," U.S. Department of Justice, May 2014 (www.dea.gov/docs/dangers-consequences-marijuana-abuse.pdf).

58. For example, Sheriff David Weaver of Douglas County, Colorado, warned in 2012, "Expect more crime, more kids using marijuana, and pot for sale everywhere." See Matt Ferner, "If Legalizing Marijuana Was Supposed to Cause More Crime, It's Not Doing a Very Good Job," *Huffington Post*, July 17, 2014 (www.huffingtonpost.com/ 2014/07/17/ marijuana-crime-denver_n_5595742.html).

59. See Jeffrey Miron, "Marijuana Policy in Colorado," Cato Institute Working Paper, October 23, 2014 (http://object.cato.org/sites/cato.org/files/pubs/pdf/working-paper-24_2.pdf).

60. See "Marijuana Is Safer Than Alcohol: It's Time to Treat It That Way," Marijuana Policy Project (www.mpp.org/marijuana-is-safer/). See also Peter Hoaken and Sherry Stewart, "Drugs of Abuse and the Elicitation of Human Aggressive Behavior," *Addictive Behaviors* 28 (2003): 1533–54 (www.ukcia.org/research/ AgressiveBehavior.pdf).

61. See Denver Police Department, Uniform Crime Reporting Program, "Monthly Citywide Data—National Incident-Based Reporting System," 2018 (www.denvergov. org/police/PoliceDepartment/CrimeInformation/CrimeStatisticsMaps/tabid/441370/Default.aspx).

62. Fort Collins crime data yield similar factual conclusions, showing no consistent rise in crime following either the November 2012 legalization or the January 2014 opening of stores.

63. See "Crime Dashboard," Seattle Police Department (www.seattle.gov/seattle-police-department/crime-data/crime-dashboard).

64. See Sierra Rayne, "Seattle's Post-Marijuana Legalization Crime Wave," *American Thinker*, November 13, 2015 (www.americanthinker.com blog/2015/11/seattles_post marijuana_legalization_crime_wave.htm).

65. Elsewhere in Washington, this conclusion seems equally robust. Tacoma, a large city in northeastern Washington where stores have opened, has generally seen stable crime trends before and after legalization. Total monthly offenses, violent crime, and property crime have shown no significant deviation from their recent trends. See Kellie Lapczynski, "Tacoma Monthly Crime Data," Washington Association of Sheriffs and Police Chiefs, pp. 377–78, 2015 (www.waspc.org/assets/CJIS/crime%20in%20washington%202015.small.pdf).

66. See "City of Portland—Neighborhood Crime Statistics," Portland Police Bureau (www.portlandonline.com/police/crimestats/).

67. In Salem, Oregon, violent crime, property crime, and drug offenses show no significant jumps post-legalization. Although Salem is farther from the border with Washington, there are no indications of major spillover effects between 2012 and 2014. See Linda Weber, "Monthly Crime Statistics," Salem Police Department, 2015 (www. cityof salem.net/Departments/Police/HowDoI2/Pages/CrimeStatistics.aspx). Alaska is not covered in this section because reliable recent crime data for major Alaskan cities were unavailable at the time of writing.

68. For a review of these issues, see Rune Elvik, "Risk of Road Accident Associated with the Use of Drugs: A Systematic Review and Meta-Analysis of Evidence from Epidemiological Studies," *Accident Analysis and Prevention* 60 (2013), pp. 254–67 (www. ncbi.nlm.nih.gov/pubmed/22785089).

69. Academic studies examining this issue have suggested a possible substitution effect. A 2015 report by the Governors Highway Safety Organization cited one study revealing that marijuana-positive fatalities rose by 4 percent after legalization in Colorado. However, another study from the same report discovered no change in total traffic fatalities in California after its decriminalization of the drug in 2011. See also

Andrew Sewell and others, "The Effect of Cannabis Compared with Alcohol on Driving," *American Journal on Addictions* 18, no. 3 (2009), pp. 185–93 (www.ncbi.nlm.nih.gov/pmc/articles/PMC2722956/).

70. See Sabet, "Colorado Will Show Why Legalizing Marijuana Is a Mistake."

71. See Associated Press, "Fatal Crashes Involving Marijuana Doubled in Washington after Legalization," *The Oregonian*, August 20, 2015 (www.oregonlive.com/marijuana/index.ssf/2015/08/fatal_crashes_involving_mariju.html).

72. See Noelle Phillips and Elizabeth Hernandez, "Colorado Still Not Sure Whether Legal Marijuana Made Roads Less Safe," *Denver Post*, December 29, 2015 (www.denverpost.com/2015/12/29/colorado-still-not-sure-whether-legal-marijuanamade-roads-less-safe/).

73. See Radley Balko, "Since Marijuana Legalization, Highway Fatalities in Colorado Are at Near Historic Lows," *Washington Post*, August 5, 2014 (www.washingtonpost.com/news/the-watch/wp/2014/08/05/since-marijuana-legalization-highway-fatalities-in-colorado-are-at-near-historic-lows/).

74. These data include any kinds of crashes on all types of roads, as recorded by each state's department of transportation. See Colorado Department of Transportation's "Fatal Accident Statistics by City and County," 2018 (www.coloradodot.info/library/traffic/traffic-manuals-guidelines/safetycrash-data/fatal-crash-data-city-county/fatalcrashes-by-city-and-county).

75. Annual crash data from the National Highway Traffic Safety Administration (NHTSA) confirm these findings. Our analysis uses state-level traffic accident data from individual state transportation departments because their data are mostly reported monthly and have a shorter reporting time lag than NHTSA data. For NHTSA data, see "State Traffic Safety Information," NHTSA, 2018 (www-nrd.nhtsa.dot.gov/departments/nrd30/ncsa/STSI/8_CO/2014/8_CO_2014.htm).

76. We additionally analyzed fatality rates for accidents involving alcohol impairment. Similarly, this time series shows no clear indications of significant swings after marijuana policy changes, suggesting that any substitution effect associated with marijuana has been small compared to overall drunk driving.

77. See "WA State Crash Data Portal," Washington Traffic Safety Commission, 2015 (https://remoteapps.wsdot.wa.gov/highwaysafety/collision/data/portal/public).

78. Washington State police routinely test drivers involved in car crashes for traces of various substances. The official legalization of marijuana use at the end of 2012 appears to have had at most a negligible effect on crash fatalities. The Washington Traffic Safety Commission recorded a total of sixty-two marijuana-related crash fatalities in 2013, compared to sixty-one in 2012. There does seem to be a temporary increase in fatalities caused by marijuana-related crashes around the same time as the establishment of Washington's first marijuana shops. Nevertheless, any sort of spike seems to have been temporary. In the first six months following the opening of stores, forty-six crash fatalities were tied to using marijuana while driving; over the following six months, that number dropped to thirty-two.

79. Monthly data on fatal crashes themselves were not available.

80. We do not observe fatal car accidents prior to and after a legal change in California.

81. For instance, Meier and others analyze a large sample of individuals tracked from birth to age thirty-eight and find that those who smoked marijuana most heavily prior to age eighteen lost an average of eight IQ points, a highly significant drop. See Madeline Meier and others, "Persistent Cannabis Users Show Neuropsychological Decline from Childhood to Midlife," *Proceedings of the National Academy of Sciences* 109, no. 40 (2012), pp. E2657–E2664 (www.ncbi.nlm.nih.gov/pubmed/22927402). However, other studies have found results that rebut Meier and others. Mokrysz and others examine an even larger sample of adolescents and, after controlling for many potentially confounding variables, discover no significant correlation between teen marijuana use and IQ change. See Claire Mokrysz and others, "Are IQ and Educational Outcomes in Teenagers Related to Their Cannabis Use? A Prospective Cohort Study," *Journal of Psychopharmacology* 30, no. 2 (2016) pp.159–68 (http://jop.sagepub.com/con tent/30/2/159).

82. Cobb-Clark and others show that much of the relationship between marijuana use and educational outcomes is likely due to selection, although there is possibly some causal effect in reducing university entrance scores. See Deborah A. Cobb-Clark and others, " 'High'-School: The Relationship between Early Marijuana Use and Educational Outcomes," *Economic Record* 91, no. 293 (June 2015), pp. 247–66. Evidence in McCaffrey and others supports this selection explanation of the association between marijuana use and educational outcomes. See Daniel F. McCaffrey and others, "Marijuana Use and High School Dropout: The Influence of Unobservables," *Health Economics* 19, no. 11 (November 2010), pp. 1281–99. Roebuck and others suggest that chronic marijuana use, not more casual use, likely drives any relationship between marijuana use and school attendance. See M. Christopher Roebuck and others, "Adolescent Marijuana Use and School Attendance," *Economics of Education Review* 23, no. 2 (2004), pp. 133–41. Marie and Zölitz estimate grade improvements are likely due to improved cognitive functioning among students whose nationalities prohibited them from consuming marijuana. See Olivier Marie and Ulf Zölitz, " 'High' Achievers? Cannabis Access and Academic Performance," Working Paper Series 5304, Center for Economic Studies and Ifo Institute (2015). van Ours and Williams review of the literature concluded that cannabis may reduce educational outcomes, particularly with early onset of use. See Jan van Ours and Jenny Williams, "Cannabis Use and Its Effects on Health, Education and Labor Market Success," *Journal of Economic Surveys* 29, no. 5 (December 2015), pp. 993–1010. For additional evidence on likely negative effects of early onset of use, see also Paolo Rungo and others, "Parental Education, Child's Grade Repetition, and the Modifier Effect of Cannabis Use," *Applied Economics Letters* 22, no. 3 (2015), pp. 199–203; Jan C. van Ours and Jenny Williams, "Why Parents Worry: Initiation into Cannabis Use by Youth and Their Educational Attainment," *Journal of Health Economics* 28, no. 1 (2009), pp. 132–42; and Pinka Chatterji, "Illicit Drug Use and Educational Attainment," *Health Economics* 15, no. 5 (2006), pp. 489–511.

83. See "Suspension/Expulsion Statistics," Colorado Department of Education, 2015 (www.cde.state.co.us/cdereval/suspend-expelcurrent).

84. See "Washington State Report Card, 2013–14 Results," Washington State Office of the Superintendent of Public Instruction (http://reportcard.ospi.k12.wa.us/summary. aspx?groupLevel=District&schoolId=1&reportLevel=State&year=2013-14&yrs=2013-14).

85. See Sarah Berger, "Colorado's Marijuana Industry Has a Big Impact on Denver Real Estate: Report," *International Business Times*, October 20, 2015 (www.ibtimes.com/colorados-marijuana-industry-has-big-impact-denver-real-estatereport-2149623).

86. See "S&P/Case-Schiller Denver Home Price Index," *S&P Dow Jones Indices*, 2018 (http://us.spindices.com/indices/real-estate/sp-case-shiller-co-denverhome-price-index/).

87. See U.S. Department of Commerce, Bureau of Economic Analysis (www.bea.gov/).

88. As an example, Oregon state legislator Ann Lininger wrote an op-ed predicting a "jobs boom" in southern Oregon after marijuana legalization. See Lininger, "Marijuana: Will Legalization Create an Economic Boom?" *Huffington Post*. October 1, 2015 (www.huffingtonpost.com/annlininger/marijuanawill-legalizati_b_8224712.html).

89. See "Local Area Unemployment Statistics," Bureau of Labor Statistics, 2018 (www.bls.gov/lau/).

90. See "National Income and Product Accounts, table 1.1.5," U.S. Department of Commerce, Bureau of Economic Analysis (https://apps.bea.gov/iTable/index_nipa.cfm).

91. See "Colorado Marijuana Tax Data," Colorado Department of Revenue (https://www.colorado.gov/pacific/revenue/colorado-marijuana-tax-data).

92. See Tom Robleski, "Up in Smoke: Colorado Pot Biz Not the Tax Windfall Many Predicted," January 2015 (www.silive.com/opinion/columns/index.ssf/2015/01/up_in_smoke_colorado_pot_biz_n.html).

93. See Washington State Department of Revenue, "Marijuana Tax Tables," 2018 (http://dor.wa.gov/Content/AboutUs/StatisticsAndReports/stats_MMJTaxes.aspx and www.502data.com/).

94. See "Washington Rakes in Revenue from Marijuana Taxes," RT (Russia Today television channel), July 13, 2015 (www.rt.com/usa/273409-washington-state-pot-taxes/).

95. See Oregon Department of Revenue, "Marijuana Tax Program Update," Joint Interim Committee on Marijuana Legalization, May 23, 2016 (https://olis.leg.state.or.us/liz/2015I1/Downloads/CommitteeMeetingDocument/90434).

3

THE SMOKE NEXT TIME

Nullification, Commandeering,
and the Future of Marijuana Regulation

Ernest A. Young

Federal law has long prohibited the cultivation, sale, and consumption of marijuana.[1] That prohibition has survived legislative and administrative efforts at modification or repeal, as well as a variety of statutory and constitutional challenges in the courts.[2] And yet, as of 2019, thirty-three states have authorized the medicinal use of marijuana, and eleven states have authorized recreational use.[3] It is commonplace to speak of this recent trend in state law as "legalization" of marijuana, but that is plainly not the case. As anyone who has taken a high school civics course could tell you, state decriminalization cannot override the federal prohibition.[4]

Nonetheless, those who speak of "legalization" or "decriminalization" are not wrong, at least as a practical matter. Although marijuana cultivation, sale, and use remain federal crimes, federal law enforcement has long depended on state and local authorities to do the heavy lifting when it comes to drug enforcement. Under the anti-commandeering doctrine,[5] Congress lacks constitutional authority to compel state or local officers to cooperate in such enforcement. And in the absence of state and local cooperation, federal authorities have so far proven unwilling to deploy sufficient resources to fill the gap. The dependence of federal drug enforcement on state cooperation has enabled states like Colorado, Washington, and California not only to sit out the federal drug war on marijuana but, effectively, to "nullify" federal law with which they disagree.[6]

This chapter begins by suggesting that state noncooperation with federal drug policy is a form of nullification that may usefully be compared with South Carolina's famous resistance to the federal tariff in the 1830s. The Supreme Court's recent decision in *Murphy v. NCAA*,[7] which affirmed New Jersey's power to remove state law prohibitions on sports gambling in contravention of federal policy, likely strengthens the hand of states wishing to facilitate the marijuana industry within their borders. I suggest, however, that the current marijuana regime remains highly unstable. Just as the cooperative structure of modern federalism gives states leverage to influence national policy on issues like marijuana, that same structure makes it difficult for states to foster a workable state legal regime for activities that remain illegal under federal law. And now that at least some national authorities are less sympathetic to marijuana legalization, this lurking instability may well flare into open conflict.

MODERN-DAY NULLIFICATION: COOPERATIVE FEDERALISM AND STATE MARIJUANA LEGALIZATION

It is a truism of modern constitutional law that no state may "nullify" federal law, so long as that law falls within Congress's (very broad) enumerated powers. That is the lesson of the famous Nullification Crisis of the 1830s.[8] In 1832, the South Carolina legislature enacted an ordinance declaring that the federal tariffs of 1828 and 1832 were null and void within the boundaries of that state.[9] Southerners viewed the tariff as not only bad policy but also unconstitutional because its purpose was not so much to raise revenue as to protect domestic industries.[10] But South Carolina's protest, which built on a strong theory of state sovereignty advanced by John C. Calhoun, went down to defeat. President Andrew Jackson rejected nullification in principle, threatened to enforce the tariff by force, then undercut the state's practical position by introducing new legislation to radically lower that same tariff.[11] No other state joined South Carolina, and, in fact, eight Southern state legislatures passed resolutions condemning the South Carolinians' action.[12] To the extent that resolution of a political dispute can settle constitutional meaning, the tariff dispute "decisively rejected" South Carolina's claimed authority to nullify federal law.[13]

So how can Colorado and other states purporting to legalize marijuana nullify the federal Controlled Substances Act? The answer has to do with changes in American federalism that, while weakening the theoretical sovereignty of the states on which Calhoun's theory relied, have rendered the national government frequently dependent on state cooperation in practice. Contemporary constitutional doctrine largely eschews the nineteenth-century notion of "dual federalism," which held that state and federal governments reign over separate and mutually exclusive spheres of authority.[14] Hence, in modern America, "virtually all governments are involved in virtually all functions," and "there is hardly any activity that does not involve the federal, state, and some local government in important responsibilities."[15] Under this regime of "cooperative federalism," federal programs like the Clean Air and Water Acts, Medicaid, and telecommunications regulation are administered by state officials working in conjunction with federal administrative agencies.[16]

Cooperative federalism is frequently seen as a tool of centralization, leading to "concentration of political powers in the national government."[17] Such regulatory regimes allow federal agencies to leverage their own limited resources, sometimes coopt state officials to adopt a more national perspective, and have gone hand in hand with an expansion of federal authority that would shock our Constitution's framers. But cooperative federalism schemes do typically have a significant amount of play in the joints, which allows state officials tasked with implementing federal mandates to put their own spin on national directives. And because cooperative federalism can leave national authorities dependent on state cooperation to implement national law, state officials can sometimes resist or undermine federal mandates. Jessica Bulman-Pozen and Heather Gerken have dubbed this sort of state behavior "uncooperative federalism."[18]

The drug enforcement regime is not technically one of cooperative federalism; in theory, state and federal authorities each enforce their own distinct set of drug laws. But at least prior to the wave of marijuana liberalizations, Congress and the states had criminalized largely the same behaviors, and federal and state law enforcement pervasively cooperated in practice. The allocation of labor was hardly equal, however; in practice, federal authorities played a decidedly secondary role. State and local law enforcement personnel outnumber federal officers in this country by a factor of roughly ten to one,[19] and drug enforcement must now compete with terrorism and other national priorities for the attention of national officials. Federal authorities have thus tended to focus on major distribution "kingpins" while leaving the overwhelming majority of minor drug offenses to state and local police.[20] In 2007, federal agents made 7,276 marijuana arrests—less than 1 percent of all American marijuana arrests that year.[21]

Federal marijuana policy thus depends heavily on state and local enforcement. But contemporary constitutional doctrine makes clear that Congress may not require state and local officials to participate in the administration of federal law if the state wishes them not to do so. Under the "anti-commandeering" rule,[22] Congress may request state assistance and offer considerable inducements to secure it, but Congress may not require or coerce state officials to participate in cooperative federalism regimes.[23] And the Court's latest anti-commandeering decision in *Murphy* makes clear that Congress may not prohibit states from repealing criminal prohibitions in their own law.[24] Hence, although federal marijuana laws remain legally binding in those states purporting to legalize the drug, state and local officials in those jurisdictions have the right to engage in the ultimate form of "uncooperative federalism"—they can, at the behest of state legislatures or referenda, simply go on strike.

Because federal authorities have insufficient resources to credibly enforce federal marijuana laws, the loss of state cooperation effectively nullifies the federal prohibition. As Rob Mikos explains, "The federal government has too few law enforcement agents to handle the large number of potential targets. Simply put, the expected sanctions for using or supplying marijuana under federal law are too low, standing alone, to deter many prospective marijuana users or suppliers."[25] This "modern day nullification" practiced by pro-marijuana states and sanctuary jurisdictions is quite different in its formal structure from Calhoun's theory that South Carolina tried to put into practice in the 1830s. The South Carolinians purported to hold the federal law legally invalid; their theory, in essence, posited that state governments had their own unreviewable authority to interpret the Constitution and to make their interpretations stick within their own borders.[26] Colorado and likeminded states make no such claim, of course. Instead, they are simply betting that, without state and local cooperation, federal authorities will be unwilling to deploy sufficient resources to enforce the national marijuana laws on their own. So far, it has been a good bet.

THE INSTABILITY OF THE CURRENT REGIME

The current "regime" of marijuana regulation—if one can call it that—has certain real advantages. Because the national government lacks the resources or political will to fill the enforcement gap, individual states have been able to experiment with liberalized drug policies. As Justice Louis Brandeis observed long ago, state-level experimentation is beneficial both because it is a means to "try novel social and economic experiments," and because it permits these experiments to be tried "without risk to the rest of the country."[27] State experiments have, in other words, something to offer both proponents and skeptics of reform. The combination of the anti-commandeering doctrine with limited national enforcement resources has allowed reform-minded states to add their voices to a debate heretofore dominated by national interests and institutions.

The present regime is considerably less attractive, however, as a practical framework for regulation. Most proponents of marijuana liberalization do not seem to envision a *laissez faire* regime for marijuana; rather, they tend to project a world in which marijuana remains restricted for certain persons (especially minors), regulated as to production, composition, sale, and circumstances of its use, and taxed. The continuing illegality of marijuana under federal law complicates all these objectives significantly. For that reason, the current *modus vivendi* appears to be highly unstable.

That instability arises from two specific sources: First, many of the regulatory measures that legalizing states have undertaken (or might desire to adopt in future) may be preempted by the federal law prohibition.[28] Second, the viability of state marijuana legalization continues to depend on the forbearance of federal law enforcement, but neither the willingness of the Justice Department to focus on other priorities nor the unwillingness of Congress to devote more resources to marijuana enforcement are guaranteed.

Consider preemption first. Preemption might operate on state marijuana

laws in at least two ways. In the early days of state legalization efforts, many believed federal law preempted states from removing their state-law prohibitions
on marijuana use. The argument was that such state repeals effectively "authorized" marijuana use, and that "affirmatively authorizing a use that federal
law prohibits stands as an obstacle to the implementation and execution of the
full purposes and objectives of the Controlled Substances Act."[29] This makes a
certain degree of sense, at least to the extent that one takes "obstacle" preemption seriously.[30] As discussed, state legalization throws an enormous practical
wrench into the gears of federal marijuana policy. The trouble with this argument, however, is that it suggests that federal law effectively compels states to
continue enforcing their laws against marijuana even if the states would like to
repeal them. As Robert Mikos has long argued, any such argument would violate the anti-commandeering doctrine by effectively requiring states to implement national policy without their consent.[31]

The Supreme Court seemed to confirm Professor Mikos's reasoning in
Murphy v. Nat'l Collegiate Athletic Assn'.[32] That decision invalidated the federal Professional and Amateur Sports Protection Act (PASPA),[33] which limited states' ability to "authorize" sports gambling. Although the United States
sought to distinguish between state laws that simply repealed state gambling
prohibitions and those that "authorized" sports gambling, Justice Samuel Alito's majority opinion held that this distinction made no difference.[34] Using state
marijuana laws as an example, the Court suggested that one might sensibly
describe state repeals of those laws as "authorizing" marijuana use.[35] Because
the federal statute in *Murphy* directed the states not to authorize sports gambling laws, it violated the anti-commandeering doctrine.[36] That doctrine, Justice Alito explained, forbids Congress "the power to issue orders directly to
the States."[37] Mikos seemed to speak for most observers when he concluded
that "the *Murphy* decision will provide states the clear precedent they need to
debunk lingering claims that their marijuana reforms are preempted because
they 'authorize' drug activities federal law forbids."[38]

Professor Mikos may well be right, but aspects of the *Murphy* opinion may
cut the other way. To invalidate the PASPA, the Court had to reject the United
States' argument that the statute was simply a "valid preemption provision."[39]
Such a provision, Justice Alito said, must meet two requirements: (1) it must be
an exercise of one of Congress's enumerated powers, and (2) it "must be best

read as [a provision] that regulates private actors."[40] This latter requirement derived from the basic principle inherent in the anti-commandeering doctrine that "the Constitution 'confers upon Congress the power to regulate individuals not States.'"[41] To underscore the point, Justice Alito noted that "regardless of the language sometimes used by Congress and this Court, every form of preemption is based on a federal law that regulates the conduct of private actors, not the States."[42] The PASPA failed this requirement. "[I]t is clear that the PASPA provision prohibiting state authorization of sports gambling is not a preemption provision," the Court said, "because there is no way in which this provision can be understood as a regulation of private actors."[43] The PASPA neither "confer[red] any federal rights on private actors interested in conducting sports gambling operations" nor "impos[ed] any federal restrictions on private actors."[44]

The trouble is that the relevant provisions of the federal CSA are not directed at the states in the way § 3702(1) of the PASPA was. The CSA regulates private actors by prohibiting them from cultivating, distributing, or consuming marijuana. The CSA's impact on state actors stems primarily from the argument that state "authorizations" of marijuana production, sale, and consumption undermine the purposes of the national prohibition. *Murphy* did not explicitly consider any implied preemption arguments of this kind. And the CSA's basic prohibition on private activity clearly passes *Murphy*'s test for a valid preemption provision. At the same time, the Court did note that the PASPA contains a prohibition on private conduct somewhat similar to the CSA's prohibition.[45] If the Court were inclined to think that such a private prohibition impliedly preempted state authorizations, one would have thought the Court would have said so.[46] But the PASPA scheme was odd enough, as it applied to both public and private entities, that one should probably resist reading *Murphy* as deciding questions it did not explicitly purport to resolve. The point here is simply that the implied preemptive effect of the CSA's general prohibition on private drug activity with respect to state efforts to authorize such activity may well be one of those unresolved questions.

In any event, even more difficult preemption questions arise as states seek to develop their own robust legal regimes to regulate the legal use of marijuana after legalization. States do not wish to leave marijuana unregulated; they seek to license distributors, regulate product quality, and restrict its use by certain persons (for example, minors) and persons engaged in certain activities (for example, driving or operating heavy machinery). They also generally seek to foster the development of a thriving marijuana industry that will provide jobs and tax revenue within the state. Certain models a state might adopt for achieving these ends seem plainly preempted under current doctrine. Several states, for example, control the distribution of alcohol and facilitate its taxation by operating state-run liquor stores. Similar state arrangements for marijuana would have the state actually conducting activity prohibited by federal law; surely this would be preempted.[47] It is not much more of a step to suggest that state laws encouraging private sellers of marijuana—perhaps through various kinds of subsidies, tax exemptions, and the like—would likewise involve state entities in directly encouraging the commission of federal crimes.[48] Preemption thus does not prevent a state from removing state-law prohibitions on marijuana use or from doing so in a more limited way that leaves many restrictions in place. But it is likely to be an impediment to efforts to derive public benefits from decriminalization by promoting a prosperous marijuana industry within a particular jurisdiction.

The second set of difficulties facing state legalization efforts arises from their continuing need for forbearance by national authorities. Federal authorities do not have sufficient resources to replace state and local officials no longer authorized to pursue marijuana producers, dealers, and users. One should not assume, however, that federal enforcement resources will remain constant. To cite an old example, Justice Joseph Story may well have thought he had fatally undercut enforcement of the Fugitive Slave Act when he held in *Prigg v. Pennsylvania*[49] that state and local law enforcement could not be required to participate in repatriating accused fugitives to the South.[50] But the national government proved willing to expand federal resources as necessary to enforce the act, creating one of the nation's earliest federal enforcement bureaucracies.[51] Such an expansion of federal resources for marijuana enforcement seems unlikely given current conditions, but those conditions could change.

In any event, a Justice Department hostile to state marijuana reforms could make life miserable for reformers through selective, high-profile prosecutions for maximum *in terrorem* effect. And resource-intensive criminal prosecutions are not the only way in which federal drug laws may bite. Nascent marijuana businesses may be unable to access the banking world on account of federal prohibitions on financial transactions involving illegal activity.[52] Although the House passed a bill easing such restrictions for marijuana businesses just as this chapter went to press, that bill faced an uncertain future in the Senate;[53] hence, "[m]ost financial institutions are staying away from the cannabis industry because of the burdensome regulations and lack of legal clarity, such as the potential for repercussions given that marijuana remains illegal on a federal basis."[54]

Similarly, marijuana businesses may face damaging federal tax consequences;[55] and state ethics rules may prevent attorneys from counseling persons who engage in activities that remain illegal under federal law.[56] Likewise, individuals using marijuana in violation of federal law may face significant employment or family law consequences, and persons on probation or parole may find that marijuana use constitutes a violation of that status.[57] All these collateral consequences of federal illegality may well combine to undermine the development of anything like a thriving market of legitimate marijuana businesses simply because state prohibitions have been removed. The development of such a market, with its attendant need for long-term investment, will depend on broad confidence that the whole range of federal regulatory and enforcement authorities—and not just the local U.S. Attorney's office—will forbear enforcement of the federal prohibition for the foreseeable future.

The Obama administration—broadly sympathetic with the goals of state reformers—was largely willing to forebear. Equally important, that administration was willing to articulate its policy of nonenforcement in official policy statements.[58] But Attorney General Jeff Sessions rescinded that guidance on January 4, 2018, and directed U.S. Attorneys to "follow well-established principles that govern all federal prosecutions" when addressing marijuana-related offenses.[59] Some U.S. Attorneys then signaled that they would not alter their post-Obama guidance approach to marijuana prosecutions, but others vowed to more vigorously pursue marijuana criminal cases.[60] Attorney General William Barr, who replaced Sessions in February of 2019, has not issued any guidance of his own and has told Congress that he favors a statutory solution over "just ignoring the enforcement of federal law."[61]

Despite these shifts under the Trump administration, we have not yet seen a spate of federal marijuana prosecutions in legalizing states. Perhaps this should not be surprising: after all, a return to pre-Obama enforcement priorities would still leave marijuana low on the list of federal priorities. And although the current Attorney General is evidently anti-legalization, he ultimately serves at the pleasure of a president who has repeatedly indicated that his sympathies lie in the opposite direction.[62] Finally, strong pro-marijuana sentiments in legalizing states no doubt lend weight and immediacy to the political safeguards of federalism on this issue.[63] With control of Congress so finely balanced and fiercely contested, one may doubt whether a Republican administration would press aggressively on this issue anytime soon.

Nonetheless, it would be hard to paint the longer-term picture as anything other than cloudy on the executive forbearance question. The present correlation of political forces makes it unlikely that federal enforcement will expand to fill the gap caused by state defections from the War on Drugs, but those forces are highly contingent. To the extent that building a viable infrastructure of legal marijuana businesses requires long-term investment, such investment remains an uncertain bet so long as marijuana remains illegal at the national level.

Finally, it is worth remembering that not everyone is Justice Oliver Wendell Holmes's "bad man"—that is, motivated only by the fear of sanctions.[64] Even if adverse legal consequences are unlikely, some persons may have strong moral or religious aversions to lawbreaking.[65] Moreover, the national government has interests in compliance with federal law that are independent of the policy objectives embodied in that law; it is not great for national authority generally, after all, if the states learn that they may ignore it with impunity. National authorities are unlikely to be indifferent to this basic institutional interest in compliance with national law indefinitely. President Dwight Eisenhower, for example, seems to have sent federal troops to Little Rock, Arkansas, in 1957 not so much out of personal support for the Supreme Court's desegregation decisions as out of a perceived need to enforce the supremacy of federal law.[66] For all these reasons, then, the current state of play on marijuana is best viewed as unstable—a temporary standoff, not an enduring settlement.[67]

THE PROSPECTS FOR STABLE STATE MARIJUANA LEGALIZATION

What might an enduring settlement look like, and what would it take to get there? To the tidy minds that seek national uniformity on every question of significance, the current patchwork of marijuana regulation and *de facto* deregulation may seem like chaos. But tidy uniformity may be overrated.[68] Moreover, I have argued in other work that federalism offers a valuable safety valve on polarizing issues like marijuana policy by allowing individual jurisdictions to satisfy the public preferences predominating within their borders without requiring a divisive fight at the national level.[69] If one agrees that the desirability of marijuana regulation is a subject upon which reasonable minds can differ, and that preferences on that question are unevenly distributed geographically among the several states, then the current flowering of state-by-state experimentation on that question may be valuable to the nation as a whole. And if that is true, then the inherent instability of those experiments should be troubling.

I thus conclude by discussing mechanisms by which state marijuana experimentation might be put on a firmer footing. Some of these mechanisms would require congressional amendments to the CSA; others could be accomplished by sub-statutory actions by federal agencies. The last would require action by the U.S. Supreme Court.

The first option would allow states affirmatively to opt out of the marijuana provisions of the CSA. The "Strengthening the Tenth Amendment by Entrusting States" (STATES) Act, introduced in the 115th Congress by Senator Elizabeth Warren, would effectively do this by carving out of the CSA's prohibitions persons using marijuana in compliance with state law (with certain exceptions).[70] Difficult questions might remain around the margins, such as the extent to which federal prohibitions might be applied to activity within an opt-out state if necessary to stop the importation of marijuana into a state that had not opted out. But an opt-out regime should go a long way toward eliminating the primary destabilizing impact of the CSA on state decriminalization efforts. It would eliminate possible federal preemption of state regulation and encouragement of marijuana businesses, redress the collateral consequences of federal illegality on marijuana businesses' access to capital markets and legal advice, and largely obviate the threat of sporadic and arbitrary federal prosecutions.

The obvious objection to opt-out rights would be that they would replace the CSA's uniform federal regime with a legal patchwork, not just as a matter of state law but of federal law as well. And surely it is strange to think of the content of federal law varying from one state to another. But the fact is that, in many areas, federal law already applies quite differently in different states. The

Clean Air Act, for example, delegates authority to the national Environmental
Protection Agency to set uniform national air quality standards[71]—except that
it also authorizes California to set more demanding standards if it so desires.[72]
Other states may then opt in to the California standards instead of the federal
ones if they wish.[73] The Voting Rights Act extensively regulates the structure
of state and local governments and the processes by which they elect their officials, but many of its provisions apply only to particular jurisdictions that have
barred African-Americans from voting in the past.[74] And the Affordable Care
Act's significant expansion of the federal Medicaid program—with its con-
comitant amendment to eligibility standards and benefit rules—applies only
to those states that have chosen to participate in the expansion.[75] To be sure,
our legal system's baseline expectation is that federal law will have the same
content in every state jurisdiction. But nothing in the Constitution requires
that this be so, and many federal statutes would be invalid if uniformity were
a constitutional mandate.

A second, less drastic option would leave the federal prohibition in place
but explicitly limit by statute the discretion of the Justice Department to prosecute violations of the CSA in states that have liberalized their own marijuana
laws. Such a limitation might reserve the option of federal CSA prosecutions
where persons have failed to comply with state marijuana regulations, thereby
allowing states the benefits of cooperation with federal law enforcement in such
cases. This sort of federal statutory reform might also set bounds beyond which
state liberalization may not go without triggering full federal enforcement; it
might state, for instance, that federal forbearance would end if a state made
marijuana use legal for minors or failed to regulate shipment of marijuana
grown in the state to other jurisdictions that continue to criminalize its use.
Such an arrangement would allow Congress to influence the course of state-
level reform while precluding federal prosecutions that might undermine that
reform. And it might minimize the risks of federal prosecutions that arbitrarily
target particular defendants.

Finally, to the extent that a non-uniform marijuana regime has become
plausible in this country, that recognition might encourage the Supreme Court
to reconsider aspects of its decision in *Gonzales v. Raich*.[76] In particular, the
Court should reconsider its conclusion in *Raich* that the existence of a state-
level regulatory regime is simply irrelevant to the constitutionality of federal

regulation.[77] Both Justice John Paul Stevens's majority opinion and Justice Antonin Scalia's concurrence emphasized the practical necessity of including even noncommercial marijuana use like Angel Raich's within the CSA's coverage to facilitate the overall enforcement of the scheme.[78] These arguments included a hearty dose of skepticism about the efficacy of California's regulatory regime.[79] But to the extent that post-legalization state regulatory regimes prove their efficacy over time, this judgment should become ripe for reexamination. More fundamentally, the necessity arguments upon which the *Raich* majority hung its hat look less and less persuasive as the *de facto* patchwork of contemporary law fails to cause chaos in the states where prohibitions are still enforced.

Reconsidering *Raich* would, of course, remove the risk of federal prosecutions for persons who, like Angel Raich herself, cultivate and consume marijuana without purchasing or carrying it across state lines. But even a Court that overruled *Raich* would surely permit federal regulation of the commercial market for marijuana. Whether or not the Court ever reconsiders *Raich*, then, hopes for a stable marijuana regime will rest primarily with Congress. Simply by repealing their own marijuana prohibitions, reform-minded states can make it unlikely that most marijuana producers, sellers, and consumers will ever face prosecution. But states cannot create a stable regulatory regime or a thriving commercial market for marijuana while the federal prohibition remains unaltered. If state-by-state experimentation on marijuana liberalization is to flourish, Congress will have to help frame the research design.

NOTES

I am grateful to Jonathan Adler for the invitation to participate in this volume, and to Mark Rothrock for outstanding research assistance. Although this chapter generally supports states' efforts to go their own way on marijuana policy, this should not be taken to endorse the liberalization of marijuana laws as a policy matter.

1. The Controlled Substances Act, 84 Stat. 1242, 21 U.S.C. § 801 et seq., enacted in 1970, classifies marijuana as a "Schedule 1" drug, 21 U.S.C. § 812(c). That classification renders the manufacture, distribution, or possession of marijuana a criminal offense, 21 U.S.C. §§ 841(a)(1), 844(a).

2. See, for example, *Gonzales v. Raich*, 545 U.S. 1, 22 (2006) (rejecting the argument that the CSA, as applied to an individual using homegrown marijuana for medicinal purposes authorized by state law, exceeded Congress's power under the Commerce Clause); *United States v. Oakland Cannabis Buyers' Cooperative*, 532 U.S. 483 (2001) (rejecting the effort to read a "medical necessity" defense into the federal CSA); *Raich v. Gonazales*, 500

F.3d 850, 861-66 (9th Cir. 2007) (rejecting substantive due process challenge to CSA based on a right to pain relief).

3. Governing the States and Localities, *State Marijuana Laws in 2019 Map*, June 25, 2019   (www.governing.com/gov-data/safety-justice/state-marijuana-laws-map-medical-recreational.html). The District of Columbia likewise purports to legalize recreational use (*see id.*), but Congress's right to exercise "exclusive legislation" over it creates problems unique to that jurisdiction (*see* U.S. Const. art. I, § 8, cl. 17).

4. U.S. Const. Art. VI, cl. 2 ("[T]he Laws of the United States . . . shall be the supreme Law of the Land; and the Judges in every State shall be bound thereby, any Thing in the Constitution or Laws of any state to the Contrary notwithstanding").

5. *New York v. United States*, 505 U.S. 144 (1992) (holding that Congress may not compel state legislatures to implement federal law); and *Printz v. United States*, 521 U.S. 898 (1997) (holding that Congress may not compel state executive officers to enforce federal law).

6. See Ernest A. Young, "Modern-Day Nullification: Marijuana and the Persistence of Federalism in an Age of Overlapping Regulatory Jurisdiction," *Case Western Reserve Law Review* 65 (2015), p. 770.

7. 138 S. Ct. 1461 (2018).

8. Daniel Walker Howe, *What Hath God Wrought: The Transformation of America, 1815–1848* (New York, 2007), pp. 395–410; Richard E. Ellis, *The Union at Risk: Jacksonian Democracy, States' Rights, and the Nullification Crisis* (New York, 1987).

9. "South Carolina Ordinance of Nullification," November 24, 1832 (www.avalon.law.yale.edu/19th_century/ordnull.asp).

10. For example, see South Carolina House of Representatives, Special Committee on the Tariff, "Exposition and Protest," December 19, 1828 (www.teachingushistory.org/documents/expositionandprotest.pdf), which was secretly drafted by John C. Calhoun; H. W. Brands, *Andrew Jackson: His Life and Times* (New York: Random House Inc., 2005), pp. 439–41; Howe, *What Hath God Wrought*, pp. 396–97.

11. Ellis, *Union at Risk*, pp. 41–73.

12. Howe, *What Hath God Wrought*, pp. 406–07.

13. Keith Whittington, *Constitutional Construction: Divided Powers and Constitutional Meaning* (USA, 2001), p. 112.

14. Edward S. Corwin, "The Passing of Dual Federalism," *Virginia Law Review* 36 (1950); Ernest A. Young, "The Puzzling Persistence of Dual Federalism," in *Nomos LV: Federalism and Subsidiarity*, edited by James E. Fleming and Jacob T. Levy (New York, 2014), pp. 34, 36–40, 53–57.

15. Morton Grodzins, "The American Federal System," in *A Nation of States: Essays on the American Federal System,* edited by Robert A. Goldwin (Chicago, 1961), pp. 1–2.

16. Philip J. Weiser, "Towards a Constitutional Architecture for Cooperative Federalism," *North Carolina Law Review* 79 (2001), pp. 663, 665.

17. Joseph F. Zimmerman, *Contemporary American Federalism: The Growth of National Power* (USA: Praeger Publishers, 1992).

18. Jessica Bulman-Pozen and Heather K. Gerken, "Uncooperative Federalism," *Yale Law Journal* 118 (2009), p. 1256.

19. Brian A. Reaves and Matthew J. Hickman, U.S. Department of Justice, Bureau of Justice Statistics Bulletin: Census of State & Local Law Enforcement Agencies, 2000 1 (2002); Reaves and Lynn M. Bauer, U.S. Department of Justice, Bureau of Justice Statistics Bulletin: Federal Law Enforcement Officers, 2002 1 (2003); William J. Stuntz, "Terrorism, Federalism, and Police Misconduct," *Harvard Journal of Law and Public Policy* 25 (2002), p. 665 ("The federal government has never employed a sizable fraction of the nation's law enforcement officers or prosecutors, nor housed a large portion of its prisoners.").

20. Robert A. Mikos, "On the Limits of Supremacy: Medical Marijuana and the States' Overlooked Power to Legalize Federal Crime," *Vanderbilt Law Review* 62 (2009), pp. 1419, 1465 (detailing how federal enforcement targets suppliers rather than minor offenders).

21. Mikos, "Limits of Supremacy," p. 1464.

22. *New York v. United States*, 505 U.S. 144 (1992) (holding that Congress may not require state legislatures to enact measures implementing federal programs); *Printz v. United States*, 521 U.S. 898 (1997) (holding that Congress may not require state executive officials to implement federal law).

23. *National Federation of Independent Business v. Sebelius*, 567 U.S. 519 (2012) (holding that Congress may not employ conditions on grants of federal money to coerce states into participating in a federal program).

24. *Murphy v. National Collegiate Athletic Association*, 138 S. Ct. 1461 (2018) (striking down a federal law provision purporting to forbid state authorization of sports gambling).

25. Mikos, "Limits of Supremacy," p. 1463.

26. Young, "Modern-Day Nullification," pp. 775–76.

27. *New State Ice Co. v. Liebmann*, 285 U.S. 262, 311 (1932) (Brandeis, J., dissenting).

28. Brannon P. Denning, "Vertical Federalism, Horizontal Federalism, and Legal Obstacles to State Marijuana Legalization Efforts," *Case Western Reserve Law Review* 65 (2015), p. 567.

29. *Emerald Steel Fabricators, Inc. v. Bureau of Labor & Industry*, 230 P.3d 518, 532 (Or. 2010) (en banc). Nebraska and Oklahoma made a similar argument in their unsuccessful attempt to challenge Colorado's legalization of marijuana in the original jurisdiction of the Supreme Court; Brief in Support of Motion for Leave to File Complaint at 15, *Nebraska & Oklahoma v. Colorado* (filed 2014) (No. 220144 ORG) (www.ok.gov/oag/documents/NE%20%20OK%20v%20%20CO%20-%20Original%20Action.pdf); Denning, "Vertical Federalism," pp. 574–75.

30. *Wyeth v. Levine*, 555 U.S. 555, 583 (2009) (Thomas, J., concurring in the judgment, suggesting that this sort of open-ended preemption analysis is unconstitutional); Caleb Nelson, "Preemption," *Virginia Law Review* 86 (2000), pp. 265–90 (developing this argument); Ernest A. Young, " 'The Ordinary Diet of the Law': The Presumption Against Preemption in the Roberts Court," *Supreme Court Review 2011* (2012), pp. 325–32 (discussing obstacle preemption).

31. Robert A. Mikos, "Preemption Under the Controlled Substances Act," *Journal of Health Care Law & Policy* 16 (2013), p. 26; Mikos, "Limits of Supremacy."

32. 138 S. Ct. 1461 (2018).

33. 28 U.S.C. § 3702(1).

34. *Murphy*, 138 S. Ct. at 1474 ("When a State completely or partially repeals old laws banning sports gambling, it 'authorize[s]' that activity.").

35. Ibid.

36. Ibid., pp. 1478–79.

37. Ibid., p. 1475.

38. See "The Implications of *Murphy v. NCAA* for State Marijuana Reforms, Marijuana Law, Policy, and Authority," 2018 (www.my.vanderbilt.edu/marijuana law/2018/05/the-implications-of-murphy-v-ncaa-for-state-marijuana-reforms/).

39. 138 S. Ct. at 1479.

40. Ibid.

41. Ibid. (quoting *New York*, 505 U.S. at 166).

42. Ibid., p. 1481.

43. Ibid.

44. Ibid.

45. Ibid., (citing 28 U.S.C. § 3702(2)). I say "somewhat" similar because § 3702(2) prohibited only sponsoring, operating, or promoting sports gambling—not simply gambling on sports per se—and it reached only private conduct that was "pursuant" to state law. See Ibid., p. 1483. The case did not present a question of the implied preemptive effect of a general prohibition on sports gambling by private persons or entities.

46. The matter is complicated by the issue that primarily divided the Justices, which was whether the private prohibition in § 3702(2) was severable from the prohibition on state authorization in § 3702(1). Ibid., p. 1482.

47. Denning, "Vertical Federalism," p. 577, supra note 27; Mikos, "Preemption," pp. 34–35.

48. As Professor Mikos points out, a considerably stronger case can be made for arguing that simply providing generally available public benefits to marijuana businesses and users would not be preempted. See Ibid., p. 35.

49. 41 U.S. (16 Pet.) 539, 615-16 (1842).

50. David C. Currie, *The Constitution in the Supreme Court, The First Hundred Years: 1789–1888,* at 245 n.54 (University of Chicago Press, 1985); Morgan D. Dowd, "Justice Story and the Slavery Conflict," *Massachusetts Law Quarterly* 52 (1967), p. 239, 251.

51. David M. Potter, *The Impending Crisis, 1848–1861* (USA: HarperCollins Publishers, 1976), pp. 138–39.

52. Julie Andersen Hill, "Banks, Marijuana, and Federalism," *Case Western Reserve Law Review* 65 (2015), p. 600; Erwin Chemerinsky, Jolene Forman, Allen Hopper, and Sam Kamin, "Cooperative Federalism and Marijuana Regulation," *UCLA Law Review* 62 (2015), pp. 91–93.

53. Jeff Smith, "Historic day: US House Passes Cannabis Banking Bill with Strong Bipartisan Support," *Marijuana Business Daily,* September 25, 2019 (https://mjbizdaily.com/historic-day-us-house-passes-cannabis-banking-bill-with-strong-bipartisan-support/); Jeff Smith, "Even without Reform, Banks Increasingly Serving Marijuana Industry," *Marijuana Business Daily,* October 8, 2019 (https://mjbizdaily.com/even-without-reform-banks-increasingly-serving-marijuana-industry/).

54. Ibid.

55. Chemerinsky, Forman, Hopper, and Kamin, "Cooperative Federalism," p. 94.

56. Ibid., pp. 95–97.

57. Ibid., pp. 98–100.

58. "Memorandum from James M. Cole, Deputy Attorney General, U.S. Department of Justice, to All United States Attorneys, "Guidance Regarding Marijuana Related Financial Crimes" 2014 (www.justice.gov/sites/default/files/usaowdwa/legacy/2014/02/14/DAG%20Memo%20-%20Guidance%20Regarding%20Marijuana%20Related%20Financial%20Crimes%202%2014%2014%20%282%29.pdf); "Memorandum from Cole, to All United States Attorneys, Guidance Regarding Marijuana Enforcement," 2013 (www.justice.gov/iso/opa/resources/3052013829132756857467.pdf); "Memorandum from Cole, Guidance Regarding the Ogden Memo in Jurisdictions Seeking to Authorize Marijuana for Medical Use," 2011 (www.justice.gov/sites/default/files/oip/legacy/2014/07/23/dag-guidance-2011-for-medical-marijuana-use. pdf); "Memorandum from David W. Ogden, Deputy Attorney General, U.S. Department of Justice, to Selected United States Attorneys, Investigations and Prosecutions in States Authorizing the Medical Use of Marijuana," 2009 (www.justice.gov/sites/default/files/opa/legacy/2009/10/19/medical-marijuana.pdf).

59. "Memorandum for All United States Attorneys: Marijuana Enforcement," 2018 (www.justice.gov/opa/press-release/file/1022196/download).

60. Sarah N. Lynch, "Trump Administration Drops Obama-Era Easing of Marijuana Prosecutions," Reuters, January 4, 2018 (www.reuters.com/article/us-usa-justice-marijuana/trump-administration-drops-obama-era-easing-of-marijuana-prosecutions-idUSKBN1ET1MU). In July 2018, the Trump administration also created the Marijuana Policy Coordination Committee, consisting of the Drug Enforcement Agency and fourteen other federal agencies, and tasked them with collecting data regarding the "negative impacts of marijuana use" to counter the "prevailing narrative" that the drug is safe. Megan Keller, "Trump Tasked Multi-Agency Committee with Countering Pro-Marijuana Message: Report," *The Hill*, August 29, 2018 (www.thehill.com/homenews/administration/404187-trump-tasked-multi-agency-committee-with-countering-pro-marijuana). That committee's efforts at countering the current narrative surrounding marijuana seemed calculated to challenge state legalization and justify more stringent federal enforcement. Ibid.

61. Kyle Jaeger, "U.S. Attorney General Says He Prefers Marijuana Reform Bill to Current Federal Law," *Marijuana Moment*, April 10, 2019 (www.marijuanamoment.net/u-s-attorney-general-says-he-prefers-marijuana-reform-bill-to-current-federal-law/).

62. See Jaeger (quoting Attorney General Barr as stating that he "would still favor one uniform federal rule against marijuana"). In 2016, then-candidate Trump stated that he supported state decisions to legalize marijuana, Nicholas Riccardi, "Trump Vows to Back Law Protecting Marijuana Industry, Breaking with Sessions," *Chicago Tribune,* April 13, 2018 (www.chicagotribune.com/news/nationworld/ct-trump-marijuana-industry-20180413-story.html). As recently as June 2018, President Trump indicated he would likely support a law to protect the marijuana industry in states that have decriminalized the drug. See Dennis Romero, "Trump Says He'll Probably Back

Marijuana Protections Bill," NBC News, June 9, 2018 (www.nbcnews.com/politics/white-house/trump-says-he-ll-probably-back-marijuana-protections-bill-n881561).

63. See generally Herbert Wechsler, "The Political Safeguards of Federalism: The Role of the States in the Composition and Selection of the National Government," *Columbia Law Review* 54 (1954), p. 543.

64. O. W. Holmes Jr., "The Path of the Law," *Harvard Law Review* 10 (1897), p. 459.

65. H. L. A. Hart, *The Concept of Law* (Great Britain, 1972), pp. 55–56 (suggesting that law binds from the "internal point of view"—that is, voluntary compliance without regard to the practical threat of sanctions).

66. Dwight D. Eisenhower, "Speech on Little Rock," September 24, 1957 (www.blackpast.org/african-american-history/1957-dwight-eisenhower-address-little-rock/).

67. Attorney General Barr, for example, has characterized the present state of affairs as "intolerable." Jaeger, supra note 63.

68. Jeffrey S. Sutton, *51 Imperfect Solutions: States and the Making of American Constitutional Law* (New York: Sheridan Books Inc., 2018) (demonstrating the virtues of state experimentation on constitutional questions); Amanda Frost, "Overvaluing Uniformity, *Virginia Law Review* 94 (2008), p. 1567 (questioning the assumption that national uniformity is always desirable).

69. Margaret H. Lemos and Ernest A. Young, "State Public Law Litigation in an Age of Polarization," *Texas Law Review* 97 (2018), pp. 60–62; Michael W. McConnell, "Federalism: Evaluating the Founders' Design," *University of Chicago Law Review* 54 (1987), pp. 1484, 1493.

70. S. 3032 – 115th Congress (2017–2018) (www.congress.gov/bill/115th-congress/senate-bill/3032/text).

71. 42 U.S.C. § 7409.

72. 42 U.S.C. § 7543(b), (e); S. Rep. No. 1196, 91st Cong., 2d Sess. 32 (1970) (stating that the provision for waiver of federal preemption was intended for California); John P. Dwyer, "The Practice of Federalism Under the Clean Air Act," *Maryland Law Review* 54 (1995), pp. 1183, 1196.

73. 42 U.S.C. § 7507.

74. Voting Rights Act of 1965, § 4(b), 79 Stat. 438; *Shelby Cty., Ala. v. Holder,* 570 U.S. 529, 537 (2013). *Shelby County* did not question the viability of applying federal law differently in different places; rather, it held that Congress had not sufficiently justified continuing to do so decades after enacting the Voting Rights Act.

75. *National Federation of Independent Business v. Sebelius,* 567 U.S. 519, 576–88 (2012).

76. 545 U.S. 1 (2005).

77. Ibid., pp. 29–33. For a critique of this aspect of *Raich,* see Ernest A. Young, "Just Blowing Smoke? Politics, Doctrine, and the Federalist Revival after *Gonzales v. Raich,*" *Supreme Court Review* 2005 (2006), pp. 33–37.

78. 545 U.S. pp. 30–33 (majority opinion); Ibid., pp. 39–42 (Scalia, J., concurring in the judgment).

79. Ibid., pp. 31–32 (majority opinion).

4

MURPHY'S MISTAKE, AND HOW TO FIX IT

Robert A. Mikos

Preemption concerns have always bedeviled state marijuana reforms. From the very start of the modern reform movement in the 1990s, supporters and opponents of these reforms have been locked in a debate over the enforceability of state laws legalizing marijuana. Invoking the Constitution's Supremacy Clause, opponents have insisted that state marijuana reforms are necessarily preempted (and thus, void) because they conflict with the federal government's strict ban on the drug. Appealing to another constitutional principle—the Supreme Court's anti-commandeering rule, supporters of reform have argued that because Congress may not compel states to enact a marijuana ban in the first instance, it may not stop them from repealing a ban they no longer wish to keep.

Each side in this ongoing debate has drawn upon (and created) precedents that ostensibly support its position. Unfortunately, the United States Supreme Court has provided little guidance on how to settle these competing constitutional claims. In particular, the Court has never clearly demarcated the boundary between permissible preemption, on the one hand, and impermissible commandeering, on the other. Indeed, until very recently, these two doctrines, though closely related, had never crossed paths at One First Street.

Murphy v. National Collegiate Athletic Association,[1] a case on the Court's docket for the 2017–2018 term, gave the Court the rare opportunity to address this glaring gap. In *Murphy,* the Court had to consider the constitutionality of a federal statute that blocked New Jersey from repealing its ban on another "vice"—sports gambling. The case cleanly pitted the state's claim that Congress had forced it to ban sports gambling, in violation of the anti-commandeering rule, against the plaintiffs' (the NCAA and other sports leagues) claim that Congress had merely preempted a state law that conflicted with one of its own, consistent with long-standing preemption jurisprudence. While the Court agreed with the state in the *Murphy* case and found a commandeering violation, it failed to explain satisfactorily why the federal statute was not a valid preemption provision, as the NCAA had claimed. This failure means that smoke continues to obscure where Congress's power to preempt state law ends and the safe harbor created by the anti-commandeering rule begins, with obvious ramifications for state marijuana reforms.

This chapter explains where *Murphy* went wrong and how to fix it. It also assesses the decision's potential implications for state marijuana reforms.

BACKGROUND: *MURPHY V. NCAA*

Murphy arose from New Jersey's campaign to relax state laws governing sports gambling. Nearly one and a half centuries ago, New Jersey enacted a prohibition against sports gambling. The statute declared unlawful "[a]ll wagers, bets or stakes made to depend upon any race or game," and it made such wagers, bets, and stakes unenforceable in a court of law.[2] That ban, and various statutes later enacted to bolster it, reflected then-prevailing concerns over the morality of gambling and the perceived threat it posed to the integrity of sporting contests.

How times have changed. In the last decade, fueled largely by a desire to inject new life into its struggling casinos and racetracks, New Jersey twice sought to legalize sports gambling in the state.

The first attempt was made in 2012. The previous year, New Jersey voters had approved a referendum—by a nearly two to one margin—that enabled the state legislature to "authorize by law" sports gambling at casinos and racetracks. Pursuant to this new authority, the New Jersey legislature passed the

Sports Wagering Act of 2012. The 2012 law repealed the aforementioned state prohibition on sports gambling as applied to the state's casinos and racetracks, and it replaced that prohibition with a "comprehensive regulatory scheme, requiring licenses for operators and individual employees, extensive documentation, minimum cash reserves, and Division of Gaming Enforcement access to security and surveillance systems."[3]

But New Jersey ran into an obstacle: the Professional and Amateur Sports Protection Act of 1992 (PASPA). Animated by the same concerns that had driven most states to ban sports gambling decades earlier, Congress made it unlawful for prohibition states to "sponsor, operate, advertise, promote, license, or authorize by law" sports gambling.[4] In other words, this federal statute seemingly barred states that had banned sports gambling from ever changing their minds.

Relying on another provision of PASPA that created a private cause of action, the National Collegiate Athletic Association (NCAA) and other sports leagues successfully sued to block implementation of New Jersey's 2012 law. Affirming a permanent injunction against the state law in *National Collegiate Athletic Association v. Christie* (*Christie I*), the U.S. Court of Appeals for the Third Circuit reasoned that the 2012 law "is precisely what PASPA says the states may not do—a purported authorization by law of sports wagering. It is therefore invalidated by PASPA."[5] At the same time, however, the *Christie I* court recognized the commandeering concern created by PASPA. It, therefore, assured the state that PASPA does not "prohibit New Jersey from repealing its ban on sports wagering. . . . All that is prohibited is the issuance of gambling 'license[s]' or the affirmative 'authoriz[ation] by law' of gambling schemes."[6]

Seemingly acting on this tip, New Jersey soon thereafter made a second attempt to legalize sports gambling. In 2014, the state legislature passed a new law that simply repealed the state's prohibition on sports gambling as applied to casinos and racetracks. In relevant part, the 2014 law declares that the state's own laws banning sports gambling:

> are repealed to the extent they apply . . . at a casino or gambling house operating in this State in Atlantic City or a running or harness horse racetrack in this State, to the placement and acceptance of wagers on professional, collegiate, or amateur sport contests or athletic events by

persons 21 years of age or older situated at such location or to the operation of a wagering pool that accepts such wagers from persons 21 years
of age or older situated at such location, provided that the operator of the
casino, gambling house, or running or harness horse racetrack consents
to the wagering or operation.[7]

Unlike its predecessor, the 2014 law did not also create a "comprehensive
regulatory scheme" to govern sports gambling at casinos and racetracks. Put
differently, the 2014 law legalized sports gambling under New Jersey law, but
it did not seek to regulate such gambling, at least directly.

Still concerned about the perceived threat that legalized sports gambling
posed to their sporting operations, the NCAA and other leagues proceeded to
challenge the 2014 law as well, arguing that New Jersey had again "authorized"
sports gambling in violation of PASPA. And once again, the Third Circuit
agreed. This time, the court found such authorization in the selective way that
New Jersey had chosen to repeal its prohibitions: "[A] state's decision to selectively remove a prohibition on sports wagering in a manner that permissively
channels wagering activity to particular locations or operators is, in essence,
'authorization' under PASPA."[8]

The *Christie II* court, therefore, affirmed a permanent injunction barring
state officials from giving effect to the 2014 law. The court, in other words, told
New Jersey that it had to keep its 150-year-old ban on sports gambling in toto,
notwithstanding changed circumstances and opinions toward sports gambling.

THE *MURPHY* DECISION IN THREE STEPS

Following *Christie II*, New Jersey petitioned the Supreme Court to hear its
claim (first broached in *Christie I*) that PASPA effectively forced the state to
prohibit sports gambling and, thus, violated the Court's anti-commandeering
rule. The Supreme Court granted certiorari in *Murphy*, so renamed because
New Jersey had elected a new governor.

This time, New Jersey prevailed. The *Murphy* Court reversed the Third
Circuit's decision in *Christie II*. It found that PASPA, indeed, violated the anti-
commandeering rule because it effectively forced New Jersey to ban sports
gambling under state law. It also found that PASPA could not be salvaged as

a valid preemption provision. Justice Alito wrote the opinion for the Court, which, while divided six to three on the issue of severability, was arguably unanimous on the commandeering and preemption issues.

Justice Alito's opinion for the Court proceeded in three steps. I will walk through each of these steps in turn and then explain the implications of each for state marijuana reforms.

Step One: To Repeal a Ban Is to Authorize Activity

In the first step, Justice Alito had to interpret the meaning of "authorize," as that term is used in PASPA. The parties had offered competing definitions of the term. As described by Justice Alito:

> Petitioners argue that the anti-authorization provision requires States to maintain their existing laws against sports gambling without alteration. One of the accepted meanings of the term "authorize," they point out, is "permit." . . . They therefore contend that any state law that has the effect of permitting sports gambling, including a law totally or partially repealing a prior prohibition, amounts to an authorization. . . .
> Respondents interpret the provision more narrowly. They claim that the primary definition of "authorize" requires affirmative action. To authorize, they maintain, means "to empower; to give a right or authority to act; to endow with authority." And this, they say, is precisely what the 2014 Act does: It empowers a defined group of entities, and it endows them with the authority to conduct sports gambling operations.[9]

Ultimately, the Court adopted the definition favored by New Jersey, although it suggested the 2014 law had "authorized" sports gambling under either party's definition of the term:

> When a State completely or partially repeals old laws banning sports gambling, it "authorize[s]" that activity. This is clear when the state-law landscape at the time of PASPA's enactment is taken into account. At that time, all forms of sports gambling were illegal in the great majority of States, and in that context, the competing definitions offered by the parties lead to the same conclusion. The repeal of a state law

banning sports gambling not only "permits" sports gambling (petitioners' favored definition); it also gives those now free to conduct a sports
betting operation the "right or authority to act"; it "empowers" them
(respondents' and the United States's definition).

The concept of state "authorization" makes sense only against a back-
drop of prohibition or regulation. A State is not regarded as authorizing
everything that it does not prohibit or regulate. No one would use the
term in that way. For example, no one would say that a State "authorizes" its residents to brush their teeth or eat apples or sing in the shower.
We commonly speak of state authorization only if the activity in question would otherwise be restricted.[10]

Step Two: To Block Authorization Qua Repeal Is to Commandeer . . .

The Court's first conclusion meant it could not dodge the constitutional claim
raised by New Jersey. Namely, because the state had plainly violated the express
terms of PASPA by authorizing sports gambling, the Court now had to decide
whether PASPA was constitutional; that is, whether it had impermissibly com-
mandeered New Jersey.

The NCAA had argued that the anti-commandeering rule was inapplicable to the case because PASPA did not compel New Jersey to take any affirmative action—such as to pass a new law banning sports gambling. But the
Court refused to draw a distinction between compelling action and compelling
inaction: "This distinction is empty. It was a matter of happenstance that the
laws challenged in *New York* and *Printz* commanded 'affirmative' action as
opposed to imposing a prohibition. The basic principle—that Congress cannot
issue direct orders to state legislatures—applies in either event."[11]

The Court also offered an illustration to drive home the point:

> PASPA includes an exemption for States that permitted sports betting
> at the time of enactment . . . but suppose Congress did not adopt such
> an exemption. Suppose Congress ordered States with legalized sports
> betting to take the affirmative step of criminalizing that activity and
> ordered the remaining States to retain their laws prohibiting sports
> betting. There is no good reason why the former would intrude more
> deeply on state sovereignty than the latter.[12]

The Court's reasoning on this second step is sound. It is well-accepted that the anti-commandeering rule prevents Congress from directly ordering states to "enact or administer a federal regulatory program."[13] Thus, Congress may not command the states to adopt a prohibition on sports gambling by private actors. As a logical corollary, however, the rule must also prevent Congress from accomplishing the same end indirectly, namely, by blocking a state from repealing a prohibition it had already adopted but no longer wished to keep. After all, allowing Congress to block such a repeal would arbitrarily limit the protections of the anti-commandeering rule. It would enable Congress to require a state to keep a prohibition Congress could not have required the state to adopt in the first instance.[14] To avoid such arbitrariness, the anti-commandeering rule must be read to prevent Congress from preempting the repeal of a state prohibition, even if such repeal amounts to affirmative action that "authorizes" conduct forbidden by federal law.

While not openly disagreeing with the foregoing logic, the *Christie II* court had, nonetheless, rejected it by suggesting that the partial repeal of a state prohibition was somehow distinguishable from the complete repeal of the prohibition. To bolster this distinction, it used an elegant variety of terms to describe the effect of the 2014 law: For example, the court suggested the state had formally "approved," "affirmatively permitted," "sanctioned," and "empowered" sports gambling in New Jersey. Even if these descriptions of the 2014 law are accurate, however, the *Christie II* court failed to explain why they exposed the state law to congressional override. All these descriptions of the statute merely restate the fact that the 2014 law repealed the state's prohibitions on sports gambling. In other words, the court provided no reason to conclude that the 2014 law did anything more than what the anti-commandeering rule entitles the state to do—namely, to repeal a state law banning an activity.

The flaw in the *Christie II* court's reasoning becomes all the more apparent when considering the effects of the court's decision. *Christie II* quite literally compelled New Jersey to reinstate its prohibitions on sports gambling in casinos and racetracks. The ruling meant that casinos, racetracks, and their patrons once again would face stiff sanctions under state law for engaging in sports gambling, notwithstanding two state attempts to repeal those sanctions. The ruling thereby threatened to raise all the accountability concerns the anti-commandeering rule is intended to address. Had the resuscitation of the state's prohibition on sports gambling proven unpopular (as seems likely, given strong public support for the 2011 referendum), voters would have faced difficulty sorting out who was to blame. The state legislature for failing to successfully repeal the state's prohibitions on sports gambling? The state Casino Control Commission, Racing Commission, or county prosecutors for continuing to enforce those unwanted prohibitions? State courts for refusing to enforce disputed sports wagers? Or Congress for blocking state officials from vindicating the interests of their constituents? By blurring the lines of accountability the anti-commandeering rule was designed to sharpen, PASPA threatened to make New Jersey officials "bear the brunt of public disapproval, while the federal officials who devised the regulatory program may remain insulated from the electoral ramifications of their decision."[15]

By recognizing the practical equivalence between passing a new ban and leaving an existing ban in place, the *Murphy* Court gave states the green light to permit sports gambling under state law. Significantly, the Court also held that such permission extended to licensing sports gambling. The issue arose because the NCAA claimed the 2014 law not only "authorized" sports gambling, but "licensed" it as well, thereby violating a separate prohibition found in Section 3702(1), one that makes it unlawful for a state to "license" sports gambling. The league had a point—the 2014 law permitted sports gambling only at casinos and racetracks that were separately licensed by the state, suggesting that the 2014 law had effectively licensed sports gambling. Nonetheless, the *Murphy* Court found no constitutionally significant distinction between "licensing" and "authorizing" an activity.[16] Both actions merely signify that the government will not punish some activity that it normally restricts. Thus, New Jersey was free not only to authorize sports gambling but to license it as well.

Step Three: . . . Unless Congress Also Regulates Private Actors

Notwithstanding its defeat in step two, the NCAA had another card up its sleeve: preemption. The NCAA insisted that PASPA was a "valid preemption provision," and thus (somehow) beyond the purview of the anti-commandeering rule.[17] In its brief for the Court, for example, the NCAA had argued: "PASPA preempts state laws authorizing casinos and racetracks to violate the federal policy against offering sports-gambling schemes. It would be 'a radical departure from long-established precedent . . . to hold that the Tenth Amendment prohibits Congress from displacing state police power laws regulating private activity.' "[18]

Thus, the *Murphy* Court had to take a third step and, finally, opine on the relationship between the anti-commandeering rule and preemption. To that end, the Court announced a two-part test for determining whether a federal statute, like PASPA, permissibly preempts state law and, thus, escapes censure under the anti-commandeering rule:

> In order for the PASPA provision to preempt state law, it must satisfy two requirements. First, it must represent the exercise of a power conferred on Congress by the Constitution . . . Second, since the Constitution "confers upon Congress the power to regulate individuals, not States," *New York*, 505 U.S. at 166 . . . , the PASPA provision at issue must be best read as one that regulates private actors.[19]

Notably, Justice Alito did not further discuss the first prong of this test—the constitutional power requirement. Rather, in his opinion, he focused entirely on the second prong—the regulation of private actors test. According to Justice Alito, all instances of preemption the Court had previously upheld "work in the same way: Congress enacts a law that imposes restrictions or confers rights on private actors; a state law confers rights or imposes restrictions that conflict with the federal law; and therefore the federal law takes precedence and the state law is preempted."[20] Thus, the constitutionality of PASPA—that is, whether it constituted a valid act of preemption rather than an invalid act of commandeering—seemingly hinged on whether Section 3702(1) is "best read" as a statute that "regulates private actors."

This reasoning doomed PASPA because the statute (or at least, the provision at issue in the case) did not regulate private actors. It was directed exclusively at the states, as a way to entrench the sports gambling bans nearly all of them had adopted by the time Congress enacted PASPA in 1992. As the Court explained:

> There is no way in which [Section 3702(1)] can be understood as a regulation of private actors. It certainly does not confer any federal rights on

private actors interested in conducting sports gambling operations. (It does not give them a federal right to engage in sports gambling.) Nor does it impose any federal restrictions on private actors. . . . Thus, there is simply no way to understand the provision prohibiting state authorization as anything other than a direct command to the States. And that is exactly what the anticommandeering rule does not allow.[21]

The Court's holding in step three meant that New Jersey could keep its winnings from the first two steps. In fact, in a separate portion of the opinion not directly relevant here, a six to three majority of the Court proceeded to find the remainder of PASPA inseverable from the constitutionally defective portions. In other words, New Jersey had scored a complete victory. It was free not only to "authorize" and "license" sports gambling, but to "sponsor, operate, advertise, [or] promote" it as well.[22]

MURPHY'S MISTAKE

Notwithstanding New Jersey's complete victory with respect to sports gambling, *Murphy* may be far less protective of state authority than it would first appear. Indeed, the Court's reasoning in step three could unwittingly curtail the scope of the anti-commandeering rule it defended in step two, with potentially far-reaching consequences in other contested policy domains—especially marijuana policy.

The problem arises from the second prong of the *Murphy* Court's test for preemption. Per Justice Alito's opinion, under this prong, Congress could seemingly evade the restrictions imposed by the anti-commandeering rule simply by embedding a command to the states in a law that also regulates private parties. Rick Hills, while not necessarily anticipating the implications of his argument, explains that: "To avoid *Murphy*, federal laws merely need to create a cause of action against a private party for engaging in some federally forbidden activity accompanied by a preemption clause barring any state law from authorizing that which federal law forbids. The problem with PASPA is that it did not contain this 'direct' federal prohibition on private gambling."[23]

To illustrate how this could be done, and why it undermines the anti-commandeering rule, suppose Congress added the following language to PAS-

PA's Section 3702(1): "It is unlawful for any private actor to sponsor, operate, advertise, or promote sports gambling."[24]

Coupled with the private cause of action already created by PASPA in 28 U.S.C. Section 3703, this language would seemingly satisfy the second prong of Justice Alito's preemption test. It would both "impose restrictions" on sports books and "confer rights" on sports leagues. Thus, under Justice Alito's preemption test, any state law that obstructed this federal regime, say, by authorizing gambling on sporting events, could be preempted—even if this would effectively block the state from repealing a prohibition it no longer wanted.

I doubt the *Murphy* Court meant to create such a loophole in the protections afforded by the anti-commandeering rule—protections the Court itself affirmed in step two of Justice Alito's opinion. After all, this revised version of PASPA would impose the same costs on the states as did the version invalidated by the *Murphy* Court. Namely, by preventing the state from repealing its ban on sports gambling, the revised statute would still blur the lines of political accountability for a sports gambling ban, and it would foist the costs of the ban onto state officials. Those problems do not go away just because Congress also regulates private actors, for example, just because it also bans sports gambling.

Unfortunately, however, *Murphy* fails to close this loophole. Indeed, *Murphy* has already sparked a lively academic debate, with commentators reaching wildly different conclusions about the broader implications of the decision.[25]

The *Murphy* Court erred in using federal law—namely, whether Congress "imposes restrictions or confers benefits on private actors"—to judge whether Congress has the power to preempt state law. Justice Alito suggested this criterion was gleaned from preemption precedents, but all the precedents upon which he relied addressed a conceptually distinct inquiry: whether Congress wanted to preempt a state law.[26] Whether a federal statute imposes restrictions or confers rights on private actors is clearly relevant for that inquiry. For example, if Congress gives private actors a right to engage in some activity, it suggests a congressional desire to preempt any state law that restricts that activity. But conferring such a right (or, conversely, imposing a restriction) on private parties cannot expand the scope of Congress's power vis-à-vis the states, that is, its power to preempt state law.

THE IMPLICATIONS FOR STATE MARIJUANA REFORMS

The effects of the Court's mistake were muted in *Murphy* itself, because PASPA did not regulate private actors. However, *Murphy*'s reasoning could easily lead courts astray in cases involving other state laws, including state marijuana reforms.

State marijuana reforms bear a striking resemblance to New Jersey's 2014 law. Like the 2014 law, state marijuana reforms "selectively repeal" prohibitions the states had previously applied to all possession, manufacture, and distribution of marijuana. For example, Colorado's Amendment 64 repeals the state's prohibition as applied to adults (but not minors), and it repeals that prohibition only with respect to relatively small quantities of the drug (one ounce).[27] In other words, Amendment 64 appears to authorize certain marijuana behaviors, much like the 2014 law authorizes sports gambling. In fact, several states have expressly declared that their reforms "authorize" individuals to possess, manufacture, and/ or distribute marijuana pursuant to state law,[28] and the Supreme Court itself has even described state reforms as "authoriz[ing] the use of marijuana."[29]

To be sure, unlike PASPA, the federal Controlled Substances Act (CSA) does not expressly prohibit states from authorizing marijuana possession and related activities. Rather, the CSA preempts state law only to the extent it poses a "positive conflict" with the CSA, "so that the two cannot consistently stand together."[30] Nonetheless, it is easy to make the argument that state "authorization" of marijuana activities poses a conflict with and is, thus, preempted by the federal CSA. Indeed, some courts have previously used this very argument to block implementation of state reforms. In *Emerald Steel Fabricators, Inc. v. Bureau of Labor & Indus.*, for example, the Oregon Supreme Court found that a state law purporting to ban employment discrimination against employees participating in the state's medical marijuana program was preempted. To reach that conclusion, the Court reasoned: "To the extent that [state law] *authorizes* persons holding medical marijuana licenses to engage in conduct that the Controlled Substances Act explicitly prohibits, it poses [an] obstacle to the full accomplishment of Congress's purposes (preventing all use of marijuana, including medical uses)," and is thus void.[31] Similar reasoning has been employed in other prominent lawsuits challenging the legal status of state marijuana reforms.[32]

Despite the similarities, however, *Murphy* may prove far less protective of state prerogatives over marijuana than sports gambling. On the one hand, the *Murphy* Court's reasoning in step two would seemingly give states the green light to legalize marijuana under state law. After all, if a state is constitutionally entitled to repeal its own ban on sports gambling (in whole or part), it naturally follows that the state is also constitutionally entitled to repeal its ban on the possession, manufacture, and distribution of marijuana, as well. Thus, this portion of the *Murphy* decision should quell claims that marijuana reforms are preempted merely because they "authorize" activities federal law forbids. Characterizing state reforms in this way, as the Court held in *Murphy*, does not somehow make them vulnerable to congressional override.

Indeed, Justice Alito's opinion in *Murphy* also seemingly gives the states the green light to license the commercial supply of marijuana—a big shot in the arm for state reforms. Every state that has authorized businesses to produce and sell marijuana requires those businesses first to obtain a license from the state.[33] Without such a license, the manufacture and distribution of marijuana for commercial purposes remain strictly prohibited under state law. The licensing requirement not only helps states vet who may produce and sell marijuana, it also provides a framework for a host of regulations states have imposed on the commercial marijuana industry, including, for example, restrictions on how the industry promotes its products.[34] Given that Justice Alito seemingly equated licensing with authorization, state marijuana licensing requirements should likewise be immune from preemption challenges.

On the other hand, the Court's reasoning in step three could be used to block state legalization of marijuana. As noted, *Murphy* suggests that Congress may preempt state authorization as long as it (Congress) also regulates private actors in the process. Although PASPA failed to do that, the federal CSA *does* regulate private actors. It bans outright their possession, manufacture, and distribution of marijuana (among many other activities).[35] Thus, under Justice Alito's reasoning in step three, one could reasonably argue that Congress has permissibly preempted state authorization of marijuana related activities, because Congress itself took the added step of banning those activities. Put another way, opponents of state reforms could argue that states may not repeal their state bans on marijuana, even though they may repeal their bans on sports gambling. The *Murphy* decision, at the very least, needlessly gives that argument a second wind and keeps alive long-standing doubts about the legal status of state laws legalizing marijuana—doubts the Court had seemingly quashed in step two.

HOW TO FIX *MURPHY*'S MISTAKE

Such doubts about state marijuana reforms should not have survived *Murphy*. Fortunately, there is a way to fix *Murphy*'s preemption test, one that not only respects Congress's power to preempt state law but also respects the limits imposed on that power by the anti-commandeering rule. Here's how: To determine whether Congress has the power to preempt a given state law, the Court should focus exclusively on the content of that *state* law. More particularly, the Court must ask whether the state law imposes a restriction or confers a right on private actors. Congress may preempt state law only to the extent the *state* law imposes restrictions or confers rights—that is, only to the extent *state* law regulates private actors. Congress may not preempt state law if it, instead, removes such restrictions or rights—that is, if the state law deregulates private actors. After all, as the *Murphy* Court correctly held in step two, to preempt the latter type of state law would effectively force the state to impose restrictions or confer rights on private actors, in plain violation of the anti-commandeering rule.

To illustrate this distinction, imagine a state law that does two separate things. First, the law repeals the state's long-standing criminal prohibition on the commercial distribution of marijuana. Second, the law imposes a tax of 10 percent on all sales of marijuana. In this example, only the second provision could be preempted by Congress. It imposes a restriction on private marijuana vendors; the tax might be less onerous than the criminal bans the state previously imposed on marijuana distributors, but it is a restriction nonetheless. By contrast, the first provision merely authorizes private actors to distribute marijuana; in other words, it removes a restriction rather than imposes one. For the reasons discussed in step two, it would contravene the anti-commandeering rule for Congress to preempt the first provision because it would force the state to retain its ban on marijuana distribution, an odd result if Congress could not force the state to adopt the ban in the first instance.

This reformulation of the *Murphy* preemption test must not be confused with the action/inaction test proposed by the NCAA and rejected by the

Murphy Court in step two. The action/inaction test fails to recognize that any given "action," such as the passage of a law, can have wildly different consequences.[36] The hypothetical two-part state law just discussed illustrates the problem. The same "action"—that is, the passage of this single law—imposed a restriction (the tax), but also removed a restriction (the criminal prohibition). The action/inaction test would empower Congress to block the whole law, thereby forcing the state to continue to ban marijuana. By contrast, if we focus on the effect of the state law—namely, whether it imposes a restriction or confers a right—Congress could block only the part of it that imposes the tax, leaving the state free to legalize marijuana.

All the cases in which the Supreme Court has held a state law preempted are consistent with this limitation of federal supremacy.[37] In other words, the state actions that have been successfully challenged as preempted in these, and myriad other, cases all interfered with an activity—broadly speaking, they made that activity more, or less, costly by imposing restrictions or conferring rights on the private actors who engage in it. Prior to *Christie I* and its progeny, no court had ever found that state action was preempted when it merely repealed a preexisting state restriction.[38]

This reformulated preemption test is also consistent with the holding in *Murphy*. New Jersey's 2014 law merely repealed certain restrictions the state had previously imposed on sports gambling. As the Court itself recognized, Congress could not block that repeal because doing so would have forced New Jersey to ban sports gambling in perpetuity (or at least until the state got Congress's blessing to lift the state ban). It is important, however, to acknowledge that the reformulated test would close the loophole created by *Murphy*. Congress could no longer transform this prohibited act of commandeering into a permissible act of preemption merely by recasting it as part of a federal regulation of private actors, for example, by adding another provision of the statute that would ban sports gambling by private actors.

Now consider how this preemption test would apply to state marijuana reforms. To the extent these reforms merely authorize—and perhaps even license—marijuana activities, they would be spared from preemption. As explained, these actions do not impose restrictions but, rather, remove them. The reforms declare that certain private actors are no longer subject to state bans on activities like producing, distributing, or possessing marijuana. Just as important, however, other state reforms that seek to regulate marijuana activities—by imposing restrictions or conferring rights on them—would remain vulnerable to preemption under this test. Sundry reforms do, indeed, impose restrictions or confer benefits on marijuana activities. For example, Colorado's Retail Marijuana Code imposes a variety of product testing, packaging, and labeling requirements on state licensed marijuana suppliers.[39] Because such requirements go beyond merely repealing prohibitions on the production and sale of marijuana, they are vulnerable to congressional override. (For similar reasons, New Jersey's 2012 sports gambling law would remain vulnerable to preemption, at least to the extent it imposed comprehensive regulations on sports gambling.) Of course, whether these state reforms are, in fact, preempted depends on congressional intent; for a variety of reasons explored elsewhere,[40] it seems doubtful Congress would want to preempt many of them.

In sum, focusing on the content of state law provides a much more satisfactory description of the boundary between preemption and commandeering and provides some much needed guidance for resolving debates over the legal status of state marijuana reforms.

CONCLUSION

Murphy v. NCAA held the promise of illuminating the elusive boundary between competing constitutional principles. In the process, the decision could have resolved long-standing debates over the legal status of many state marijuana reforms. *Murphy*, however, failed to live up to that lofty promise. While it upheld state legalization of sports gambling, it did so on grounds that muddle the decision's implications for other areas of law, including state marijuana reforms. Thus, whether the decision will help remove the preemption shadow now looming over many state marijuana reforms is, well, anyone's bet.

NOTES

1. 138 S.Ct. 1461 (2018).

2. P.L. 1871 § 1, later codified at N.J. Stat. Ann. § 2A:40-1 et seq.

3. *Nat'l Collegiate Athletic Ass'n v. Christie*, 832 F.3d 389, 393 (3d Cir. 2016) (*Christie II*) (describing law).

4. 28 U.S.C. § 3702(1). For ease of exposition, the term "sports gambling" is used as shorthand for all the wagering activities regulated by PASPA, including a "lottery,

sweepstakes, or other betting, gambling, or wagering scheme based, directly or indirectly (through the use of geographical references or otherwise), on one or more competitive games in which amateur or professional athletes participate, or are intended to participate, or on one or more performances of such athletes in such games." 28 U.S.C. § 3702(2). PASPA exempted sports gambling authorized by a handful of states, including Nevada, but not New Jersey.

5. 730 F.3d 208, 227 (3d Cir. 2013).

6. Ibid., p. 232.

7. 2014 N.J. Sess. Law Serv. Ch. 62, codified at N.J. Stat. Ann. §§ 5:12A-7(1) (2014 Law).

8. *Christie II*, 832 F.3d at 401. See also Ibid., p. 396 ("The 2014 Law authorizes sports gambling by selectively dictating where sports gambling may occur, who may place bets in such gambling, and which athletic contests are permissible subjects for such gambling.").

9. *Murphy,* 138 S.Ct. at 1473.

10. Ibid., p. 1474.

11. Ibid., p. 1478.

12. Ibid.

13. *New York v. United States*, 505 U.S. 144, 188 (1992).

14. See Robert A. Mikos, On the Limits of Supremacy: Medical Marijuana and the States' Overlooked Power to Legalize Federal Crime, 62 *Vanderbilt Law Review* 1442, 1446 (2009) ("When state law simply permits private conduct to occur . . . preemption of such a law would be tantamount to commandeering.").

15. *New York,* 505 U.S. at 169. See also *Printz v. United States,* 521 U.S. 898, 930 (1997) ("Under the [Brady Act,] it will be the [Chief Law Enforcement Officer] and not some federal official who stands between the gun purchaser and immediate possession of his gun. And it will likely be the CLEO, not some federal official, who will be blamed for any error (even one in the designated federal database) that causes a purchaser to be mistakenly rejected.").

16. *Murphy,* 138 S.Ct. at 1481-82 ("PASPA's prohibition of state 'licens[ing]' . . . suffers from the same defect as the prohibition of state authorization. It issues a direct order to the state legislature. Just as Congress lacks the power to order a state legislature not to enact a law authorizing sports gambling, it may not order a state legislature to refrain from enacting a law licensing sports gambling.").

17. Ibid., p. 1479.

18. Brief for Respondents, *Christie v. Nat'l Collegiate Athletic Ass'n*, 2017 WL 4684747, 48 (2017) (citations omitted).

19. *Murphy,* 138 S.Ct. at 1479.

20. Ibid., p. 1480.

21. Ibid., p. 1481. PASPA did have a second provision, 28 U.S.C. § 3702(2), that made it unlawful for private actors "to sponsor, operate, advertise, or promote, pursuant to the law or compact of a governmental entity" sports gambling. But the *Murphy* Court brushed that provision aside as it "is not the provision challenged by petitioner." 138 S.Ct. at 1481. The Court later found this prohibition inseverable from § 3702(1), thus gutting the entire statute.

22. 28 U.S.C. § 3702(1).

23. Roderick Hills, "*Murphy v. NCAA's* Escape from Baseline Hell," Prawfsblawg, May 16, 2018 (https://prawfsblawg.blogs.com/prawfsblawg/2018/05/murphy-v-ncaas-escape-from-baseline-hell.html) (emphasis added).

24. This revised version of the statute is, in fact, similar to the language of Section 3702(2); it simply omits the limiting language "pursuant to the law or compact of any government entity."

25. For example, Professor Daniel Hemel has suggested that the Court's language actually restricts (not expands) Congress's preemption power, because a laundry list of express preemption provisions simply cannot "be understood as a regulation of private actors." See Daniel Hemel, "Justice Alito, State Tax Hero?" Medium, May 15, 2018 (https://medium.com/whatever-source-derived/justice-alito-state-tax-hero-3338 30d097ab). By contrast, Rick Hills suggests the decision "is best understood as leaving old-fashioned preemption unscathed." Hills, "*Murphy v. NCAA's* Escape from Baseline Hell," supra.

26. See, for example, *Morales v. Trans World Airlines, Inc.*, 504 U.S. 374, 383 (1992) (noting that the question confronted by the Court, "at bottom, is one of statutory intent").

27. See generally Colo. Const. art. XVIII, § 16.

28. For example, Me. Rev. Stat. Ann. § 2423-A ("*Authorized* conduct for the medical use of marijuana. (1). . . . a qualifying patient *may* [inter alia] . . . [p]ossess up to 2 ½ ounces of prepared marijuana") (emphases added).

29. *Gonzales v. Raich*, 545 U.S. 1, 5 (2005) ("California is one of at least nine States that *authorize* the use of marijuana for medicinal purposes") (emphasis added).

30. 21 U.S.C. § 903. For a thorough discussion of the meaning of this provision, see Robert A. Mikos, "Preemption Under the Controlled Substances Act," 16 *Journal of Health Care Law & Policy* 5 (2013).

31. 230 P.3d 518, 531 (Or. 2010). Ibid., p. 529 ("Affirmatively authorizing a use [of marijuana] that federal law prohibits stands as an obstacle to the implementation and execution of the full purposes and objectives of the Controlled Substances Act."); Ibid., p. 531 ("[T]here is no dispute that Congress has the authority under the Supremacy Clause to preempt state laws that affirmatively authorize the use of medical marijuana.").

32. For example, Brief in Support of Motion to File Complaint, *Nebraska v. Colorado*, 136 S. Ct. 1034 (2016) (No. 144, Orig.) (claiming that Colorado's Amendment 64 is preempted, in part, because it "affirmatively *authorizes* conduct prohibited by federal law") (emphasis added). See also Mikos, "Preemption," pp. 16–17 (discussing cases).

33. Robert A. Mikos, *Marijuana Law, Policy, and Authority* (New York: Wolters Kluwer, 2017), p. 444.

34. The requirement to get a license (like the one upheld by the *Murphy* Court) is not the same as the requirements imposed on licensees. I explained the distinction in an Amicus Brief before the *Murphy* Court: "Just like authorization, licensure merely provides the state's permission to engage in activity. If that is all licensing does, then it is not preemptible, for the same reasons authorization qua repeal is not preemptible. But if the license imposes additional restrictions that interfere with activity—such as requiring a retail licensee to collect sales taxes—those additional restrictions likely would be subject

to preemption, even if the underlying license (permission) is not." Brief of Constitutional Law Scholars as Amici Curiae in Support of Petitioners, *Christie v. National Collegiate Athletic Association*, 2017 WL 4004531 p.6, n.3.

35. See 21 U.S.C. §§ 841-844, 856.

36. See Mikos, "On the Limits," pp. 1446–49 (demonstrating the problems with making the preemption inquiry turn on an action/inaction distinction, and suggesting that courts must instead focus on the effects of a challenged state law to determine whether or not Congress may preempt it).

37. For example, *Arizona v. United States*, 567 U.S. 387 (2012) (state law barring undocumented immigrants from seeking work); *Geier v. Am. Honda Motor Co.*, 529 U.S. 861 (2000) (state tort suit claiming manufacturer had a duty to install airbags); *Ableman v. Booth*, 62 U.S. 506 (1858) (state court writ demanding release of prisoner being held under the federal Fugitive Slave Act).

38. See Mikos, "On the Limits," p. 1449 ("The Court has found myriad state laws preempted, but only when the states have punished or subsidized (broadly defined) behavior Congress sought to foster or deter. . ."); Ibid., p. 1449 ("The Court has never held that Congress could block states from merely allowing some private behavior to occur, even if that behavior is forbidden by Congress.").

39. See Colo. Code Reg. 212-2.1501 & .1503 (2016).

40. See Mikos, "Preemption," pp. 17–21 (suggesting that many state reforms create only "false conflicts" with the CSA).

5

FEDERAL NONENFORCEMENT

A Dubious Precedent

Zachary S. Price

Federal marijuana nonenforcement may turn out to be one of the Obama administration's most consequential policies. By announcing publicly that state-compliant marijuana sellers and consumers would be low priorities for federal enforcement, the Obama Justice Department effectively opened the door to state-level experimentation with marijuana legalization. In consequence, a multibillion-dollar marijuana industry now operates openly in many states, apparently undeterred by its blatant criminality under federal law.

To the extent federal marijuana prohibitions were outdated, unpopular, and only sporadically and inequitably enforced, this outcome may seem a victory for both federalism and democracy. After all, the Obama administration's choices produced a legal landscape more in line with popular preferences, both nationally and in individual states. From the perspective of governing norms and separation of powers, however, the example is unsettling. Although the administration's enforcement policy was ultimately within its authority, the episode dramatically highlighted executive capacity to reshape effective legal requirements through enforcement policy. The policy, thus, set an example that other administrations might follow in still more contentious areas, as, indeed, the Trump administration has arguably done with respect to a number of regulatory statutes. At the same time, the policy raises a host of difficult questions about judicial review, reliance, and congressional authority with respect to such permissive executive policies.

Drawing from my own prior work on these questions, this chapter offers a brief analysis of salient legal issues presented by federal marijuana nonenforcement. The first section provides an overview of the marijuana policies of both the Obama and the Trump administrations, their on-the-ground effects, and Congress's limited interventions. The next section turns to some key legal issues. It explains, first, why the Obama administration's policies were defensible, if only marginally so, in terms of the president's constitutional obligation to ensure "faithful execution" of federal laws. The policy's permissibility, however, only raises a tangle of further issues, including, above all, whether relying on the policy may afford private parties any effective defense to future prosecution. This section argues that, as a general matter, no such defense should be available, for the simple reason that recognizing a defense would enable executive officials to cancel statutory prohibitions by inviting reliance on promised enforcement forbearance.

The third section reflects on some broader implications of the marijuana example. Although federal marijuana nonenforcement has proven relatively stable so far in the Trump administration, Obama's example (and some others set by the new administration) could augur a new era of whipsaw enforcement, in which conduct invited by one administration is singled out for retribution by the next. To the extent that prediction proves accurate, three key legal constraints on executive policy will be important. First, although courts generally lack competence to assess executive enforcement priorities, they can police the boundary between priority-setting and lawmaking, as, indeed, courts have done recently by invalidating unduly permissive environmental policies from the Trump administration. Second, even without recognizing any general reliance defense, courts can, and should, protect reliance on nonenforcement assurances in certain limited contexts that involve especially acute unfairness and limited harm to separation-of-powers constraints on executive authority.

Finally, Congress holds authority to adjust executive enforcement priorities by either restricting or mandating particular enforcement expenditures. Congress has used this power in recent years to forbid certain marijuana investigations and prosecutions. To the extent other presidents follow Obama's lead—and notwithstanding a signing statement by President Trump raising misguided constitutional concerns—Congress should employ its power of the purse to maintain an active legislative constraint on executive enforcement policies.

FEDERAL POLICY DURING THE OBAMA AND TRUMP ADMINISTRATIONS

Possessing any amount of marijuana is a federal crime, and has been for decades. Outside of large-scale distribution or trafficking, however, the federal government appears to have rarely enforced this prohibition in recent years; it, instead, largely left the question of enforcement vigor to state and local authorities enforcing their own parallel marijuana prohibitions. As more and more states relaxed their own restrictions on either medical or recreational marijuana, federal authorities faced a new choice: should the federal government actively assert the federal prohibition's continuing force, or should it, instead, keep deferring to state and local preferences despite the dramatic change in state and local policy?

After some waffling, the Justice Department under President Obama opted for the latter course. In 2013, just as the first two states were implementing state-level legalization of recreational (as opposed to medical) marijuana, the Justice Department issued a memorandum to all U.S. Attorneys indicating that federal prosecutors should generally treat as low priority any possession or distribution in compliance with state law, concentrating enforcement efforts, instead, on specified federal priorities.[1] The department, however, framed this guidance in noncommittal terms; the memo merely announced relative priorities for enforcement, not any form of absolute permission, and, in fact, some sporadic enforcement continued. Ultimately, concerns about continued federal enforcement despite the policy prompted Congress to adopt a recurrent rider forbidding use of Justice Department funds against state-compliant medical (though not recreational) marijuana users and businesses.[2]

For its part, the Trump administration revoked the Obama Justice Department's 2013 guidance and announced a new policy of leaving the exercise of prosecutorial discretion with respect to marijuana up to individual U.S. Attorneys.[3] In addition, in a signing statement, President Trump raised constitutional doubts about the congressional appropriations limits on federal law enforcement.[4]

President Trump himself, however, apparently gave assurances to a Colorado senator that his administration would not crack down on the state's recreational marijuana industry.[5] As a matter of on-the-ground practice, furthermore, the administration appears not to have departed sharply from the priorities set out in the Obama administration policy. Although some Trump-appointed U.S. Attorneys have brought or threatened to bring some marijuana prosecutions, they appear not to have launched any concerted nation-wide effort to obstruct or roll back state-level legalization.[6] What is more, President Trump's current Attorney General, William Barr, who took office in February 2019, indicated during his Senate confirmation proceedings that he did "not intend to go after parties who have complied with state law in reliance on" Obama administration policies.[7] The private marijuana industry, meanwhile, has continued to grow apace as more and more jurisdictions have relaxed or eliminated state and local marijuana prohibitions.[8]

WAS THE OBAMA POLICY LAWFUL?

At the moment, then, marijuana legalization appears to be moving forward almost inexorably in an increasing number of states. Absent some dramatic shift in public opinion or the political environment, it seems unlikely that any politically realistic level of federal enforcement could succeed in putting all this toothpaste back in the tube. In all likelihood, marijuana legalization is here to stay for the foreseeable future, its federal-law criminalization notwithstanding.

Insofar as the Obama administration's choice to announce a permissive enforcement approach helped enable these developments, the administration's action might seem to set a positive example of executive-branch democratic majoritarianism. Blanket federal marijuana prohibition appears quite unpopular; some even view it as a clear example of federal overreach.[9] In effect, then, President Obama's executive policy helped unstick a frozen issue, overcoming congressional paralysis to generate an on-the-ground reality more in line with public preferences. By the same token, the policy might be considered a win for federalism. By clearing away a largely unenforced and arguably unjustified federal prohibition, the Obama Justice Department opened up space for state-level experimentation and regional variation in policy, resulting in a pattern of on-the-ground law more in line with local public preferences.

These perspectives, however, miss another important dimension of the problem. From a separation-of-powers point of view, the Obama administration's policies were troubling, if not altogether inexcusable (for reasons explained below). The federal Constitution presumes an executive branch that executes acts of Congress, not one that picks and chooses which laws to give effect. After all, the Constitution not only allows Congress to enact statutes over a presidential veto, but also expressly obligates the president to "take care that the Laws be faithfully executed."[10]

Furthermore, most scholars agree that, whatever else it means, this so-called Take Care Clause bars executive officials from "suspending" federal laws by affirmatively permitting what the law forbids.[11] Executive officials, to be sure, may have some discretion over enforcement. Indeed, I have argued that the Constitution supports presuming authority to decline enforcement in particular cases for case-specific reasons.[12] In addition, insofar as resource constraints or practical challenges preclude full enforcement, executive officials may hold broader authority to set priorities for enforcement, emphasizing certain types of cases rather than others because they lack the time and money to pursue both.[13] As a practical matter, however, the Obama administration's policies ended up yielding an effective suspension of federal marijuana prohibitions in large portions of the country.

It is even possible that federal law on marijuana would be clearer today if the administration had taken a harder line, before states and their citizens placed such heavy bets on federal forbearance. Congress's imposition of appropriations limits appears to have been motivated in part by concerns about continued enforcement,[14] and the U.S. House of Representatives, following lobbying by banks, in September 2019 passed legislation that would remove penalties for providing banking services to illegal marijuana businesses.[15] Perhaps a more stubborn executive would have stimulated still more significant reforms. Ulysses Grant, at the least, thought there was "no method to secure the repeal of bad or obnoxious laws so effective as their stringent execution."[16]

Such practical concerns notwithstanding, as a legal matter, the Obama administration's action was "dubious but defensible," as I argued at the time.[17] Although the policy came close to authorizing conduct Congress prohibited by statute—and although, again, it may have effectively ended up doing so in practice—the policy itself stopped short of that key limitation on executive authority. Offering only a noncommittal indication of internal executive priorities, the policy made no guarantees and gave no prospective license for legal violations; nor did it provide categorical assurance that those outside the stated priorities were safe from enforcement. On the contrary, the policy made clear that marijuana prohibitions remained in effect, exposing participants in state-authorized marijuana businesses to continued legal risk. In effect, then, the policy simply announced that, in allocating its limited enforcement resources, the federal government would assign low importance to marijuana possession or distribution in compliance with state law and without significant interstate effects. Those relying on the policy had clear notice that they were taking their chances.[18]

It is true that, as time went on, the policy came to appear more categorical. Even as states and private parties manifestly interpreted the policy, contrary to its letter, as a green light for extensive marijuana violations, the Justice Department made no effort to signal that criminal prohibitions remained in effect and that violators remained at risk. The Obama administration even adopted further (and still more dubious) policies aimed at enabling marijuana-related bank transactions.[19] As a point of contrast, the Trump administration, to its credit, sent clear signals in one instance that state-authorized violations of the Affordable Care Act would not be tolerated. Doing so may well have nipped in the bud state-level undermining of a federal statute President Trump appears to despise at least as much as many progressives dislike marijuana prohibitions.[20]

Even if the administration ultimately breached its duty of faithful execution, however, it did not do so in a way that courts could remedy.[21] Although courts have sometimes reviewed general enforcement policies, any such review must ultimately be highly deferential so long as the policy states a facially plausible resource-allocation rationale for its choice of priorities. Challenges regarding whether executive priorities are appropriate, or even whether executive officials are doing their best in the first place, effectively present courts with a form of political question, in the sense of the "political question doctrine":

courts generally lack principled criteria—"judicially manageable standards," as courts put it—for assessing executive judgments about different violations' relative importance. Accordingly, as with certain other core executive functions, courts may appropriately leave the choice of law enforcement intensity and focus to executive "accountab[ility]" and "conscience,"[22] not because the executive branch holds no legal responsibility but, rather, because courts lack competence to oversee executive choices. Here, after all, invalidating the marijuana policy would have accomplished little unless the court directed some affirmative level of marijuana enforcement, yet any such directive would itself have raised separation-of-powers concerns by involving courts in the performance of executive law-enforcement functions.

FURTHER LEGAL QUESTIONS

The Obama administration's enforcement policy, then, was lawful, at least as initially formulated, and even if it were unlawful (or became so), courts lacked authority to remedy the breach of faithful execution. Yet these conclusions do not exhaust the issue, as the policy has left a tangle of further questions in its wake. Are marijuana contracts enforceable, or are they, instead, either preempted or contrary to public policy due to federal law? Can landlords rent to marijuana businesses without legal jeopardy? Can marijuana businesses deduct business expenses from taxable income, and can growers access federal water resources? Above all, what legal protection, if any, can entrepreneurs and consumers who relied on the Obama administration's enforcement policy now claim if they are prosecuted for their conduct—a possibility that is at least theoretically possible under Trump administration policies?[23]

As a general matter, and subject to some exceptions addressed below, those who violated federal marijuana laws should not hold any valid reliance defense based on the prior policy. Although the Supreme Court has recognized a limited due process defense to prosecution for conduct the government erroneously indicated was lawful, this defense cannot properly extend to reliance on mere nonenforcement assurances.[24] This conclusion is admittedly harsh in real-world terms. While lawyers and sophisticated large-scale operators, perhaps, can be expected to understand the distinction between enforcement policy and statutory law, it seems doubtful that every participant in the burgeoning, openly tolerated marijuana marketplace fully appreciates the degree of risk they are assuming. Yet protecting reliance here would obliterate the distinction between law and its enforcement, enabling executive officials to wipe away statutory prohibitions by inviting reliance on assurances of enforcement forbearance. A harsh legal doctrine with respect to potential defendants is, thus, necessary to maintain essential separation-of-powers limitations on the executive.[25]

This reliance problem highlights the key dilemma President Obama's marijuana policy may leave us with. By producing such dramatic on-the-ground results with even such an indeterminate and noncommittal policy, the Obama administration highlighted how potent enforcement choices may be in reshaping effective legal obligations. What is more, by employing nonenforcement so visibly in an area of acute policy conflict, President Obama may have set a precedent for other enforcement policies aimed at relaxing laws that key constituencies would like to see repealed. At the least, the Trump administration appears to have relaxed enforcement with respect to a number of disfavored laws, particularly environmental and banking regulations.[26]

On some level, this pattern reflects an old playbook: prior deregulatory administrations have, likewise, reduced effective legal burdens on the economy by slackening regulatory enforcement.[27] But increasing political polarization and the sharpening intensity of our political disagreements may well increase the chances that those lulled into complacency during one administration will face legal repercussions in the next. In the past, although priorities shifted from one administration to another, executive officials seem to have informally protected regulated parties' reliance by forbearing from retrospective enforcement.[28] To the extent such informal, political protection is growing less likely, legal limits on executive authority may become both more important and more contested.

LEGAL LIMITS ON ENFORCEMENT

What legal limits, then, should constrain executive enforcement choices? If it is true that the marijuana example both reflects and reinforces political dynamics that may yield whipsaw policies from one administration to the next, at least three legal limitations may be particularly important.

The first is the central limit already mentioned on executive nonenforcement: that executive enforcement discretion provides no authority to change the law itself. As noted, enforcement discretion is generally a power to pursue one case rather than another because the government lacks the time and resources to pursue both; it is not a power to alter substantive legal obligations themselves by licensing prospectively what the law prohibits. Nor, by the same token, should it be a power to announce policies so categorical and definitive that they effectively authorize such legal violations.[29]

Notwithstanding the challenges already noted that attend judicial review of less determinate enforcement policies, courts should step in and invalidate policies that breach this fundamental boundary between law and its enforcement. Indeed, even when agencies hold some presumed authority to interpret the laws they administer, there is some point at which interpretation runs out and the agency must simply enforce as best it can the laws that bind it and the regulated parties. As the Supreme Court has observed, "an agency confronting resource constraints may change its own conduct, but it cannot change the law."[30] In keeping with this principle, lower courts have invalidated deregulatory Trump administration policies that purported to eliminate legal obligations without any procedurally valid change in governing substantive statutes or regulations.[31] As the marijuana example illustrates, even indefinite and noncommittal enforcement policies may be dramatic enough in their effects. Invalidating policies that go further and offer prospective license for legal violations at least holds the line on unauthorized suspensions of substantive law, thus maintaining the constitutional primacy of congressional statutes (or valid exercises of delegated lawmaking power) over executive enforcement choices. Even if an agency ultimately ends up bringing no cases enforcing a restriction it sought to suspend, regulated parties must take their chances in choosing to violate the prohibition.

A second set of judicially enforceable limits apply to the converse problem: a deliberate resumption of enforcement following a deliberate suspension. Enforcement, again, generally must remain possible, despite any assurances to the contrary, so as to prevent de facto executive suspensions of law. In the marijuana context, accordingly, businesses and consumers properly remain subject to prosecution, notwithstanding prior executive assurances that the government would focus its enforcement efforts elsewhere. By the same token, however, courts can properly protect reliance on nonenforcement policies when doing so prevents especially acute unfairness to the individual at limited cost to the anti-suspending principle dictated by separation of powers and the Take Care Clause.[32]

With respect to marijuana, I have elsewhere identified several limited examples where this balance should tip against allowing retrospective enforcement against conduct undertaken in reliance on the Obama administration's policies. For example, even if regulated parties cannot rely on nonenforcement assurances to prevent enforcement of substantive conduct rules against them, they should generally be able to rely on such assurances to prevent use of incriminating information they provide pursuant to such a policy.[33] In the marijuana context, operating state-authorized businesses often requires extensive disclosures to state authorities—disclosures that could readily be used to prove a federal case against the businesses' owners.[34] Even if such state-collected information would otherwise be accessible to federal prosecutors,[35] due process should bar federal authorities from using it. In all likelihood, regulated parties would not have disclosed such information (or even operated the business in question at all) without the federal policy of forbearance, and allowing independent federal investigation and prosecution of violations suffices to preserve federal substantive law's primacy over executive enforcement policies. Federal authorities should not come out ahead in their enforcement efforts by virtue of having invited self-incrimination with promises of forbearance.[36]

Similarly, a reliance defense should bar enforcement of prohibitions that clearly exist only to back up primary prohibitions that the federal government is declining to enforce. Leasing property for a drug operation is a federal crime, for instance, yet enforcing such prohibitions against landlords who leased property to state-authorized and federally tolerated marijuana businesses could raise particularly acute fairness concerns while only indirectly vindicating statutory prohibitions on marijuana distribution.[37] For similar reasons, at least some defendants should likewise hold a reliance defense if they violated prohibitions during a period in which Congress affirmatively prevented federal enforcement by denying appropriations for it, as Congress has done in recent years with respect to state-authorized medical marijuana violations. While some sophisticated operators might be expected to understand that the appropriations denial did not change the underlying criminal law, such appropriations denials necessarily yield a categorical suspension of federal enforcement, thus heightening the risks of confusion, and resulting unfairness, for individuals. At the same time, the cost to separation of powers in preventing retrospective enforcement is limited, as Congress, rather than the executive alone, brought about the nonenforcement in question.[38]

The appropriations limitation just mentioned highlights a last key constraint on executive policy in our polarized era: by exercising its constitutional power over appropriations, Congress may always override executive enforcement choices and assert control over federal policy. Although President Trump suggested in a signing statement that his responsibility for faithful execution of the laws might permit his administration to defy funding constraints on marijuana enforcement,[39] executive law enforcement authority is, in fact, thoroughly dependent on congressional appropriations and, thus, subject to ongoing congressional control.[40] The president's constitutional responsibility, after all, is not to execute the laws personally but, rather, to "take Care" that they are faithfully executed. As this indirect formulation reflects, the president requires some external provision of means for carrying out his or her law enforcement responsibility, and by virtue of its authority over appropriations, only Congress can provide such means. Appropriations limits, furthermore, are themselves laws whose faithful execution the president must uphold; responsibility for faithful execution, thus, cannot provide a reason for defying those limits.[41]

As a matter of practice, Congress routinely blocks enforcement of disfavored regulations in annual appropriations, just as it has done in the recent marijuana provisions.[42] Although presidents have occasionally objected to such restraints (as Trump did in his signing statement), they have not developed any substantial practice of acting on such objections.[43] History's "gloss" on the separation of powers, thus, further supports congressional authority to bar enforcement of particular laws or provisions through denial of appropriations for that purpose.[44] By the same token, although such legislation appears far less common, Congress may also hold authority to affirmatively require enforcement of particular laws. Congress, indeed, regularly requires expenditure of particular sums for particular purposes and occasionally dictates that executive agencies follow specified enforcement priorities. Such measures, too, should fall within Congress's authority to structure the executive branch and direct its activities through conditional provision of law enforcement resources.[45]

To the extent enforcement policy continues to be a focus of partisan disagreement, Congress should employ these constitutional tools to check and constrain executive policies. As the recent history of federal marijuana policy reflects, the accretion of federal crimes, civil prohibitions, and statutory delegations over time has effectively given the executive branch great power of initiative in setting federal policy. In that context, Congress's role is often largely reactive, yet its long-standing practice of appropriating funds one year at a time gives it leverage to impose ongoing constraints when it disapproves of executive policies. Insofar as Congress lacks the will or capacity to adjust the terms of substantive laws themselves, it should not shy from employing its appropriations authority to moderate those laws' on-the-ground effect, just as it has done in recent years with respect to marijuana.

CONCLUSION

The United States's political polarization has reduced congressional capacity to enact new legislation while at the same time yielding sharp disagreements over the merits of key existing laws. In responding to state-level reforms in one such area, the Obama administration's marijuana policy set a bold precedent for adjusting the effective scope of existing laws through executive enforcement choices. Though I have argued here that the administration's action was ultimately lawful, it induced many Americans to take serious legal risks without providing any basis for a valid reliance defense in future litigation. To help keep such executive action within proper limits, courts should (1) invalidate policies that go still further and seek to categorically immunize legal violations without valid delegated authority to do so, (2) recognize a due process reliance defense when doing so will not risk giving executive officials undue authority to suspend statutes, and (3) recognize Congress's authority to control enforcement efforts through conditional or restricted appropriations. While imperfect, these restraints will help prevent further erosion of the congressional primacy over lawmaking that our constitutional structure prescribes.

NOTES

I am grateful to Jonathan Adler for inviting me to participate in this book, and I thank Julia Venditti for superb research assistance. All errors are of course my own.

1. Memorandum from James M. Cole, Deputy Attorney General, U.S. Department of Justice, to All U.S. Attorneys, "Guidance Regarding Marijuana Enforcement," August

29, 2013 (www.justice.gov/iso/opa/resources/3052013829132756857467.pdf). This guidance superseded two earlier memoranda on medical marijuana enforcement. See Memorandum from James M. Cole, Deputy Attorney General, U.S. Department of Justice, to All U.S. Attorneys, "Guidance Regarding the Ogden Memo in Jurisdictions Seeking to Authorize Marijuana for Medical Use," June 29, 2011 (www.justice.gov/sites/default/files/oip/legacy/2014/07/23/dag-guidance-2011-for-medical-marijuana-use.pdf); Memorandum from David W. Ogden, Deputy Attorney General, U.S. Department of Justice, to Selected U.S. Attorneys, "Investigations and Prosecutions in States Authorizing the Medical Use of Marijuana," October 19, 2009 (www.justice.gov/sites/default/files/opa/legacy/2009/10/19/medical-marijuana.pdf).

2. See Consolidated and Further Appropriations Act, 2015, Pub. L. No. 113-235, div. B, tit. V, § 538, 128 Stat. 2130, 2217 (2014) (barring use of Justice Department funds to "prevent" specified states from "implementing their own State laws that authorize" medical marijuana). This provision has been repeatedly reenacted with minor modifications, most recently in the Consolidated Appropriations Act, 2019, Pub. L. No. 116-6, div. C, tit. V, § 537, 133 Stat. 13, 138 (2019). For discussion of the original provision's legislative history, see *United States of Am. v. Marin All. for Med. Marijuana*, 139 F. Supp. 3d 1039, 1046-1047 (N.D. Cal. 2015).

3. Memorandum from Jefferson B. Sessions, III, Attorney General, to All U.S. Attorneys, "Marijuana Enforcement," January 4, 2018 (www.justice.gov/opa/press-release/file/1022196/download).

4. Presidential Statement on Signing the Consolidated Appropriations Act 2017, 2017 Daily Comp. Pres. Doc. 312, May 5, 2017 (www.govinfo.gov/content/pkg/DCPD-2017 00312/pdf/DCPD-201700312.pdf).

5. Evan Halper, "Trump Administration Abandons Crackdown on Legal Marijuana," *Los Angeles Times*, April 13, 2018 (www.latimes.com/politics/la-na-pol-mari juana-trump-20180413-story.html).

6. See, for example, U.S. Attorney's Office, District of Vermont, Press Release: "New Hampshire Man Arrested for Possessing Firearm During Attempted Robbery of THC Products in Springfield, Vermont," March 12, 2019 (www.justice.gov/usao-vt/pr/new-hampshire-man-arrested-possessing-firearm-during-attempted-robbery-thc-products) (reporting charges for attempted robbery in connection with the sale of "tetrahydro-cannabinol [THC]-infused products"); U.S. Attorney's Office, District of Massachusetts, "Statement from U.S. Attorney Andrew Lelling Regarding the Legalization of Recreational Marijuana in Massachusetts," July 10, 2018 (www.justice.gov/usao-ma/pr/statement-us-attorney-andrew-lelling-regarding-legalization-recreational-marijuana) ("Because I have a constitutional obligation to enforce the laws passed by Congress, I will not effectively immunize the residents of the Commonwealth from federal marijuana enforcement."); Memorandum from Billy J. Williams, U.S. Attorney, District of Oregon, "Re: Priorities in Enforcement of Federal Laws Involving Marijuana in the District of Oregon," May 18, 2018 (https://media.oregonlive.com/marijuana/other/2018/05/18/US-AOR-Marijuana%20Enforcement%20Priorities-Final%20(1).pdf) ("As the primary federal law enforcement official in Oregon, I will not make broad proclamations of blanket immunity from prosecution to those who violate federal law."); Jack Moran, "Veneta

Man, Corvallis Residents Charged in Federal Marijuana Cases," *Register-Guard*, June 12, 2018 (www.registerguard.com/news/20180612/veneta-man-corvallis-residents-charged-in-federal-marijuana-cases) (describing charges in two cases and reporting assertion by· a U.S. Attorney's Office spokesperson that the cases could have been pursued under pre-2018 guidance).

7. Questions for the Record, William P. Barr, Nominee to be United States Attorney General, Senate Judiciary Committee, p. 217 (www.judiciary.senate.gov/imo/media/doc/Barr%20Responses%20to%20Booker%20QFRs1.pdf).

8. See, for example, Associated Press, "Legal Marijuana Industry Had Banner Year in 2018 with $10B Worth of Investments," NBC News, December 27, 2018 (www.nbcnews.com/news/us-news/legal-marijuana-industry-had-banner-year-2018-10b-worth-investments-n952256).

9. See, for example, Hannah Hartig and Abigail Geiger, Pew Research Center, "About Six in Ten Americans Support Marijuana Legalization," October 8, 2018 (www.pewresearch.org/fact-tank/2018/10/08/americans-support-marijuana-legalization/).

10. U.S. Constitution art. II, § 3.

11. For my own defense of this view, see Zachary S. Price, "Enforcement Discretion and Executive Duty," *Vanderbilt Law Review* 67 (2014), p. 671. See also, for example, Adam B. Cox and Cristina M. Rodriguez, "The President and Immigration Law Redux," *Yale Law Journal* 125 (2015), p. 104 (noting near-consensus on this point); but see Saikrishna Bangalore Prakash, *Imperial From the Beginning: The Constitution of the Original Executive* (Yale University Press, 2015), pp. 92–93 (doubting that the Take Care Clause bars suspensions but nonetheless deeming it "clear" that the president holds no suspending power).

12. Price, "Enforcement Discretion," p. 704.

13. Ibid., p. 754.

14. See legislative history collected in *United States of Am. v. Marin All. for Med. Marijuana*, 139 F. Supp. 3d 1039, 1046–1047 (N.D. Cal. 2015).

15. See H.R. 1595, 116th Congress (September 26, 2019) (received in Senate); Chris Hansen, "Marijuana Banking Bill Passes House in Historic Vote," *U.S. News & World Report*, September 25, 2019 (www.usnews.com/news/national-news/articles/2019-09-25/marijuana-banking-bill-passes-house-in-historic-vote).

16. Ulysses S. Grant, First Inaugural Address, March 4, 1869.

17. Price, "Enforcement Discretion," p. 759.

18. The marijuana policy was, thus, distinguishable from two controversial immigration initiatives the Obama administration adopted around the same time. Although these policies also purported to be mere exercises of enforcement discretion, they invited broad categories of deportable immigrants to apply for two- or three-year grants of "deferred action," a form of immigration relief that effectively assured non-deportation. The marijuana analogue to these policies would be a federal program inviting qualifying cannabis businesses to apply for an assurance that they could operate without interference for a period of years. For a description of the immigration policies and the administration's legal defense, see *The Department of Homeland Security's Authority to Prioritize Removal*

of Certain Aliens Unlawfully Present in the United States and to Defer Removal of Others, 38 O.L.C. (November 19, 2014).

19. Memorandum from James M. Cole, Deputy Attorney General, to U.S. Attorneys, "Guidance Regarding Marijuana Related Financial Crimes," February 14, 2014 (www.justice.gov/sites/default/files/usao-wdwa/legacy/2014/02/14/DAG%20Memo%20-%20 Guidance%20Regarding%20Marijuana%20Related%20Financial%20Crimes%202%20 14%2014%20%282%29.pdf). The U.S. House of Representatives recently passed legislation to legalize such transactions. See H.R. 1595, 116th Congress (September 26, 2019) (received in Senate).

20. See Nick Bagley, "Knock It Off, Idaho. (But Carry On, Idaho.)," Take Care Blog, March 9, 2018 (https://takecareblog.com/blog/knock-it-off-idaho-but-carry-on-idaho).

21. For a more complete exposition of the points in this paragraph, see Zachary S. Price, "Law Enforcement as Political Question," *Notre Dame Law Review* 91 (2016), p. 1571.

22. *Marbury v. Madison*, 5 U.S. (1 Cranch) 137, 165–66 (1803).

23. For my prior exploration of this last question, see Zachary S. Price, "Reliance on Nonenforcement," *William & Mary Law Review* 58 (2017), p. 937.

24. For cases recognizing such a defense, see *United States v. Pa. Indust. Chem. Corp.*, 411 U.S. 655, 674 (1973), *Cox v. Louisiana*, 379 U.S. 559, 570–71 (1965), and *Raley v. Ohio*, 360 U.S. 423, 438–39 (1959). For my own more extended discussion of why this defense must be limited, see Price, "Reliance on Nonenforcement," pp. 987–90.

25. As this chapter went to press, the Supreme Court was considering whether the government acted arbitrarily, in violation of the Administrative Procedure Act, by seeking to terminate an immigration "deferred action" program granting renewable two-year promises of non-deportation to certain immigrants. See *Dep't of Homeland Sec. v. Regents of the Univ. of California*, 139 S. Ct. 2779 (2019) (granting certiorari). Should the Court rule against the government on this question, its decision could establish a precedent supporting similar arbitrariness review of any future policy renewing enforcement against marijuana businesses. The lower-court decisions on review, however, have focused on the particular legal reasons the government gave for ending the immigration program at issue. Extending any similar Supreme Court decision to marijuana might therefore be difficult. At least one lower court, furthermore, specifically rejected arguments that reliance on the programs establishes a general due process defense to enforcement. *Regents of the Univ. of California v. U.S. Dep't of Homeland Sec.*, 908 F.3d 476, 514-15 (9th Cir. 2018), *cert. granted sub nom. Dep't of Homeland Sec. v. Regents of the Univ. of California*, 139 S. Ct. 2779 (2019).

26. Alex Leary, "Trump Administration Pushes to Deregulate with Less Enforcement," *Wall Street Journal*, June 23, 2019 (www.wsj.com/articles/trump-administration-pushes-to-deregulate-with-less-enforcement-11561291201); Eric Lipton and Danielle Ivory, "Under Trump, E.P.A. Has Slowed Actions Against Polluters, and Put Limits on Enforcement Officers," *New York Times*, December 10, 2017 (www.nytimes.com/2017/12/10/us/politics/pollution-epa-regulations.html).

27. For my brief account of such prior actions, see Zachary S. Price, "Politics of Nonenforcement," *Case Western Law Review* 65 (2015), p. 1119.

28. Price, "Reliance on Nonenforcement," p. 961.

29. Price, "Enforcement Discretion," p. 704.

30. *Utility Air Regulatory Group v. EPA*, 573 U.S. 302, 327 (2014).

31. See, for example, *Air Alliance Houston v. EPA*, 906 F.3d 1049, 1060–61 (D.C. Cir. 2018) (per curiam); *Clean Air Council v. Pruitt*, 862 F.3d 1, 4 (D.C. Cir. 2017) (per curiam).

32. See Price, "Reliance on Nonenforcement," p. 945–46.

33. Ibid., pp. 1007–08.

34. Ibid.

35. For an argument against federal authority to obtain such information, see Robert A. Mikos, "Can the States Keep Secrets from the Federal Government?," *University of Pennsylvania Law Review* 161 (2012), p. 103.

36. Price, "Reliance on Nonenforcement," pp. 1007–08.

37. Ibid., pp. 1008–10.

38. Ibid., pp. 1010–15. I have also advocated recognizing a desuetude defense based on long-standing, overt adherence to a federal nonenforcement policy, but the Trump administration's revocation of any express marijuana nonenforcement policy makes any such desuetude principle inapplicable here. Ibid., pp. 1015–16.

39. "Presidential Statement on Signing the Consolidated Appropriations Act 2017," *2017 Daily Compilation of Presidential Documents*, May 5, 2017, p. 312 (www.govinfo.gov/content/pkg/DCPD-201700312/pdf/DCPD-201700312.pdf).

40. For my elaboration of this argument, see Zachary S. Price, "Funding Restrictions and Separation of Powers," *Vanderbilt Law Review* 71 (2018), p. 357.

41. Ibid., p. 438.

42. See Jason A. MacDonald, "Limitation Riders and Congressional Influence over Bureaucratic Policy Decisions," *American Political Science Review* 104 (2010), p. 766.

43. For discussion of examples, see Price, "Funding Restrictions," pp. 440–45.

44. *Youngstown Sheet & Tube Co. v. Sawyer*, 343 U.S. 579, 610 (1952) (Frankfurter, J., concurring); see also Curtis A. Bradley and Trevor W. Morrison, "Historical Gloss and the Separation of Powers," *Harvard Law Review* 126 (2012), p. 411.

45. Price, "Funding Restrictions," pp. 446–47.

6

BANKS AND THE MARIJUANA INDUSTRY

Julie Andersen Hill

In states that have legalized marijuana, the marijuana industry is flourishing. You might expect that, as the marijuana industry finds success, banks would compete for its business. But the legal limbo created by conflicting state and federal laws keeps most financial institutions from serving marijuana-related customers.[1] As a Bank of America spokesperson Mark Pipitone explained: "We abide by federal law and do not bank marijuana-related businesses."[2] Even people and entities not directly involved in cultivating or selling marijuana can have banking trouble. For example, Wells Fargo closed the campaign account of a Florida politician after she admitted receiving donations from the medical marijuana industry.[3]

Lack of banking services is a formidable barrier to growth of the state-legal marijuana industry. Marijuana businesses must conduct transactions in cash and spend an inordinate amount of time and resources on cash management. From vaults to security personnel to finding suppliers that accept cash payment, managing cash can quickly become a logistical and security nightmare. In Colorado, a marijuana retailer described cash management as "a full-time job."[4]

At the same time, lack of banking services equates to a lack of capital for the marijuana industry. Banks are the traditional backbone of small business financing, but most banks will not lend to marijuana-related businesses. The industry must, instead, "rely on short-term loans from individuals, usually with higher interest rates."[5] Even if a marijuana-related business finds financing, there is still the problem of not having a bank account. As a marijuana retailer hoping to finance the $1 million-dollar purchase of a new building explains, "What do you say? . . . I want it in cash, guys?"[6]

The banking problem also raises hurdles for states seeking to tax and regulate marijuana use. Notwithstanding the security efforts of marijuana businesses themselves, the combination of marijuana and cash raises local law enforcement concerns. Armed robberies are common. Marijuana industry employees have been injured and killed.[7] States often plan to fund the monitoring and registration of marijuana growers, distributors, retailers, and medical users by taxing the marijuana industry.[8] But cash businesses have opportunities and incentives to underreport taxes.[9] Without anticipated tax revenues, states could have trouble funding their regulatory structures. Cash businesses may also be more likely to funnel earnings to illicit activities.[10] Finally, tax authorities (including federal tax authorities) prefer to be paid by check, credit card, or electronic deposit, rather than with bags of cash smelling of weed.[11]

BANKING MARIJUANA MONEY IS ILLEGAL

So why do marijuana businesses have difficulty getting banking services? The short answer is the one Bank of America, Citigroup, J.P. Morgan Chase, and Wells Fargo all provide when explaining why they will not bank the marijuana industry: federal law—more specifically, the Controlled Substances Act (CSA) and anti-money laundering laws.[12]

The CSA prohibits manufacturing, distributing, or dispensing marijuana.[13] Criminal liability extends beyond directly handling marijuana. It is illegal to conspire to violate the act and to aid and abet violations of the act.[14] Financial institutions operating in the marijuana space violate these laws. Suppose a marijuana retailer in Colorado comes to a bank and forthrightly explains that her business needs a small inventory loan, a checking account, and credit card processing services. By providing the loan and placing the proceeds in the checking account, the bank would be conspiring to distribute marijuana. By facilitating customers' credit card payments and providing checking account services, the bank would be aiding and abetting the distribution of marijuana.

Money laundering is also illegal. In general, money laundering occurs when money from a criminal activity is used for noncriminal purposes or vice versa. There are several ways to commit the offense of money laundering, but two are especially relevant to financial institutions considering marijuana banking. First, a bank commits money laundering by conducting a financial transaction involving the proceeds of a "specified unlawful activity" (like offenses involving marijuana) while "knowing that the transaction is designed in whole or in part to conceal the nature, the location, the source, the ownership or the control of the proceeds of specified unlawful activity."[15] Second, a bank commits money laundering if it "knowingly engages or attempts to engage in a monetary transaction in criminally derived property of a value greater than $10,000."[16]

Banks cannot avoid sanctions by turning a blind eye to money laundering. Under the Bank Secrecy Act and USA Patriot Act, financial institutions must maintain robust compliance programs. They must make reasonable efforts to "verify the identity of any person seeking to open an account."[17] They must also know the purpose of each account, the source of funds in the account, and the customer's primary trade area.[18] And they must watch for suspicious transactions and report those to the federal Financial Crimes Enforcement Network (FinCEN).[19]

Violations of the CSA and anti-money laundering laws are punishable by imprisonment and fines.[20] These are daunting penalties for both financial institutions and their employees.

FEDERAL CONTROL OF BANKS

Of course, those who operate marijuana-related businesses also face potential criminal liability for violations of the CSA and anti-money laundering laws. Why are these businesses and individuals willing to take the risk when most financial institutions will not?

Marijuana-related businesses recognize the federal government lacks the resources to prosecute most marijuana-related offenses.[21] Financial institutions, however, are in a more precarious position. Anti-money laundering laws were implemented because it is easier for law enforcement to cut off access to money than to prosecute those who deal directly with illegal drugs.[22] In addition, financial institutions are supervised by a variety of federal regulators with plenty of resources to punish wrongdoing. While these regulators do not have the power to send people to jail, they do have the authority to impose costly penalties. The two nearly unavoidable areas of federal control over financial institutions are (1) federal deposit insurance and (2) federal payment systems administration. Some banks have even more federal oversight.

The vast majority of financial institutions, whether federal- or state-chartered, are federally insured. Banks are insured by the Federal Deposit Insurance Corporation (FDIC), and credit unions are insured by National Credit Union Administration (NCUA).[23] With the benefit of federal insurance comes the burden of federal regulation. FDIC and NCUA examinations scrutinize financial institutions' compliance with the Bank Secrecy Act and anti-money laundering laws. The federal insurers can bring civil money penalty actions for violations.[24] They can also impose the "death penalty," revocation of deposit insurance, effectively forcing the closure of the institution.[25] Finally, financial institution employees who violate the Bank Secrecy Act or anti-money laundering laws face regulatory suspension or prohibition from the banking industry.[26]

The federal government also wields power over all financial institutions (both banks and credit unions) through its control of access to payment systems. The Federal Reserve provides four payment services: (1) a centralized check collection system, (2) the Automated Clearinghouse (ACH) network for processing batched electronics small-dollar payments, (3) the Fedwire system for larger electronic payments, and (4) coin and currency services.[27] Financial institutions use these systems to provide customers payment services. Under normal circumstances, once a financial institution receives a charter, the Federal Reserve grants the institution a "master account" and access to payment services.[28] This process makes sense because the prospective financial institution has already been vetted by the chartering authority (either a state or federal regulator) and the deposit or share insurer. If, however, the Federal Reserve learned that a financial institution was using its systems to process payments that violate federal law, the Federal Reserve could deny access to the system.[29] After all, if the Federal Reserve knowingly processes transactions that violate anti-money laundering laws, it, too, commits the crime of money laundering.

Some banks have even more federal oversight. Most banks are organized in a holding company structure, and the Federal Reserve oversees all bank holding companies. Many banks, including all very large banks, are chartered and supervised by the federal Office of the Controller of the Currency (OCC). Finally, the Federal Reserve supervises state-chartered banks that have chosen to be members of the Federal Reserve System. These regulators have authority to issue cease-and-desist orders and impose civil money penalties for money laundering violations.[30]

FEDERAL GUIDANCE

Although the FDIC, Federal Reserve, NCUA, and OCC have the authority to punish banks that deal with state-legal marijuana businesses, these regulators can also choose to ignore violations. For this reason, financial institutions and state officials have repeatedly requested that the federal regulators issue guidance describing the extent to which they allow financial institutions to serve the marijuana industry. Federal officials have provided some guidance, but that guidance is subject to change.

The FDIC, Federal Reserve, NCUA, and OCC view themselves as secondary actors in crafting marijuana banking policies. In 2013, they declined to issue guidance, noting that the federal FinCEN and the Department of Justice were working together to resolve "the uncertainties that continue to surround the issue of providing banking services to marijuana dispensaries." The regulators explained that because "FinCEN is the Administrator of the Bank Secrecy Act," it would be "premature to provide guidance to the banking industry."[31]

As the regulators had suggested, DOJ and FinCEN guidance was forthcoming. On Valentine's Day 2014, the DOJ and FinCEN both released guidance covering marijuana-related financial transactions. The DOJ's guidance built on earlier DOJ guidance containing eight federal criminal enforcement priorities. Those priorities included preventing the distribution of marijuana to minors, preventing revenue from the sale of marijuana from going to criminal enterprises, and preventing the diversion of marijuana from states where it is legal under state law to states where it is not.[32] The DOJ's 2014 guidance explained that enforcement of marijuana-related financial crimes "should be subject to the same consideration and prioritization."[33] Thus, "if a financial institution or individual offers services to a marijuana-related business whose activities do not implicate any of the eight priority factors, prosecution for [money-laundering] offenses may not be appropriate."[34] The guidance advised that financial institutions take care to ensure customers' activities do not violate the enforcement priorities. It warned that a financial institution could face prosecution for inadequate due diligence.[35]

Because FinCEN is the administrator of the Bank Secrecy Act, its guidance focused on when financial institutions should file suspicious activity reports. It clarified that transactions conducted by a state-legal marijuana business "involve funds derived from illegal activities" as described in the Bank Secrecy Act.[36] Thus, financial institutions must prepare suspicious activity reports for most marijuana-related transactions. Run-of-the-mill marijuana-related transactions warrant only "Marijuana Limited" suspicious activity reports. These reports identify the parties involved, state that "the filing institution is filing the [report] solely because the subject is engaged in a marijuana-related business," and represent that "no additional suspicious activity has been identified."[37] For a customer whose marijuana activity continues, a financial institution must regularly refile and update "Marijuana Limited" suspicious activity reports.[38] However, FinCEN expects financial institutions to conduct due diligence to determine whether the marijuana-related transactions implicate any of the DOJ's enforcement priorities or state law. If an institution discovers transactions that might violate those priorities or state law, the institution must file a "Marijuana Priority" suspicious activity report.[39] Finally, a financial institution must provide a "Marijuana Termination" suspicious activity report when the institution determines "it necessary to terminate a relationship with a marijuana-related business in order to maintain an effective anti-money laundering compliance program."[40]

As a practical matter, the FinCEN guidance sets a high compliance bar, especially for businesses that sell marijuana to consumers. The guidance explains financial institutions should determine whether their customers' activities implicate the federal enforcement priorities. Institutions must ensure that their customers do not sell marijuana to minors and do not sell marijuana to customers who may transport it across state lines. Such due diligence is time-consuming and costly.

Following the FinCEN guidance, the FDIC, Federal Reserve, NCUA, and OCC jointly announced they "incorporate" the FinCEN guidance "into [their] supervisory process."[41] The regulators evaluate whether banks are filing appropriate reports and conducting sufficient due diligence. The regulators explained that "generally the decision to open, close or decline a particular account or relationship is made by a bank or credit union, without involvement by its supervisor."[42] However, they offered no additional guidance and stopped short of saying that financial institutions complying with the DOJ and FinCEN guidance need not fear regulatory enforcement. Instead, the letter explained: "Further clarity from Congress on the legal treatment of state-licensed marijuana-related businesses under federal law would provide greater legal certainty for both marijuana-related businesses and banks and credit unions."[43]

Financial institutions, however, would soon be faced with greater legal uncertainty. In 2018, under a new attorney general, the DOJ rescinded its earlier marijuana guidance. The new attorney general, a long-time opponent of marijuana, explained that "guidance specific to marijuana enforcement is unnecessary."[44] Instead, he instructed prosecutors to "weigh all relevant considerations, including federal law enforcement priorities set by the Attorney General, the seriousness of the crime, the deterrent effect of criminal prosecution, and the cumulative impact of particular crimes on the community" in deciding whether to bring a case.[45]

The rescission of the DOJ marijuana guidance raised questions about the status of FinCEN's 2014 marijuana guidance. FinCEN's guidance was drafted in conjunction with the DOJ and relied on the DOJ's now-rescinded enforcement priorities. Amid speculation that the FinCEN guidance was effectively repealed, the Department of the Treasury clarified that the suspicious activity reporting structure in FinCEN's guidance remains in effect until further notice. However, Treasury explained: "we are reviewing the [FinCEN] guidance in light of the Attorney General's announcement and are consulting with law enforcement."[46] More than a year later, FinCEN, FDIC, Federal Reserve, NCUA, and OCC had not offered further instruction for financial institutions. Although the FinCEN guidance remains in place, some commentators believe the repeal of the DOJ guidance increases the risk of banking marijuana businesses.[47]

The DOJ's rescission of its marijuana guidance illustrates the danger in relying on agency guidance. Guidance alone cannot make marijuana banking legal. Law enforcement officials and banking regulators are free to enforce the law. While guidance may give financial institutions some assurance that current officials will not fully enforce the law, there is no guarantee that future officials will be similarly tolerant.

CURRENT MARIJUANA BANKING

Despite the lack of a clear safe harbor, some financial institutions provide services to marijuana businesses. In June 2018, FinCEN reported that suspicious activity reports indicated 334 banks and 107 credit unions are providing services to marijuana related businesses.[48] This represents less than 1 percent of the financial institutions in the United States.[49]

FinCEN does not disclose the names of the financial institutions serving the marijuana industry and does not describe the services those institutions provide. There is some evidence that although the largest banks publicly state that they do not service marijuana-related businesses, they sometimes do. In Massachusetts, applicants seeking a license to operate medical marijuana dispensaries are asked to list their bank accounts. Of the eighty-four applications filed between June 2015 and September 2016, "29 reported having access to funds in at least one account at Bank of America, Citi, Wells [Fargo], JPMorgan [Chase], or at one of their subsidiaries."[50] In at least some cases, it is likely that the bank knew the nature of its customer's business. Of course, there is also evidence that these banks sometimes close accounts, even in cases where the accountholder is not directly involved in marijuana.[51] At a minimum, marijuana-related businesses with accounts at the largest U.S. banks have tenuous banking relationships.

Only a small number of financial institutions openly offer account-related services to marijuana-related businesses.[52] Most of these are small, state-chartered banks or credit unions. They typically provide only account-related services, not loans.[53] Because of heightened due diligence requirements, financial institutions charge marijuana-related business thousands of dollars in fees per month for accounts.[54]

Financial institutions that openly court marijuana money do not necessarily serve the entire state-legal marijuana industry. Businesses that do not directly deal with marijuana have the easiest time finding banking services.[55] Consider, for example, a landlord that rents space to a marijuana dispensary. The landlord poses some risk to the financial institution. If the dispensary pays rent with money from the sale of marijuana and the landlord deposits the rent in its account, prosecutors and regulators could conclude that the bank violated the law. However, because the landlord does not directly touch marijuana, a financial institution can reasonably perform due diligence to assure itself that the landlord is not directly engaging in any activity that would require a "Marijuana Priority" suspicious activity report. The FinCEN guidance notes that in such cases the financial institution is "not well-positioned" to determine whether the dispensary is violating state law. "In such circumstances where services are being provided indirectly, the financial institution may file a [report] based on existing regulations and guidance without distinguishing between 'marijuana limited' and 'marijuana priority.'"[56] At the other end of the spectrum are marijuana retailers. Even with robust due diligence, it is nearly impossible for financial institutions to confirm that retailers never sell marijuana to minors and never sell marijuana that will later be transported across state lines. Consequently, when marijuana retailers do find a financial institution, the account fees may be substantially higher than for other marijuana-related businesses.[57]

In sum, although there is some marijuana banking, most marijuana-related businesses, particularly those that deal directly with the plant, are likely to encounter banking problems. Indeed, the only entities that handle marijuana money but do not have banking problems are governments that collect marijuana taxes. Financial institutions seem to have no qualms accepting tax revenue, even from marijuana.[58]

WORK AROUNDS

Current law leaves marijuana-related businesses and state officials looking for answers. However, private businesses and state governments cannot change the underlying federal law.

Some marijuana banking "fixes" just disguise the source of money. Marijuana-related businesses set up holding companies with innocuous names that open bank accounts without disclosing ties to the marijuana industry.[59] They turn to third-party payment processors that do not fully disclose the nature of the money to financial institution partners.[60] They install third-party cashless ATM machines in their stores where customers use a debit or credit card to withdraw credit that can be spent in the store.[61] Or they have customers purchase bitcoin with a credit card and use the bitcoin to buy marijuana. The business then converts the bitcoin to cash.[62] If a marijuana business or its partners disguise the illegal source of their funds, they violate anti-money laundering laws. In addition, these schemes work only as long as financial institutions do not discover the marijuana connection. If banks discover the money laundering, they typically close the related accounts.[63]

Some hope that technology will bridge the gap between marijuana-related businesses and banks. Payment processors specializing in high-risk payments offer technology that lets customers electronically pay for retail marijuana. The processors can also help financial institutions meet due diligence and compliance requirements. For example, the processors might file suspicious activity reports or provide technology that allows banks to watch marijuana sales happen in real time.[64] With this assistance, some financial institutions will accept the risk of banking marijuana-related businesses. But even for these institutions, risk remains. Regulators expect banks to rigorously vet and monitor third-party payment processors and other service providers.[65] And the technology, while helpful, still relies on financial institutions that will accept the risk of processing illegal payments.

Others see cryptocurrencies or blockchain technology as offering a non-bank alternative for payment processing. Marijuana businesses could "take an existing digital currency and simply use it as a method of transaction business to avoid the need to rely on banks."[66] Or entrepreneurs could create a "new token . . . specifically for the marijuana industry."[67] This would "eliminate the use of cash and integrate blockchain technology into the compliance and other needs of marijuana businesses."[68] So far, these approaches have not gained significant traction. Because virtual currency is not widely accepted outside the marijuana industry, marijuana-related businesses prefer to have traditional money. Trading virtual currency for traditional money in a bank implicates all of the marijuana banking concerns. Moreover, because virtual currencies themselves do not have a pristine reputation, some businesses worry that using virtual currency will attract law enforcement and regulatory scrutiny.[69]

Finally, some states are exploring whether a state-owned bank could solve the marijuana banking problem.[70] The basic idea is that the state would charter and fund a financial institution to provide account services to marijuana-related businesses. There are several barriers to this solution. First, to the extent that a state-chartered bank wants to directly process payments using the Federal Reserve's systems, the bank would need approval from the Federal Reserve.[71] It is not clear that the Federal Reserve would grant access. Private organizers of Fourth Corner Credit Union in Colorado asked the Federal Reserve Bank of Kansas City for a master account. The Kansas City Fed. denied the account citing the Credit Union's "focus on serving marijuana-related businesses."[72] Perhaps another regional Federal Reserve Bank might be more lenient.[73] Or perhaps the Federal Reserve would be more receptive to an application from a state as opposed to a private party.[74] However, the Federal Reserve could still deny a state-owned bank access because marijuana banking is illegal under federal law. Second, if the state-owned bank wants federal insurance, the FDIC would have to grant approval, and it is not clear the FDIC would approve, because marijuana is illegal under federal law. Third, establishing a public bank will be time-consuming and costly. Fourth, like private marijuana banking, public marijuana banking relies on federal forbearance. Even if a state-owned bank successfully opened, it (and its employees) could, in the future, be targeted for violating federal law.

PATH FORWARD

Although marijuana-related businesses and state officials have invested significant time and effort to solve the marijuana banking access problem, they cannot. Congress holds the keys to marijuana banking for two reasons. First, marijuana is illegal under federal law. Second, federal law enforcement and financial regulators have significant power to punish institutions that do not comply with federal law. Unless Congress acts to remove one or both of those barriers, most financial institutions will not provide services to the marijuana industry. In considering legislation, Congress should be mindful of the compliance burden imposed on banks. Congress or regulators may be tempted to require that banks and credit unions police the marijuana industry's compliance with state and federal law. However, if compliance costs are too high, or the risk of punishment too great, financial institutions will continue to avoid marijuana.

NOTES

Portions of this chapter draw on work originally published in Julie Andersen Hill, "Banks, Marijuana, and Federalism," Case Western Reserve Law Review 65 (2015), pp. 597–647.

1. Nathan DiCamillo, "How to Tell If You're Banking a Pot Business," *American Banker*, August 27, 2018 (available at 2018 WLNR 2592192).

2. Quoted in Steven A. Rosenberg, "Marijuana Businesses May Be Cash Only," *Boston Globe*, August 10, 2014, p. Z1.

3. Emily Flitter, "Wells Fargo Shut Account of Marijuana Candidate," *New York Times*, August 20, 2018, p. B4.

4. Eric Gorski, "Herb Empire: A Series About the Recreational Marijuana Industry—Holding the Bags," *Denver Post*, June 15, 2014, p. 1A.

5. Serge F. Kovaleski, "Banks Say No to Marijuana Money," *New York Times*, January 11, 2014, p. A1.

6. Gorski, "Herb Empire," p. 1A.

7. Alex Altman, "Pot's Money Problem," *Time*, January 27, 2014, p. 32.

8. Colorado Revised Statutes §§ 24-32-119, 39-28.8-203, 44-11-501 (2018); Washington Revised Code § 69.50.540(4) (2018).

9. Leandra Lederman, "The Interplay Between Norms and Enforcement in Tax Compliance," *Ohio State Law Journal* 64 (2003), pp. 1504–05.

10. Aloke Chakravarty, "Feeding Humanity, Starving Terror: The Utility of Aid in a Comprehensive Antiterrorism Financing Strategy," *Western New England Law Review* 3 (2010), p. 307 n.35.

11. The IRS charges a 10 percent penalty for taxes not paid electronically unless the taxpayer has "undertaken reasonable efforts to obtain a bank account" and has been "unable to do so." Internal Revenue Service, Interim Guidance on the Failure to Deposit Penalty Under Section 6656 for Taxpayers Unable to Get a Bank Account, June 9, 2016 (www.irs.gov/pub/foia/ig/spder/SBSE-04-0615-0045%5B1%5D.pdf).

12. Kevin Wack, "Big Banks Worked with Pot Industry, Despite Denials, Records Show," *American Banker*, January 11, 2017 (available at 2017 WLNR 1007182).

13. United States Code, vol. 21, §§ 841(a)(1), 802(6), 812 (2012).

14. United States Code, vol. 18, §§ 2, 3, 371 (2012).

15. United States Code, vol. 18, § 1956(a)(1)(B) (2012).

16. United States Code, vol. 18, § 1957(a) (2012).

17. United States Code, vol. 31, § 5318(l) (2012); Code of Federal Regulations, vol. 31, § 1020.220 (2018).

18. Federal Financial Institutions Examination Council, Bank Secrecy Act/Anti-Money Laundering Examination Manual (2014), pp. 22, 57–59.

19. Code of Federal Regulations, vol. 31, §§ 1010.311, 1020.320(a)(2) (2018).

20. United States Code, vol. 18, §§ 1956(a), 1957(b) (2012) (money laundering); United States Code, vol. 18, § 841(b)(1)(A) (2012) (Controlled Substances Act); United States Code, vol. 31, §§ 5322, 5324(d) (2012) (Bank Secrecy Act).

21. Sam Kamin, "Disjointed Regulation: State Efforts to Legalize Marijuana," *University of California Davis Law Review* 50 (2016), p. 627.

22. See generally Senate Report 433, 99th Cong., 2nd Sess. (1986).

23. U.S. Government Accountability Office, Private Deposit Insurance: Credit Unions Largely Complied with Disclosure Rules, But Rules Should Be Clarified, GAO-17-259 (2017), pp. 5, 27.

24. United States Code, vol. 12, §§ 1786(k), 1818(i) (2012).

25. United States Code, vol. 12, §§ 1786, 1818(a)(2) (2012)

26. United States Code, vol. 12, § 1818(e)(2) (2012).

27. Board of Governors of the Federal Reserve System, Federal Reserve's Key Policies for the Provision of Financial Services, November 5, 2018 (www.federalreserve.gov/paymentsystems/pfs_policies.htm).

28. *Fourth Corner Credit Union v. Fed. Reserve Bank of Kansas City*, 861 F.3d 1052, 1064 (10th Cir. 2017) (Bacharach, C. J., concurring). Rather than establishing a master account, a bank may, instead, contract with a correspondent bank to conduct transactions with the Federal Reserve. However, for many of the same reasons banks are reluctant to serve marijuana-related businesses, banks will be reluctant to provide correspondent banking services for institutions that do. Ibid. p. 1053 (Moritz, C. J., concurring) (noting that Fourth Corner Credit Union "tried and failed to secure a correspondent relationship").

29. Ibid. p. 1055 (Moritz, C. J., concurring) ("Even if [marijuana-related] businesses are 'compliant' with Colorado law, their conduct plainly violates [federal law.] By providing banking services to these businesses, the Credit Union would—by its own admission—facilitate their illegal activity. . . .").

30. United States Code, vol. 12, §§ 1818, 1847 (2012).

31. Letter from Board of Governors of the Federal Reserve System and others, to Washington Governor Jay Inslee, November 14, 2013 (https://dfi.wa.gov/documents/banks/fed-letter-to-gov-inslee-11-15-2013.pdf).

32. Memorandum from Deputy Attorney General James M. Cole to United States Attorneys, Guidance Regarding Marijuana Enforcement, August 29, 2013.

33. Memorandum from Deputy Attorney General James M. Cole to United States Attorneys, Guidance Regarding Marijuana Related Financial Crimes, February 14, 2014.

34. Ibid.

35. Ibid.

36. Financial Crimes Enforcement Network, Department of the Treasury, FIN-2014-G001, BSA Expectations Regarding Marijuana-Related Businesses, 2014.

37. Ibid.

38. Ibid.

39. Ibid.

40. Ibid.

41. Letter from Board of Governors of the Federal Reserve System and others to Washington Governor Jay Inslee, August 13, 2014 (https://dfi.wa.gov/documents/banks/gov-inslee-interagency-response.pdf).

42. Ibid.

43. Ibid.

44. Memorandum from Attorney General Jefferson B. Sessions, III, to United States Attorneys, Marijuana Enforcement, January 4, 2018.

45. Ibid.

46. Letter from Drew Maloney, Assistant Secretary for Legislative Affairs, Department of the Treasury, to Representative Denny Heck, January 31, 2018 (https://denny heck.house.gov/sites/dennyheck.house.gov/files/documents/Treasury%20Response%20 1.31.18_Heck.pdf).

47. See Dorsey & Whitney LLP, FinCEN Guidance on Banking Marijuana – Increased Legal Risk to Banks, January 23, 2018 (www.dorsey.com/newsresources/ publications/client-alerts/2018/01/fincen-guidance-on-banking-marijuana).

48. FinCEN, Marijuana Banking Update, June 2018 (www.fincen.gov/sites/default/ files/shared/3rd%20Q%20MJ%20Stats.pdf).

49. At the end of 2017, there were 5,573 federally insured credit unions and 5,738 banks in the United States Federal Deposit Insurance Corporation, Annual Report (2017), p. 5; National Credit Union Administration, Annual Report (2017), p. 195.

50. Wack, "Big Banks Worked With Pot Industry, Despite Denials, Records Show."

51. Flitter, "Wells Fargo Shut Account of Marijuana Candidate," p. B4.

52. See, for example, Jessica Bartlett, "Seeing Green: Why a Mass. Credit Union Jumped Into the Marijuana Business," *Boston Business Journal*, September 18, 2018 (available at 2018 WLNR 28726135) (GFA Federal Credit Union in Massachusetts); Nathan DiCamillo, "Despite DOJ's Marijuana Moves, It's 'Business as Usual' for Partner Colorado," *Credit Union Journal*, January 10, 2018 (available at 2018 WLNR 887577) (Partner Colorado Credit Union in Colorado); Ashley Stewart, "No More Lies: Banks and Credit Unions Take a Risk to Serve the Budding Legal Marijuana Industry," *Puget Sound Business Journal*, September 26, 2018 (available at 2018 WLNR 22815206) (Salal Credit Union, Timberland Bank, Numerica Credit Union, and O Bee Credit Union in Washington).

53. Monica Mendoza, "A Money Matchmaker for the Legal Pot Industry," *Denver Business Journal*, March 14, 2017 (available at 2017 WLNR 8046630).

54. Robb Mandelbaum, "High Finance," *New York Times Magazine*, January 7, 2018, p. 51 (reporting that Partner Colorado, a credit union in Colorado, charges its new marijuana customers $450 in fees for each $100,000 deposited); Aaron Gregg, "Bank Eases Pot World's Cash-Only Handicap," *Washington Post*, January 3, 2018, p. B1 (reporting that one marijuana-related business "paid $3,000 to open an account . . . and pays monthly fees of $1,750"); James Rufus Koren, "Hard to Stash: Most Banks Won't Work With Marijuana Businesses," *Los Angeles Times*, July 7, 2017, p. 1 (reporting that an unnamed California credit union charges marijuana growers $5,000 per month and dispensaries $7,500 per month for a bank account).

55. A 2015 Marijuana Business Daily surveyed more than 400 marijuana businesses. The survey found that 30 percent of "plant-touching" cannabis companies had banks accounts while 51 percent of "ancillary" marijuana-businesses had bank accounts. Becky Olson, "Chart of the Week: 60% of Cannabis Companies Don't Have Bank Accounts," Marijuana Business Daily, December 14, 2015 (https://mjbizdaily.com/chart-week-60-cannabis-companies-dont-bank-accounts/).

56. Financial Crimes Enforcement Network, Department of the Treasury, FIN-2014-G001, BSA Expectations Regarding Marijuana-Related Businesses, 2014.

57. Koren, "Hard to Stash," p. 1.

58. David Migoya, "State Can Deposit Cash, But It's Hazy," *Denver Post*, January 5, 2015, p. 10K (reporting that Colorado deposits its tax revenue at JPMorgan Chase and Washington deposits its tax revenue at Bank of America).

59. Kristina Davis, "Banking Barriers For Legal Pot Businesses," *San Diego Union-Tribune*, February 18, 2017, p. 1.

60. Annie Nova, "Bitcoin Offers the Cannabis Industry An Alternative to Banks," CNBC, December 15, 2017 (www.cnbc.com/2017/12/15/bitcoin-offers-the-cannabis-industry-an-alternative-to-banks.html) (reporting that SinglePoint offered a mobile app that would accept debit cards, but that SinglePoint's partner banks withdrew once the nature of the payments was identified).

61. Sarah Wynn, "Cashless ATMs: An Imperfect Solution to Legal Pot's Bank Problem," *American Banker*, August 14, 2017 (available at 2017 WLNR 24806462).

62. Charles Alvisetti, Opinion, "Pipe Dreams: Bitcoin Won't Solve Pot Industry's Banking Problem," *CoinDesk*, November 11, 2017 (www.coindesk.com/pipe-dreams-bitcoin-wont-solve-pot-industrys-banking-problem/).

63. David Migoya, "Bank Pulls ATMs' Plugs," *Denver Post*, October 23, 2014, p. 1A (describing how "hundreds of ATMs located in medical marijuana dispensaries" were turned off after a sponsoring bank discovered the nature of the businesses).

64. Nathan DiCamillo, "Pot Banking Regtech is Ready For Its Moment," *American Banker*, July 24, 2018 (available at 2018 WLNR 22519172) (discussing payment processors Hypur and PayQwik).

65. FDIC, Payment Processor Relationships: Revised Guidance, FIL-2-2012 (January 31, 2012).

66. Alvisetti, "Pipe Dreams: Bitcoin Won't Solve Pot Industry's Banking Problem."

67. Ibid.

68. Ibid.

69. Ibid.

70. Laura Alix, "A Public Bank For Pot Firms? Mass. Regulator Likes the Idea," *American Banker Magazine*, April 1, 2018, p. 5 (Massachusetts); James Rufus Koren, "State Explores Creating Bank to Serve Pot Firms," *Los Angeles Times*, January 31, 2018, p. 1 (California); Jake Zuckerman, "Legislators Mull Fix for Banking," *Charleston Gazette-Mail* (West Virginia), September 18, 2018, p. 3A (West Virginia).

71. A state-owned bank could, instead, process payments through a correspondent bank. Banks may be more willing to serve as a correspondent for a state-owned bank than for a privately-owned bank. After all, banks routinely process transactions involving government-collected marijuana taxes. Migoya, "State Can Deposit Cash, But It's Hazy," p. 10K.

72. *Fourth Corner Credit Union v. Fed. Reserve Bank of Kansas City*, 861 F.3d 1052, 1054 (10th Cir. 2017 (Moritz, C. J. concurring). After Fourth Corner modified its business plan and agreed not to accept deposits from marijuana-related businesses that violate federal law, the Kansas City Fed. granted the credit union a master account. Alicia Wallace, "Federal Reserve Gives OK to Pot-Focused Credit Union," *Denver Post*, February 7, 2018, p. 12A.

73. Master accounts are acted on by the regional Federal Reserve bank in the region

where the financial institution is headquartered. Some observers believe the Federal Reserve Bank of San Francisco is more receptive to the idea of marijuana banking that the Federal Reserve Bank of Kansas City. See Aaron Klein and Kristofer Readling, "Marijuana Legalization: Raising Novel Banking Questions," Bipartisan Policy Center, November 5, 2015 (https://bipartisanpolicy.org/blog/marijuana-legalization-banking-questions/) (noting that the San Francisco Fed. has offered some guidance on marijuana banking and even announced the number of banks in its region providing services to marijuana related businesses, while the Kansas City Fed. has not).

74. As one proponent of a state-owned bank in California put it: "There's a big difference between an application from a tiny credit union and an application from the sixth-largest economy in the world." James Rufus Koren, "Public Bank for Pot Businesses? It Wouldn't Be Easy," *Los Angeles Times*, August 6, 2017, p. 1.

7

LEGAL ADVICE FOR MARIJUANA BUSINESS ENTITIES

Cassandra Burke Robertson

To what extent should lawyers be able to assist cannabis businesses in states with legalized marijuana? The need for legal counsel seems obvious given how rapidly the legal status of the marijuana industry is changing. It was only in 1996 that California became the first state to authorize the use of marijuana in medical treatment. By early 2020, a majority of the states had passed legislation approving medical marijuana, and eleven states had approved the sale and use of recreational marijuana. Perhaps no other industry has seen its legal and regulatory environment change quite so fast.

Given these rapid changes, it is only natural that businesses entering this space would need legal assistance. Some legal needs are predictable from the beginning: for example, an entity might need help drafting sales contracts and supplier agreements—and it would need legal counsel to ensure that the business dealt only with authorized suppliers. Other legal needs are less obvious and may depend on quirks of individual state law. For example, Ohio's marijuana law contained a requirement that at least 15 percent of cultivation licenses go to minority-owned businesses.[1] When a medical marijuana company challenged that restriction on constitutional grounds, marijuana business entities on both sides of the case needed legal assistance.[2] Under Ohio law, as in most other states, business entities have no right to represent themselves in court.[3] Without the assistance of lawyers, the constitutional challenge could not have gone forward.

Lawyers' assistance is needed not just to test the validity of state enactments but also to help firms navigate the boundaries of state and federal authority. States' willingness to experiment with marijuana legalization calls to mind Justice Louis Brandeis' famous description of the states as "laborator[ies] of democracy" capable of making "novel social and economic experiments without risk to the rest of the country."[4] But, of course, the states are not acting on a blank slate; they are acting within a constitutional system that gives supremacy to federal law, and federal law currently prohibits the manufacture, distribution, and possession of marijuana under the Controlled Substances Act of 1970. Any action the states take, therefore, raises significant questions about the balance of regulatory authority under federalism.[5]

What is more, these legal questions must be analyzed under federal law that itself lacks consistency. Although the CSA offers a flat prohibition of all marijuana-related activity, later acts of Congress and the executive branch have shown some tolerance for state experimentation. Congress enacted an appropriations rider in 2014—and renewed it each year for five years—restricting the Department of Justice from using federal funds to prosecute conduct that complies with state medical-marijuana laws.[6] And under the Obama administration, the Department of Justice itself issued the Cole Memorandum, announcing a hands-off policy with regard to state legalization of marijuana.[7]

The DOJ rescinded that memorandum under the Trump administration in early 2018, vowing, instead, to "return to the rule of law" by directing "all U.S. Attorneys to enforce the laws enacted by Congress and to follow well-established principles when pursuing prosecutions related to marijuana activities."[8] But the directive did not order an immediate crackdown on state legalization efforts; instead, it ordered federal officials to "deploy Justice Department resources most effectively to reduce violent crime, stem the tide of the drug crisis, and dismantle criminal gangs." In the words of one commentator, "the policy shift merely gives prosecutors *the option* of enforcing federal marijuana law against those who violate it, whereas previously prosecutors were directed to respect state marijuana laws."[9] Nearly a year later, enforcement actions have not significantly increased, suggesting that activities consistent with state legalization programs are not a priority for federal law enforcement.

PROVIDING LEGAL ADVICE TO MARIJUANA BUSINESS ENTITIES

Given the rapidly changing legal and regulatory environment for marijuana, it is unsurprising that people in both the government and private industry agree there is a real need for legal advice. Start-up companies need lawyers to advise them about how to comply with brand new state regulations, and they need lawyers to advise them about how to work in a complicated federal regulatory environment. Banks, real estate companies, and other established businesses need advice about how to protect themselves as they consider engaging in transactions with marijuana companies. All businesses, whether start-ups or established businesses, need advice about risk management, including avoiding business practices that might increase the risk of harm to third parties and, thereby, increase the risk of civil or criminal liability. But there are significant questions about whether lawyers may ethically provide this assistance and whether they would be subject to civil or criminal liability if they did.

Defining Criminal Conduct

Marijuana's legal status—legal to possess and sell under some states' laws, illegal to possesses or sell under federal law—has created difficulty for lawyers who might otherwise be able to advise marijuana businesses. The Model Rules of Professional Conduct, followed by most states, provide that lawyers "shall not counsel a client to engage, or assist a client, in conduct that the lawyer knows is criminal or fraudulent."[10] The rule allows lawyers to "discuss the legal consequences of any proposed course of conduct with a client" and to "counsel or assist a client to make a good faith effort to determine the validity, scope, meaning or application of the law."[11] But it does not allow lawyers to assist with conduct deemed criminal under the law.

The current status of marijuana in American society does not fit easily into the ordinary criminal framework. Society criminalizes conduct that it considers morally or socially wrongful.[12] When societal views change, the law

may undergo a period of chaos or confusion before settling on new param-
eters.[13] During that period of flux, there are likely to be questions about how
to define—and whether to punish—conduct that is nominally still criminal.

Such a change seems to be in progress for marijuana. In 1969, only 12 percent of Americans believed marijuana should be legalized. By 2017, 61 percent
of Americans (70 percent of those under forty) favored legalization.[14] As with
other matters, support for legalization is not geographically uniform. In the
2018 elections, for example, voters in Michigan supported legalization of recreational marijuana but voters in North Dakota did not. Given the ongoing
(though uneven) shift in public opinion, it is understandable that the federal
government would want to hold back, waiting to let state experiments play
out—a policy that so far transcends the change in administration in practice,
even after rescission of the Cole Memorandum. Informally, at least, the law
criminalizing marijuana is in the process of weakening. States have moved
toward legalization, public opinion supports legalization, and the federal government does not have a clear policy condemning those efforts.

The problem for lawyers, however, is that even with some degree of federal
tolerance of state legalization efforts, the possession and sale of marijuana is
still a criminal offense under federal law. Furthermore, federal law supersedes
conflicting state law under the U.S. Constitution's Supremacy Clause—and
lawyers swear an oath upon admission to the bar vowing to uphold the Constitution.[15] As a result, lawyers find themselves in a difficult position. The U.S.
Constitution, which they have sworn to uphold, requires them to recognize the
primacy of federal law. And the federal CSA is quite clear that the cultivation,
possession, and distribution of marijuana are criminal acts.

After Initial Hesitation, States Encourage Legal Assistance

As a result of the discord between state and federal law, a number of the
state ethics committees have been asked to opine whether lawyers can ethically assist marijuana-related businesses. The states have struggled with that
question and have arrived at conflicting answers. Opinions from several states,
including Maine,[16] Connecticut,[17] and Ohio,[18] initially suggested that lawyers
could "advise" marijuana entities but could not "assist" them—that is, attorneys could not offer the kind of strategic and tactical legal advice that start-
up companies so often need. Instead, they could ethically offer only limited

advice, mostly to inform their clients that their desired course of action is illegal under federal law. Legal assistance that went further—for example, executing sales agreements for cannabis products—would be prohibited under this view.[19] As a result of these decisions, experts advised attorneys that they "ought to limit their conversations with medical marijuana patients to mere advice that does not encourage the client to take action . . . being careful to avoid any language that may suggest actions the client should take in order to ensure protection under state medical marijuana laws."[20] Of course, such limited advice is of equally limited utility to clients. Non-lawyers can read the text of the law themselves, after all. The lawyer's primary value is in providing strategic advice and counsel to ensure protection under the law—but that is the very activity that lawyers are being warned away from.

Furthermore, the line between "advice" and "assistance" is far from clear. As one commentator pointed out, "most authorities discern a critical distinction between on the one hand presenting a client with an analysis of the legal aspects of questionable conduct and on the other hand recommending the means by which a crime or fraud may be committed with impunity."[21] Even accepting for the sake of argument that state-authorized marijuana commerce is a "crime," there is still much room in the middle of those two poles. That room in the middle is where legal advice is the most important.

As a result, these early negative opinions were often superseded by changes in the state rules of professional conduct. After all, most states have adopted the view that "the primary purpose of lawyer regulation proceedings is to protect the public, not to punish the offending lawyer."[22] If the state has adopted a program of marijuana legalization, the public is not protected by forbidding lawyers from assisting in the new businesses—to the contrary, the public suffers harm when state-authorized businesses cannot obtain advice about their rights and responsibilities under the law.[23] As a result, states such as Colorado, Connecticut, and Ohio each amended the state rules of professional conduct to permit lawyers to assist with conduct legal under state law, as long as the lawyers also advised clients about federal law and policy.[24]

Maine similarly changed course, concluding after further review that, "to subject lawyers to discipline for counseling or assisting clients to engage in Maine's testing of this area would be, in practical effect, to shut down this particular approach to development of the law."[25] The board concluded that "the public's need for legal assistance and right to receive it are substantial, and concerns about upholding respect for the law and legal institutions are not significant enough to outweigh those considerations in this circumstance." It consequently adopted a revised opinion providing that "Rule 1.2 is not a bar to assisting clients to engage in conduct that the attorney reasonably believes is permitted by Maine laws regarding medical and recreational marijuana, including the statutes, regulations, Orders and other state or local provisions implementing them."[26]

In other states, including Alaska, Illinois, Nevada, Hawaii, Oregon, and Washington, the state supreme court adopted rule changes specifically permitting attorneys to assist in-state marijuana businesses.[27] One state acted through the legislative branch rather than the judicial branch: Minnesota adopted a statutory provision barring attorney discipline for attorneys' advice to state-authorized marijuana entities.[28]

Committees in several other states reached more permissive results even without rule or statute changes. A New York ethics committee, for example, concluded that New York lawyers may give legal assistance "that goes beyond a mere discussion of the legality of the client's proposed course of conduct."[29] Likewise, the State Bar of Arizona concluded that state ethics rules should not prohibit lawyers from assisting marijuana businesses legal under state law, at least as long as there has been no "judicial determination" concluding that the state law is preempted by contrary federal law.[30] Two other states, Florida and Massachusetts, issued opinions stating that lawyers would not be subject to discipline for assisting marijuana entities. As others have noted, however, such a policy "is, of course, subject to the whim of the administrator and therefore provides lawyers less protection than a rule change."[31]

Ethical Questions Remain After a Shift in Federal Policy

Although states have largely moved toward allowing lawyers to advise state-authorized marijuana businesses without fear of professional discipline, there are still many open questions—questions that are significant enough to make lawyers think twice about representing such entities. First, of course, is the problem that not all states legalizing marijuana have issued any guidance at all. And although it is likely that other states would follow the trend of allowing lawyer representation, there is no guarantee of that. For example, as of 2019,

New Mexico still maintains the position that lawyers may not assist clients with marijuana-related activity.[32] Thus, the threat of state disciplinary proceedings remains real in states that have not provided a safe harbor to attorneys.

Even those states that have provided a safe harbor from state disciplinary processes cannot protect against the possibility that federal courts will take a different—and less deferential—approach. After the Colorado Supreme Court amended the rules of professional conduct to clarify that lawyers could assist state-authorized entities, the federal district court in Colorado amended its own rules.[33] Previously, the court had adopted the Colorado Rules of Professional Conduct as standards of professional responsibility of attorneys appearing before it. But now, the court specifically excluded the amended comment to Colorado RPC 1.2(d) to the extent that it allowed attorneys to "assist" state-authorized marijuana businesses.[34] As a result, lawyers face an "uncertain playing field" in Colorado, where the state rules permit assistance to marijuana business but federal court rules imply the prohibition of it.[35]

Finally, even some states adopting a permissive view of lawyers' assistance have depended at least to some extent on the existence of a deferential federal policy under the Cole Memorandum. The rule change in at least one case (Washington) explicitly depended on that policy. Washington adopted a comment to its rules of professional conduct allowing lawyer assistance with state marijuana businesses, but it provided in a comment that such practice was authorized "at least until there is a change in federal enforcement policy."[36] It, thus, left open the question of whether Washington's rules of professional conduct would still protect lawyers' assistance now that the Cole Memorandum has been rescinded.

Other permissive ethics opinions came with similar caveats. The New York opinion, for example, was based explicitly on the federal hands-off position adopted by the Cole Memo. It pointed out that both state and federal interests were served by encouraging robust legal advice, noting that the "federal forbearance" policy relied on "strong and effective regulatory and enforcement systems" in the states and that implementing such systems necessarily required legal assistance. The committee warned, however, that if the federal government's position were to "change materially" then its opinion "might need to be reconsidered." The disavowal of the Cole Memorandum raises a significant question about the continuing validity of the New York opinion as well.

BARRIERS TO THE AVAILABILITY OF LEGAL COUNSEL

A lack of clarity in the state ethics rules creates a barrier to industry members' efforts to obtain legal services. The risk of disciplinary consequences may be small, as "no attorney to date has faced ethics proceedings related to his representation of recreational marijuana clients."[37] Even so, the chilling effect on lawyers' willingness to provide this counsel is real. Sometimes, even the possibility of disciplinary action is enough to make lawyers turn away cases. One attorney in New Mexico, for example, terminated "four or five" clients after a New Mexico ethics opinion concluded that lawyers assisting marijuana operations could face discipline.[38] In other cases, however, lawyers may be reluctant to accept such representation even when they have no significant fear of discipline. Out of respect for a constitutional order that gives primacy to federal law, for example, a lawyer may be reluctant to engage in conduct that could violate state ethical rules even when the risk of facing discipline for doing so is small or nonexistent.

Furthermore, the threat of attorney discipline is only one of the potential consequences lawyers need to worry about. A related possibility is the threat that the lawyer's malpractice insurance will not protect against potential liability. Most policies, after all, exclude lawyer conduct that amounts to a crime. Of course, once a liability claim is brought against a lawyer, the insurance company would have a powerful economic incentive to argue that coverage was excluded under this exception—and the withdrawal of the Cole Memorandum takes away the attorney's strongest counterargument for deference to state laws decriminalizing marijuana activity.

A review of legal malpractice policies suggests that insurance companies would be on strong ground to deny claims arising from the representation of marijuana-industry clients. One reviewer found that "all policies exclude" coverage for intentional criminal activity.[39] Some policies will pay to defend such a claim, and some will cover colleagues unaware of the criminal act, but none of the policies would provide indemnity to an attorney found to have engaged in intentional criminal wrongdoing. As a result, some insurance carriers have dropped law firms that do any work at all in the marijuana industry.[40] Other carriers continue to provide policies, but those policies might not cover a claim arising from legal assistance to state-authorized marijuana businesses.[41]

An even more serious risk is the threat of being criminally charged in conjunction with client activity. As other scholars have noted, "it is not clear whether lawyers can advise in-state dispensaries without being guilty of criminal conspiracy or accomplice liability."[42] Commentators have mostly expressed concern about the possibility of federal charges. But state charges are also a possibility, as the contours of the new state marijuana laws leave ambiguity about what activity is protected under the state statutes and what activity could still sustain criminal charges.

The threat of accomplice liability is a real one. Attorney Jessica McElfresh, who represents marijuana clients, was recently charged with assisting a client in hiding evidence of an illegal cannabis-product manufacturing operation. Her client had been openly engaged in a medical marijuana business authorized by California law for two years.[43] But the San Diego district attorney charged the client with exceeding permissible activity under state law by "illegally manufacturing and distributing $3.2 million worth of hash oil, a type of marijuana concentrate made with flammable chemicals."[44] He was charged with fifteen separate felony counts. McElfresh, his lawyer, had her home and office raided and her mother and boyfriend placed in handcuffs.[45] She originally faced thirteen felony counts for assisting her client. Even more seriously, prosecutors argued that attorney-client privilege should not protect McElfresh's communications with her client, as she was allegedly assisting him in criminal activity.

Ultimately, McElfresh's client pleaded guilty only to two misdemeanor counts. McElfresh herself pleaded guilty only to the violation of a San Diego city ordinance—an infraction that did not even rise to the misdemeanor level.[46] Both lawyer and client were largely vindicated. But the case demonstrated the vulnerability of both lawyers and clients working in the cannabis industry. With new and untested state laws, it can be difficult to discern where the line is drawn between state-authorized and non-state-authorized activity.

The precarious legal position of the marijuana industry makes it difficult for the legal system to determine where the line between legal and illegal conduct should be drawn. This is certainly true with the variance between state and federal law, but as the McElfresh prosecution demonstrated, it is also true even within the supposedly easier question of state-law interpretation. A client trying to navigate these waters needs quality legal advice to stay within state-

authorized bounds—and needs legal assistance to defend against overly aggressive prosecution. But when providing that very advice and assistance makes
lawyers themselves vulnerable to prosecution, attorneys will be less likely to
take those cases.

THE DOWNSIDE OF DISCOURAGING LEGAL ADVICE

The barriers just described combine to create a powerful disincentive for lawyers to represent clients in the cannabis industry. The possibility of disciplinary
action is fairly remote but not nonexistent. The likelihood that the lawyer's
work will not be covered by malpractice insurance is much higher. And the
risk of criminal charges, though still rare, comes with consequences so severe
that many attorneys would think twice about accepting even a remote risk of
charges.

Of course, neither the states legalizing marijuana nor the federal government have any interest in keeping marijuana companies from getting robust
legal advice. Those who support the states' efforts on marijuana legalization understand that quality legal advice can facilitate commerce—and poor
or absent legal advice can greatly hinder it.[47] But even those who believe the
states are acting presumptuously in the absence of proper federal authorization
would almost certainly prefer that such state experimentation be done with
legal advice and assistance rather than without it.

Our knowledge about how often lawyers are, in fact, deterred from providing representation is limited and anecdotal. But what we do know is troubling.
Some lawyers, after all, have withdrawn from representing marijuana-industry
clients over even the remote threat of attorney discipline. And we know that
some insurance companies have refused to renew policies for firms accepting
cannabis clients. It is not a huge leap to conclude that even a single high-profile
story about an attorney being charged as an accessory to a client's crime is likely
to further deter lawyers from entering the marketplace.

With fewer attorneys left in the market for cannabis clients, those who are
brave enough to take such cases can likely charge a higher premium for their
work. Indeed, they may need to do so, to self-insure against the risk of financial
loss not covered by a malpractice policy. Perhaps industry clients can afford to
pay a higher price for legal counsel. But it adds a level of inefficiency into the

business that makes it harder to properly evaluate the results of state experimentation.

There is also another, more worrying possibility. It is possible that the lawyers with the most to lose will be so deterred from the marketplace that those left are significantly less qualified to provide counsel. One obvious outcome of such a scenario is that such lawyers might give less-than-optimal legal advice. Businesses getting bad legal advice may violate state regulations, which would, in turn, increase state administrative costs on enforcement actions. Bad legal advice can also scuttle otherwise beneficial transactions, as parties decline to enter into flawed contracts or must later litigate ambiguous terms.

Beyond these direct risks, there is also a more indirect risk that unscrupulous attorneys will use the federal prohibition on marijuana to create leverage over dissatisfied clients who contest the attorney's bill. In one case arising out of Arizona, for example, the client—a medical-marijuana consulting business—sought advice from a lawyer about the possibility of suing a customer who had failed to pay. The lawyer failed to have the client sign a fee agreement at the outset. After the marijuana business settled the claim without the lawyer's involvement, the business refused to pay for the consultation and initial work the attorney's firm had completed, arguing that it had never authorized such work to begin.[48] Trying to push for payment, the lawyer communicated to the client in what the disciplinary board later termed "increasingly insulting and off-color" language that focused on the uncertain legality of the business's marijuana work. In one email, the lawyer disparagingly referred to the client as a "drug dealer" and stated that the lawyer looked forward to "the many nights and mornings" in which the client would, the lawyer implied, suffer incarceration and associated abuse. The lawyer was ultimately given probation through the attorney discipline process and was required to attend an anger-management treatment program. Although this example presents a somewhat extreme case, even one such egregious case may discourage marijuana-industry clients from seeking representation.

CONCLUSION

The American public's view of marijuana is undergoing rapid and major change. A majority of the public no longer believes marijuana use should be criminalized. More than half the population supports legalizing recreational marijuana, and more than 80 percent supports legalizing medical marijuana. Conditions are, therefore, ripe for allowing states to adopt marijuana policies tailored to the needs of the state population.

If the states are to serve as laboratories of democracy, however, they will need legal assistance to succeed in that endeavor. Marijuana's current status— illegal under federal law but authorized to a greater or lesser degree by most states' law—creates significant disincentives for lawyers to provide that assistance. This leaves a distorted marketplace, where legal assistance can be difficult to obtain and may be both more expensive and of lesser quality than legal assistance in other industries. As Dean Chemerinsky concluded in a recent article, "the tension between federal law and state laws with regard to marijuana enforcement generates an untenable status quo."[49]

This is not a problem that can be solved at the state level. Some authors have suggested that states should make clear in their ethics rules that attorneys do not violate the rules of professional ethics when they assist state-regulated businesses to engage in activities authorized by state law.[50] While this would be a good idea and would certainly provide some measure of protection to attorneys, it would not counteract other disincentives to legal assistance: the lack of malpractice insurance coverage and the possibility of criminal liability.

But neither is this a problem that requires the federal government to legalize marijuana nationwide. After all, even as public attitudes toward marijuana are shifting, that shift is not happening uniformly nationwide. It would likely be politically difficult to get the needed level of support for that legislation, and even members of Congress who agree on broad principles would likely disagree on the details of how such a change in policy should be implemented.

A change in federal law that authorizes states to opt out of the CSA's prohibition on marijuana is likely to be much more politically feasible. Such a strategy would protect the ability of states to serve as laboratories of democracy—and it would allow lawyers to assist in those experiments. By eliminating the argument that lawyers are assisting "illegal" conduct, the change would both avoid questions under state ethics laws and protect the availability of malpractice insurance. It would also significantly reduce the possibility that the lawyer would be charged as an accomplice or a co-conspirator. It would not entirely eliminate the possibility of criminal charges, as it is always possible that client conduct (and lawyer assistance) might exceed what is permitted under state law. But even when such issues arise, lawyers would be better positioned to help develop and clarify the contours of state law. By reducing the disincentives for lawyer assistance, such a change in the law would ultimately promote the availability of lower-cost and higher-quality legal counsel to an emerging industry.

NOTES

1. Ohio Rev. Code § 3796.09(c).

2. Jackie Borchardt, "Medical Marijuana Company Sues Ohio Over Cultivator License 'Racial Quota,'" *Cleveland Plain Dealer*, December 13, 2017.

3. *Cincinnati Bar Ass'n v. Foreclosure Sols., L.L.C.*, 914 N.E.2d 386, 390 (Ohio 2009).

4. *New State Ice Co. v. Liebmann*, 285 U.S. 262, 311 (1932) (Brandeis, J., dissenting).

5. William Baude, "State Regulation and the Necessary and Proper Clause," *Case Western Reserve Law Review* 65 (2015), p. 517.

6. H. R. Res. 1370, 115th Cong. (2017) (enacted); Consolidated Appropriations Act, 2018, Pub L. No. 115-141, § 538 (March 23, 2018).

7. Memorandum from James M. Cole, Deputy Attorney General, to U.S. Attorneys, at 3 (August 29, 2013); see also Bradley E. Markano, Note, "Enabling State Deregulation of Marijuana Through Executive Branch Nonenforcement," *New York University Law Review* 90 (2015), p. 291.

8. Department of Justice, Office of Public Affairs, Justice Department Issues Memo on Marijuana Enforcement, January 4, 2018 (www.justice.gov/opa/pr/justice-department-issues-memo-marijuana-enforcement).

9. Anna El-Zein, Note, "Caught in A Haze: Ethical Issues for Attorneys Advising on Marijuana," *Missouri Law Review* 82 (2017), p. 1190. Emphasis in original.

10. Model R. Prof'l Conduct 1.2(d).

11. Ibid.

12. John L. Diamond, The Myth of Morality and Fault in Criminal Law Doctrine, *American Criminal Law Review* 34 (1996), pp. 130–31 ("The criminal law's deterrence . . . is in psychologically and culturally indoctrinating values and boundaries of conduct so that society and individuals perceive such behavior as wrong and condemnable.").

13. See Kevin F. Ryan, "A Flawed Performance," *Vermont Bar Journal*, Fall 2003, pp. 5, 11 (noting that the Supreme Court's reversal on the constitutionality of sodomy law "simply recognized where society had already moved and pushed over a handful of laws that were already on their last legs").

14. Pew Research, *U.S. Public Opinion on Legalizing Marijuana, 1969–2017*, January

5, 2018 (www.pewresearch.org/fact-tank/2018/10/08/americans-support-marijuana-legal
ization/ft_18-01-05_marijuana_line_update/).

15. See, for example, *Cole v. Richardson*, 405 U.S. 676, 681 (1972) ("The oath taken by attorneys as a condition of admission to the Bar of this Court . . . provides in part 'that I will support the Constitution of the United States' "); Lawyer's Oath, State Bar of Michigan ("I do solemnly swear [or affirm]: I will support the Constitution of the United States and the Constitution of the State of Michigan . . .).

16. Prof'l Ethics Comm'n, Opinion 199. Advising Clients Concerning Maine's Medical Marijuana Act, Board Overseers Bd. (July 7, 2010).

17. Informal Opinion 2013-02: Providing Legal Services to Clients Seeking Licenses under the Connecticut Medical Marijuana Law (January 16, 2013).

18. Bd. Of Prof'l Conduct, Supreme Court of Ohio, Opinion 2016-6: Ethical Implications For Lawyers Under Ohio's Medical Marijuana Law 1 (August 5, 2016),

19. Ibid.

20. A. Claire Frezza, "Counseling Clients on Medical Marijuana: Ethics Caught in Smoke," *Georgetown Journal of Legal Ethics* 25 (2012), p. 553.

21. Tom Feher, "Representing Clients In The Marijuana Industry: Greener Grass?," *Law for Lawyers Today*, July 23, 2014 (www.thelawforlawyerstoday.com/2014/07/repre senting-clients-in-the-marijuana-industry-greener-grass/).

22. *In re Cardwell*, 50 P.3d 897, 904 (Colo. 2002).

23. Francis J. Mootz III, "Ethical Cannabis Lawyering in California," *St. Mary's Journal of Legal Malpractice & Ethics* 9 (2018), p. 63.

24. Colorado R. Prof'l Conduct 1.2, cmt. [14]; Connecticut R. Prof'l Conduct 1.2(d)(3); Ohio R. Prof'l Conduct 1.2(d)(2).

25. Prof'l Ethics Comm'n, Opinion 215. Attorneys' Assistance To Clients Under Rule 1.2 Regarding The Use And Sale Of Medical And Recreational Marijuana, Board Overseers Bd. March 1, 2017.

26. Ibid..

27. Alaska R. Prof'l Conduct 1.2(f); Illinois R. Prof'l Conduct 1.2(d)(3); Nev. R. Prof'l Conduct 1.2, cmt. [1]; Hawaii R. Prof'l Conduct 1.2(d); Oregon R. Prof'l Conduct 1.2(d); Wash. R. Prof'l Conduct 1.2, cmt. [18];

28. Minn Stat. Ann. § 152.32(2)(i).

29. N.Y. Eth. Op. 1024 (September 29, 2014).

30. Minn. Ethics Op. 23 (April 3, 2015).

31. Philip Cherner and Dina Rollman, "Marijuana and Your License to Practice Law: A Trip Through the Ethical Rules, Halfway to Decriminalization," *Journal of the Legal Profession* 41 (2016), p. 31.

32. State Bar of N.M.'s Ethics Advisory Comm., Formal Opinion: 2016-1 at 18 (August 10, 2015). This may change in the near future, however, as the governor of New Mexico has appointed a committee to study the legalization of marijuana in the state. They are expected to produce a recommendation in 2020. See Dan Boyd, "Gov. Lujan Grisham Creates Cannabis Legalization Task Force," *Albuquerque Journal*, June 28, 2019.

33. El-Zein, Note, "Caught in A Haze: Ethical Issues for Attorneys Advising on

Marijuana"; see also Peter A. Joy and Kevin C. McMunigal, "Lawyers, Marijuana, and Ethics," *American Bar Association Journal, Criminal Justice* 32 (Spring 2017), p. 29.

34. See Attorney Rules for the District of Colorado, U.S. District Ct.: District Colo. (www.cod.uscourts.gov/CourtOperations/RulesProcedures/LocalRules/AttorneyRules. aspx).

35. Eli Wald, Eric Liebman, and Amanda Bertrand, "Representing Clients in the Marijuana Industry: Navigating State and Federal Rules," *Colorado Law* (August 2015), p. 61.

36. Wash. R. Prof'l Conduct 1.2, cmt. [18].

37. Eric Mitchell Schumann, "Clearing the Smoke: The Ethics of Multistate Legal Practice for Recreational Marijuana Dispensaries," *St. Mary's Journal of Legal Malpractice & Ethics* 6 (2016), pp. 364–65.

38. Brian Melley, "Lawyers Handling Marijuana Business Operate in Hazy Legal Zone," *Insurance Journal,* December 12, 2017.

39. L Squared Insurance Agency, "Attorney Malpractice—Coverage for Marijuana Practice Up in Smoke?" December 14, 2017 (www.l2insuranceagency.com/blog/attorney-malpracticecoverage-for-marijuana-practice-up-in-smoke.aspx).

40. Raffi Kodikian, "Insuring Law Firms with Cannabis Clientele," Founders Professional, September 21, 2018 (www.founderspro.com/2018/09/21/insuring-law-firms-with-cannabis-clientele/).

41. Mootz, "Ethical Cannabis Lawyering in California," p. 42.

42. Baude, "State Regulation and the Necessary and Proper Clause."

43. Renee Flaherty, "VICTORY for the Slatic Family in California," *Institute for Justice*, August 2017 (https://ij.org/ll/august-2017-volume-26-issue-4/victory-slatic-family-california/).

44. Will Yakowicz, "After 2 Years, This Marijuana Entrepreneur's 'Nightmare' Legal Issues Are Finally Over," Inc., November 14, 2017 (www.inc.com/will-yakowicz/james-slatic-med-west-takes-plea-deal.html).

45. Benjamin N. Adams, "Charges Dropped against San Diego Cannabis Attorney," San Diego CityBeat, July 31, 2018 (http://sdcitybeat.com/culture/cannabeat/charges-dropped-against-san-diego-cannabis-attorney/).

46. Ibid.

47. Sam Kamin and Eli Wald, "Marijuana Lawyers: Outlaws or Crusaders?," *Oregon Law Review* 91 (2013), p. 920.

48. *In re Wilenchik,* Arizona Supreme Court Disciplinary Commission, No. PDJ 2015-9011 (January 29, 2015).

49. Erwin Chemerinsky and others, "Cooperative Federalism and Marijuana Regulation," *UCLA Law Review* 62 (2015), p. 113

50. See Joy and McMunigal, supra note 33.

8

THE CONTINGENT FEDERAL POWER
TO REGULATE MARIJUANA

William Baude

The United States has half-heartedly decentralized the regulation of marijuana. Many states have legalized it for some or all purposes, but it remains contraband at the federal level. The result is that neither business investments nor state regulatory institutions are secure from federal enforcement, and the marijuana industry faces potential civil liability and difficulties accessing ordinary commercial services.

It does not have to be this way. In 2005, the Supreme Court upheld the federal ban on marijuana in *Gonzales v. Raich*.[1] In the course of doing so, it denied that state law was ever relevant to the scope of Congress's power under the Commerce Clause or the Necessary and Proper Clause. That conclusion was misguided, was not required by the text or structure of the Constitution, and should be cast aside.

As a matter of constitutional federalism, state regulation should have a role in determining how far the federal drug laws may reach. Congress's power to reach purely in-state conduct is premised on the possibility of interstate spillovers. If a state legalizes and regulates a drug in a way that minimizes the risk of spillovers into the interstate black market, the federal drug laws should not be able to reach within that state. This better squares with the basic premises of federal power and provides better incentives for states to responsibly manage local behavior.

THE NEW MARIJUANA FEDERALISM

Federal law bans the distribution or possession of marijuana. That has been true since the Controlled Substances Act[2] was enacted in 1970 and remains unchanged today. The major blip was a constitutional challenge to the scope of the federal ban, which was ultimately rejected by the Supreme Court in *Gonzales v. Raich*.[3]

State marijuana law, however, has changed dramatically. Twenty-five years ago, marijuana was illegal in every state. In 2005, when the Court decided *Raich*, there were up to eleven states that authorized the use of marijuana for medical purposes.[4] Despite *Raich*'s affirmation of the federal ban, marijuana legalization has continued unabated: thirty-three states now permit medical uses of marijuana,[5] and nine states permit its use for recreational purposes.[6]

The federal ban, although vindicated, has never been aggressively enforced in legalizing states. This was initially the case as a matter of express policy[7] but remains true now as a matter of practice even after Attorney General Sessions formally nullified earlier DOJ guidance.[8] Thus, as a practical matter, states have been given some room to make decisions about whether marijuana should be legal and how its use should be managed. For those who accept the standard policy arguments for decentralization—diversity of preferences, localizing externalities, and policy innovation[9]—this might seem like a happy outcome.

The results have been mixed. Some studies point to positive effects from legalization—even aside from the sheer gain in liberty.[10] And even states that have legalized recreational marijuana have sometimes taken steps to control the diversion of marijuana outside of the state-legalized market.[11]

Nonetheless, both academic and law-enforcement reports suggest there is substantial diversion from recreational marijuana states like Colorado.[12] Indeed, two neighboring states even filed suit against Colorado in the Supreme Court's original jurisdiction, seeking to enjoin the state's regulatory approach.[13]

Moreover, the looming shadow of the federal ban creates problems for an orderly marketplace. Federal law does not allow banks to safely serve the industry.[14] Lawyers who advise in-state dispensaries may be guilty of criminal complicity.[15] Dispensaries face potential civil liability under the federal racketeering statute.[16] And some report that the federal ban makes it "hard to form any contractual relationship" relating to marijuana at all.[17]

It is, therefore, something of a surprise that marijuana federalism has been working as well as it has. If one thinks decentralization has benefits, constitutional federalism doctrine can and should be structured to encourage the states to succeed. States have taken at least some steps to reduce spillovers and diversion, even without any incentive to do so. A sounder constitutional federalism doctrine would actually harness and encourage such state responsibility by making the constitutionality of federal law turn in part on what the state has accomplished.

A CONSTITUTIONAL ROLE FOR STATE LAW

Let's start, as the Supreme Court once said, "with first principles."[18] The federal marijuana laws, like any federal law, are constitutionally permissible only to the extent that they fall within Congress's enumerated powers. While those powers probably give Congress some power, even a broad power, to prohibit marijuana, there are some limits to that power. In particular, Congress's power to regulate in-state marijuana calls for some inquiry into whether that regulation is actually necessary. While the Court's cases do not always adopt this framework clearly, almost all of them are consistent with it.[19]

Congress has no affirmative, explicit power to regulate marijuana generally, or even all national commerce. Rather, its enumerated powers are "to regulate commerce . . . among the several States" and to "make all Laws which shall be necessary and proper for carrying into Execution" that power.[20] In-state marijuana is outside the direct scope of the federal commerce power, and its prohibition must be justified as "necessary and proper" instead. Even if we grant several well-established assumptions that enhance the scope of the government's commerce power—the assumptions that Congress has the power to categorically prohibit interstate trade in marijuana[21] and to reach in-state commerce as necessary to its interstate prohibition[22]—it does not follow that its ancillary power is quite so categorical. Rather, the regulation must also be "necessary"—that is, "convenient, or useful, or essential"[23]—to Congress's powers over interstate commerce. It must be a "means calculated to produce the end."[24]

The argument that the broad prohibitions of the Controlled Substances Act are "necessary and proper" to the interstate commerce power relies on potential spillovers from the in-state market to the interstate market. The claim about spillovers might or might not be valid. It should be taken as a question of reality, not an article of faith.

In the ordinary case, respect for the political branches of the federal government might lead us to presume that there really are spillovers addressed by the federal law. But what happens if the political branches of a state make a different judgment and maintain that spillovers can be contained? If they do, the CSA's categorical prohibition on in-state marijuana will be "convenient, or useful, or essential,"[25] and therefore constitutional, only if the state-law regime will not work. That might be true, but it should not be irrebuttably presumed.

In other words, the federal power to reach in-state commerce is, ultimately, contingent. It depends on how that in-state commerce relates to the federal government's enumerated powers. The effects of a state regulatory regime are simply one such kind of circumstance. Such state regulations have sometimes been regarded with a wary eye, but as this chapter explains, they ought to be tolerated—even welcomed—instead.

The same analysis ought to hold if the case is looked at through the lens of the Commerce Clause alone rather than the Necessary and Proper Clause. As Alison LaCroix has noted, the Supreme Court's decision in *Raich* "blended the commerce and necessary and proper discussions to such a degree that [the] opinion reads as though they were a single unit of analysis."[26] And the same is true more generally of much of its twentieth-century Commerce Clause jurisprudence.[27]

Some founding-era materials engage in a similar blending. Alexander Hamilton and James Madison both argued that the Necessary and Proper Clause was only "declaratory" of how the enumerated powers would have been construed on their own.[28] The Court's analysis in *M'Culloch v. Maryland*[29] proceeds the same way.[30]

So, regardless of whether the analysis is located, as a formal matter, in the Necessary and Proper Clause or in the Commerce Clause itself,[31] the point remains: Congress has no power to regulate in-state commerce as such. Rather, Congress can regulate it only to the extent it is part of the core power to regulate interstate commerce. Therefore, when in-state commerce has been separated from the interstate market over which Congress has power, Congress ought not to have the power to regulate in-state commerce.

The claim that state regulatory regimes should matter to federal power under the Necessary and Proper Clause is, thus, a subset of the claim that actual facts should matter. One could reject this claim if one thinks federal power can never depend on any facts or developments after a law has been enacted. There is a hint of this view in *Raich*'s reference to "shifting" developments "uncontrolled" by Congress. This extends the Necessary and Proper Clause beyond even the broad logic of the twentieth-century cases.

Alternatively, one might reject this claim because of a suspicion about states. The idea might be that allowing state action to be relevant to federal power would be a wedge for nullification, secession, and the usual bogeymen of constitutional federalism. But constitutional history and structure suggest there is good reason for state law to matter.

Most fundamentally, there is nothing wrong with federal authorities occasionally yielding to state institutions. As Heather Gerken has written, the Supreme Court's most successful federalism doctrines "look to the states in describing the limits of *federal* power."[32] Gerken acknowledges that this "might seem odd . . . but the Court does so for a reason. It marks the outer limits of federal authority by identifying the bounds of state power, much the way an artist designates a shape using negative space."[33]

A rule that made federal power turn on state law would also create good incentives for states to affirmatively address potential problems. It is fortunate that marijuana federalism has been working as well as it has, but there are certainly incentives working against it. Strong federal enforcement can resume at any time, depending on executive grace and the political winds. (Remember "Hamsterdam"?)[34] And the federal statutory ban, even if it is not enforced criminally, threatens to put marijuana businesses outside the normal tools of law and order like banks, lawyers, and contracts.

A constitutional ruling based on state law would provide both incentives and protection for well-regulated state experiments. The possibility of freedom from federal regulation would inspire lawmakers to address potentially problematic spillovers rather than ignoring them as somebody else's problem. It would also encourage state officials to continue to ensure, over time, that the safeguards were effective in reality, not just on paper. In other words, states would have a reason to be responsible.

Such a constitutional ruling would also provide protection for investments in those experiments once they succeeded. It takes economic capital and political capital to create a well-functioning market, especially where there has not been one before. The shadowy legal status of marijuana, thus, deters financial investment.[35] It also takes political will to allow such local experiments to proceed when they are contrary to the political fortunes of the ruling majority.[36]

To be sure, not every state's current marijuana regime would obviously satisfy the appropriate constitutional test. As I have noted, for instance, there are arguments that Colorado's marijuana market sees a substantial amount of diversion to interstate black markets.[37] Rather, my point is that constitutional doctrine should have given states more of an incentive to take charge of their own policies and markets. Indeed, the potential tragedy of the current approach is that we may not ever see what kind of creative and effective regulatory approaches states are capable of, because they are given no particular reason to pursue them.

Finally, it is important to be clear that this is not a call for nullification.[38] It is not even a denial of Congress's power to regulate in-state marijuana in some circumstances. It would simply hold that the constitutionality of federal law under the Necessary and Proper Clause must be judged under the circumstances, and those circumstances should include a state's own success at solving the problem Congress has the power to address.

SOME COUNTERARGUMENTS

One challenge confronted by the plaintiffs in *Raich* was how to face down the Supreme Court's precedent in *Wickard v. Filburn*.[39] In *Wickard*, the Supreme Court upheld federal regulations of wheat extending even to wheat that was grown and consumed on a single farm and, therefore, never entered commerce—interstate or otherwise.[40] While many have suggested that *Wickard*'s view of federal power may be overly enthusiastic, the Supreme Court does not seem to be interested in overturning it.

Nothing about the state-law view of the Necessary and Proper Clause challenges *Wickard*. The Court could have continued to assume that Congress can regulate the in-state production and consumption of an agricultural commodity because of its relationship to the interstate market.

In *Wickard*, the Court held that "even if appellee's activity be local and though it may not be regarded as commerce, it may still, whatever its nature, be reached by Congress if it exerts a substantial economic effect on interstate commerce."[41] In *Raich*, however, California law sought to eliminate this effect. It attempted to cut medical marijuana off from the interstate drug market by limiting consumption to Californians and to medical purposes,[42] by imposing individual ID requirements,[43] and by requiring the intervention of doctors, who could be sanctioned for failing to enforce the state's rules.[44]

By contrast, there was no sign of such a state attempt in *Wickard*. So there was nothing to push against the broad conclusion by the federal government that it needed to regulate "all that may be sold without penalty but also what may be consumed on the premises."[45]

That leads us to *Raich*. The dissents in *Raich* did argue that California state law was relevant, though this point was entangled with some of their larger disputes with the majority. Justice Sandra Day O'Connor argued that "the Government ha[d] not overcome empirical doubt" that legal California marijuana had an effect on the interstate market.[46] Justice Clarence Thomas argued that California law "set[] respondents' conduct apart from other intrastate producers and users of marijuana," which made "this class of intrastate users . . . distinguishable from others."[47] But because of their broader disputes with the majority, the dissents did not articulate the role of states under the Necessary and Proper Clause in detail.

The majority's chief response to this point was contained in one sentence of the text: "Just as state acquiescence to federal regulation cannot expand the bounds of the Commerce Clause, so too state action cannot circumscribe Congress' plenary commerce power."[48] The Court further elaborated this reasoning in a long footnote, arguing that considering state law would "retroactively divest Congress of its authority under the Commerce Clause," "turn the Supremacy Clause on its head," and "resurrect limits on congressional power" that have been rejected since *M'Culloch*.[49] The Court also rejected the state-law view of the Clause because it would leave Congress unable to prohibit recreational intrastate marijuana possession, use, and cultivation—"an activity which all States 'strictly contro[l]' "—or, more broadly, any area of commerce a state regulates under its police powers.[50]

As for the majority's chief response, from the body of the opinion,[51] it is a non sequitur. The question is not whether state desire is relevant to the Necessary and Proper Clause but, rather, whether state action can change the referents of the Clause. As for the footnote, the holding and reasoning of *M'Culloch* do not require one to categorically reject the relevance of state enforcement regimes. *M'Culloch* gives Congress broad discretion to choose the means necessary for achieving its permissible ends; but the discretion is not unlimited, and *M'Culloch* repeatedly emphasized the connection between means and ends.

M'Culloch repeatedly stresses that the federal government's powers cannot result in "a dependence . . . on [the governments] of the States," or on "the necessity of resorting to means . . . which another government may furnish or withhold. . . ."[52] But the proposed state-law doctrine would not do that. Federal law would become unconstitutional only if a state law actually addressed the harm to any federal interests (to the satisfaction of the relevant interpreter). There would be no state power to "withhold" effective federal enforcement and no "dependence," because federal law remains available as a backstop.

In that context, I would add that *M'Culloch*'s statement (not quoted in *Raich*) that "the existence of state banks can have no possible influence on the question"[53] should not be extended to the modern spillover context. It suggests a formal separation between state and federal spheres of activity that predates the twentieth-century cases that allowed Congress to reach in-state commerce in the first place. Since the premise of modern regulation of in-state commerce is its relationship to interstate commerce, it no longer makes sense to ignore state institutions that are relevant to that relationship.

As for the *Raich* majority's complaint that this logic could "equally" extend to the "use of marijuana for *recreational* purposes,"[54] that might be so. It is true that the state-law theory would apply as much to state laws about recreational marijuana as to state laws about medical marijuana. It is unclear why the Court deemed that so implausible.

That said, as a practical matter, medical marijuana laws seem more likely to be upheld under a state-influenced theory. Medical marijuana laws involve doctors and other professionals as part of the state distribution regime. Medicine is already regulated, meaning that there is an existing network of enforcement to tap. Moreover, doctors hold lucrative professional licenses and, therefore, have more to lose if they misbehave. So perhaps medical marijuana regimes are more likely to be spillover-free.

APPLYING THE REVISED DOCTRINE

It is possible that *Raich*'s rejection of state law does not really derive from a first-order view about the scope of constitutional power but, rather, from a view about judicial capacity. If so, then the more relevant question is how, as a practical matter, courts could account for state regulation under the Necessary and Proper Clause.

There are, no doubt, many ways courts could admit the relevance of state law. One way is to ask the following two questions: First, does the state have a regime that seems likely, on its face, to eliminate whatever spillover problem Congress would otherwise have the power to address? For instance, does the state limit the purchase of marijuana to residents, limit the purchase quantities in a way that makes straw buyers infeasible, and also regulate production and sale in a way that makes diversion unlikely?

Second, if the regime seems likely to work on its face, is there also evidence that it works in practice? For example, does the state allocate significant resources to enforcement at the border or other relevant nexus? Do studies or reports demonstrate a large amount of diversion?[55] States that have any interest in the preservation of their regulatory authority could themselves be the ones to amass some of this evidence and provide it to the court, whether as litigants or intervenors or amici.

Answering these questions should be no harder in principle than any other judgment about the scope of necessity. If one thinks the judiciary had the capacity to say, as it did in *United States v. Lopez*[56] and *United States v. Morrison*,[57] that the law was too attenuated from any enumerated power, then in principle it should have the same ability when the attenuation is caused by state regulation. Contrariwise, if one is dubious of the entire project of judicially enforced limits on the enumerated powers, then one does not have any special complaint about the role of state law, and one does not need to rely on that part of *Raich*. Either way, the point is that looking to state law and state institutions does not pose a special judicial capacity problem.

There are also simpler ways to give relevance to the role of state law. The Court often says that its review of Congress's enumerated powers judgments is subject only to "rational basis" scrutiny.[58] As Ernie Young has observed, that standard usually assumes there is only one political decision to defer to.[59] Courts might, instead, shift the level of scrutiny in cases where two governments have made differing considered judgments, as in *Raich*. If the state has its own enforcement regime that seems plausibly designed to eliminate spillovers (we might say there must be a "rational basis" for believing it will do so), then perhaps the court would apply some variation of "intermediate" scrutiny instead. This method would use state law to frame the amount of deference before proceeding to the court's other doctrinal tools.

One can imagine other variations on this approach, as well. For instance, one might wish to give more deference to Congress when it has made a specific judgment that the specific state-law regime is not likely to be effective and less deference when it has not considered the problem. The CSA categorically banned marijuana more than twenty-five years before any state introduced an attempt to regulate in-state marijuana and control interstate spillovers. And Congress has never given any formal indication that it thinks the state regimes are unlikely to be effective, since it has not returned to marijuana's classification at all since the act's enactment. Courts might respond to this dynamic by adopting an approach like so: When a state introduces a plausible regime for controlling spillovers, the federal law is presumptively judged under a stricter standard of scrutiny. If Congress responds with a specific, plausible doubt about the state regime, the level of scrutiny recedes back to the lower level.[60]

CONCLUSION

It is probably clear by now that none of these constitutional principles are really limited to marijuana or even to drug prohibition. Marijuana legalization is simply a policy context that currently happens to cast this problem in sharp relief.

The current doctrinal is, thus, a twofold tragedy. It is first the loss of the chance to harness state energy and creativity to responsibly regulate marijuana and control interstate spillovers. But it is also the loss of the chance to, more generally, give states a proactive and responsible role in future challenges to federal policy. The contours of those debates are hard to even guess at now, just as the *Raich* Court probably did not guess that more than one state would legalize recreational marijuana less than ten years later.

Let us hope the future does not give federalism such short shrift.

NOTES

This chapter was adapted from "State Regulation and the Necessary and Proper Clause," Case Western Reserve Law Review *513 (2015), with the always excellent assistance of Sarah Welch and the omnipresent research support of the SNR Denton and Alumni Faculty Funds.*

1. 545 U.S. 1, 29 n.38 (2005).

2. 21 U.S.C. ch.13, § 801.

3. 545 U.S. 1. See Ibid., pp. 10–15 for the statutory scheme and historical background. The minor blips are the federal "Compassionate IND" program, which supplies four people with medical marijuana as the result of an old lawsuit, and a handful of research programs. Gerald Uelmen, Victor Haddox, and Alex Kreit, Drug Abuse and the Law Sourcebook §§ 1:22, 3:88 (2017 update).

4. *Raich*, 545 U.S. at 5 n.1. I say "up to eleven" because the Court appeared uncertain about two states: Arizona and Montana; Ibid.

5. See National Conference of State Legislatures, "State Medical Marijuana Laws" (2018) (www.ncsl.org/research/health/state-medical-marijuana-laws.asp).

6. See National Conference of State Legislatures, "Marijuana Overview" (2018) (www.ncsl.org/research/civil-and-criminal-justice/marijuana-overview.aspx).

7. Memorandum from David W. Ogden, Deputy Attorney General to Selected U.S. Attorneys, "Investigations and Prosecutions in States Authorizing the Medical Use of Marijuana 2" (2009) (www.justice.gov/sites/default/files/opa/legacy/2009/10/19/medical-marijuana.pdf); Memorandum from James M. Cole, Deputy Attorney General to All U.S. Attorneys, "Guidance Regarding the Ogden Memo in Jurisdictions Seeking to Authorize Marijuana for Medical Use 2" (2011) (www.drugpolicy.org/sites/default/files/DOJ_Guidance_on_Medicinal_Marijuana_1.pdf).

8. Memorandum from Jefferson B. Sessions, III, Attorney General to all United States Attorneys, "Medical Marijuana" (2018) (www.justice.gov/opa/pressrelease/file/1022196/download) (rescinding Ogden and Cole memos and instructing federal prosecutors to instead "follow the well-established principles that govern all federal prosecutions"). Still, Attorney General Sessions later clarified in a speech that "federal prosecutors 'haven't been working small marijuana cases before, they are not going to be working them now.'" "Jeff Sessions says prosecutors won't pursue 'small marijuana cases,'" CBS, 2018 (www.cbsnews.com/news/jeff-sessions-doj-prosecutors-will-not-pursue-small-marijuana-cases).

9. Michael W. McConnell, "Federalism: Evaluating the Founders' Design," *University of Chicago Law Review* 54 (1987), pp. 1484, 1493–1500.

10. D. Mark Anderson, Benjamin Hansen, and Daniel I. Rees, "Medical Marijuana Laws, Traffic Fatalities, and Alcohol Consumption," *Journal of Law and Economy* 56 (2013), p. 333; See David A. Makin and others, "Marijuana Legalization and Crime

Clearance Rates: Testing Proponent Assertions in Colorado and Washington State," *Police Quarterly* (2018) (www.doi.org/10.1177/1098611118786255).

11. John Hudak, "Colorado's Rollout of Legal Marijuana Is Succeeding: A Report on the State's Implementation of Legalization," *Case Western Reserve Law Review* 65 (2015), pp. 649, 660–63, 678–85; Alex Kreit, "Marijuana Legalization and Nosy Neighbor States," *Boston College Law Review* 58 (2017), pp. 1059, 1062 (arguing that "as currently constituted, state marijuana legalization laws are unlikely to have anything more than a negligible effect on neighboring states").

12. Zhuang Hao and Benjamin Cowan, "The Cross-Border Effects of Recreational Marijuana Legalization," Working Paper 23426 (NBER, October 2017) (www.nber.org/papers/w23426); Rocky Mountain High Intensity Drug Trafficking Area, "The Legalization of Marijuana in Colorado: The Impact," pp. 37–49 (2013); Rocky Mountain High Intensity Drug Trafficking Area, "The Legalization of Marijuana in Colorado: The Impact" 5, pp. 59–62 (Update September 2018); but see Kreit, supra note 12, pp. 1066–70 (criticizing the Rocky Mountain High Intensity Drug Trafficking Area reports).

13. *Nebraska & Oklahoma v. Colorado*, 136 S. Ct. 1034 (2016) (denying leave to file, over dissent by two justices).

14. Julie Andersen Hill, "Banks, Marijuana, and Federalism," *Case Western Reserve Law Review* 65 (2015), p. 597.

15. Sam Kamin and Eli Wald, "Marijuana Lawyers: Outlaws or Crusaders?" *Oregon Law Rev*iew 91 (2013), pp. 869, 886–99.

16. Robert A. Mikos, "A Critical Appraisal of the Department of Justice's New Approach to Medical Marijuana," *Stanford Law & Policy Review* 22 (2011), pp. 633, 649–56.

17. Sam Kamin, "Marijuana at the Crossroads: Keynote Address," *Denver University Law Review* 89 (2012), pp. 977, 985.

18. *United States v. Lopez,* 514 U.S. 549, 552 (1995).

19. See infra for a discussion of the chief exception, *Raich*.

20. U.S. Const. art I, § 8, cl. 3, 18.

21. *Champion v. Ames*, 188 U.S. 321, 357 (1903); *States v. Darby*, 312 U.S. 100, 120 n.3 (1941). But see Barry Friedman and Genevieve Lakier, " 'To Regulate,' Not 'To Prohibit': Limiting the Commerce Power," *Supreme Court Review* (2012), pp. 255, 257.

22. *Houston E. and W. Tex. Ry. Co. v. United States* (Shreveport Rate Cases), 234 U.S. pp. 342, 351–52 (1914); *Darby*, 312 U.S. at 122. But see *M'Culloch* v. Maryland, 17 U.S. (4 Wheat.) 316, 411 (1819) ("The power of . . . regulating commerce . . . cannot be implied as incidental to other powers").

23. *M'Culloch*, 17 U.S. (4 Wheat.) at 413.

24. Ibid., pp. 413–14.

25. Ibid., p. 413.

26. Alison L. LaCroix, "The Shadow Powers of Article I," *Yale Law Journal* 123 (2014), pp. 2044, 2069.

27. Ibid.; also, Gary Lawson and David B. Kopel, "The PPACA in Wonderland," *American Journal of Law and Medicine* 38 (2012), pp. 269, 282 (arguing that the two should be untangled).

28. William Baude, "Rethinking the Federal Eminent Domain Power," *Yale Law Journal* 122 (2013), pp. 1738, 1750 (citing The Federalist No. 33 at 158 [Alexander Hamilton], George W. Carey and James McClellan, eds., 2001; and James Madison, Speech on February 2, 1791, reprinted in *Legislative and Documentary History of the Bank of the United States* 39, no. 42 (photo reprint 2008 (1832)).

29. 17 U.S. (4 Wheat.) 316 (1819).

30. Baude, supra note 29, pp. 1753–54 (discussing *M'Culloch*, 17 U.S. (4 Wheat) pp. 409–12.

31. I am putting to one side the question of whether the federal government could use the treaty power to support its marijuana ban, which was not discussed in *Raich*, Jim Leitzel, *Regulating Vice: Misguided Prohibitions and Realistic Controls* (New York, 2008), pp. 262–64. That question would depend on the exact requirements of the treaties the United States has signed, Steven B. Duke, "The Future of Marijuana in the United States," *Oregon Law Review* 91 (2013), pp. 1301, 1316–18; Michael Tackeff, "Constructing A 'Creative Reading': Will US State Cannabis Legislation Threaten the Fate of the International Drug Control Treaties?" *Vanderbilt Journal of Transnational Law* 51 (2018), pp. 247, 249 on the resolution of the constitutional question avoided in *Bond v. United States*, 134 S. Ct. 2077 (2014), and perhaps on the same questions of state implementation discussed in this Article. *Cf. Gonzales v. O Centro Espirita Beneficente Uniao do Vegetal*, 546 U.S. 418, 438 (2006) (requiring more than "invocation of . . . general interests" in alleged conflict between treaties and religious exemption from the CSA).

32. Heather K. Gerken, "Slipping the Bonds of Federalism," *Harvard Law Review* 128 (2014), pp. 85, 96. Emphasis in original.

33. Ibid. To be sure, Gerken also says the theory of state sovereignty that underlies these negative-space cases is "mostly claptrap," but even then she acknowledges that "one should give the devil his due. The sovereignty account has managed to generate reasonably coherent doctrine." Ibid., p. 99.

34. *The Wire: Hamsterdam* (HBO television broadcast October 10, 2004).

35. Adrian A. Ohmer, "Investing in Cannabis: Inconsistent Government Regulation and Constraints on Capital," *Michigan Journal of Private Equity and Venture Cap. Law* 3 (2013), pp. 97, 108–18.

36. Lance McMillian, "Drug Markets, Fringe Markets, and the Lessons of Hamsterdam," *Washington and & Lee Law* Review 69 (2012), pp. 849, 882–91.

37. Ibid., see supra note 13.

38. For thoughts on nullification, Ernest Young, "Modern-Day Nullification: Marijuana and the Persistence of Federalism in an Age of Overlapping Regulatory Jurisdiction," *Case Western Reserve Law Review* 65 (2015), pp. 769, 794. ("Nullification is dead . . . Long live nullification").

39. 317 U.S. 111 (1942).

40. Ibid., p. 125.

41. Ibid.

42. Cal. Health & Safety Code §1 1362.5(b)(1)(A), (b)(2) (West Supp. 2005).

43. Health & Safety §§ 11362.715–11362.76.

44. Health & Safety § 11362.5(d); see *People v. Spark*, 16 Cal. Rptr. 3d 840, 843 (Cal. Ct. App. 5th 2004) (noting that a doctor's license was suspended at the recommendation of undercover police officers).

45. *Wickard*, 317 U.S. at 119.

46. *Gonzales v. Raich*, 545 U.S. 1, 52–56 (2005) (O'Connor, J., dissenting).

47. Ibid., pp. 62–63 (Thomas, J., dissenting).

48. Ibid., p. 29 (majority opinion) (citations omitted). It did go on to provide some speculation that the state scheme was still likely to have an effect on the interstate market. Ibid., pp. at 30–32.

49. Ibid., p. 29 note 38.

50. Ibid.

51. The text also contained a citation to *United States v. Darby*, 312 U.S. 100 (1941), which says, like many similar cases from the period, that Congress's Commerce "power can neither be enlarged nor diminished by the exercise or non-exercise of state power." *Raich*, 545 U.S. p. 29 (quoting *Darby*, 312 U.S. at 114). But as discussed earlier, the marijuana cases present the different question of whether the in-state activity falls within that non-enlarged, non-diminished power.

52. *M'Culloch v. Maryland*, 17 U.S. (4 Wheat) 316, 424 (1819).

53. Ibid.

54. *Raich*, 545 U.S. p. 29 n.38 (2005) (emphasis in original).

55. One can also imagine different ways to calibrate how much of the spillover problem the state must control. One possibility is that the state must eliminate all but *de minimis* spillovers. Another is that it must do so at least as well as the proposed federal rule would.

56. 514 U.S. 549 (1995).

57. See *United States v. Morrison*, 529 U.S. 598, 614 (2000) ("Simply because Congress may conclude that a particular activity substantially affects interstate commerce does not necessarily make it so," quoting *Lopez*, 514 U.S. at 557 n.2 (citation omitted)).

58. *Raich*, 545 U.S. at 22, citing *Lopez*, 514 U.S. 549, 557 (1995).

59. Ernest A. Young, "Just Blowing Smoke? Politics, Doctrine, and the Federalist Revival After *Gonzales v. Raich*," *Sup. Ct. Rev.* (2005), pp. 1, 32–33 (explaining that rational basis "has its impetus in the institutional advantages that legislative bodies enjoy over courts" but noting the complication in unique situations where the case "involves not one legislature but two").

60. See Ibid., pp. 31–32 (suggesting a "process-based" "clear statement" rule); see also Guido Calabresi, "Antidiscrimination and Constitutional Accountability (What the Bork-Brennan Debate Ignores)," *Harvard Law Review* 105 (1991), pp. 80, 103–08 (proposing that acts of Congress that implicate fundamental rights without adequate consideration be remanded to Congress).

CONTRIBUTORS

JONATHAN H. ADLER is the inaugural Johan Verheij Memorial Professor of Law and director of the Coleman P. Burke Center for Environmental Law at the Case Western Reserve University School of Law. His previous books include *Business and the Roberts Court* (2016).

WILLIAM BAUDE is professor of law and Aaron Director Research Scholar at the University of Chicago Law School.

ANGELA DILLS is the Gimelstob-Landry Distinguished Professor of Regional Economic Development at Western Carolina University.

SIETSE GOFFARD is a researcher in the Department of Economics at Harvard University and a current Schwarzman Scholar at Tsinghua University.

JULIE ANDERSEN HILL is the Alton C. and Cecile Cunningham Craig Professor of Law at the University of Alabama.

JOHN HUDAK is deputy director of the Center for Effective Public Management, a senior fellow in governance studies at the Brookings Institution, and the author of *Marijuana: A Short History* (2016).

ROBERT A. MIKOS is professor of law at Vanderbilt University and the author of *Marijuana Law, Policy and Authority* (2017).

JEFFREY MIRON is director of economic studies at the Cato Institute and director of undergraduate and graduate studies in the Department of Economics at Harvard University.

ZACHARY S. PRICE is a professor at the University of California Hastings College of the Law in San Francisco.

CASSANDRA BURKE ROBERTSON is the John Deaver Drinko-BakerHostetler Professor of Law and director of the Center for Professional Ethics at the Case Western Reserve University School of Law.

CHRISTINE STENGLEIN is a research analyst at the Brookings Institution.

ERNEST A. YOUNG is the Alston & Bird Professor at Duke Law School.

INDEX

Figures at the end of chapter 2 are indicated by "f"